AN INTRODUCTION TO PSYCHOLINGUISTICS

AN INTRODUCTION TO PSYCHOLINGUISTICS

Jean Caron

University of Poitiers

Translated by Tim Pownall

University of Toronto Press

Toronto Buffalo

Précis de psycholinguistique © Presses Universitaire de France, 1989;
this translation © Harvester Wheatsheaf, 1992

First published in North America by
University of Toronto Press Incorporated 1992
ISBN 0–8020–5026–3 (hbk)
   0–8020–7743–9 (pbk)

Typeset in 10/12 pt Times

Printed and bound in Great Britain

A CIP catalogue record is available from the publisher

Contents

Foreword   vii

1. *The Objectives and Methods of Psycholinguistics*   1
   The birth and evolution of psycholinguistics   1
   The methods   12
   Recommended reading   15

2. *The Levels of Analysis*   16
   Comprehension of the verbal message   16
   Levels of processing and interactions   27
   Verbal production   29
   Conclusion   30
   Recommended reading   31

3. *The Perception of Speech*   32
   General problems   32
   The perception of phonemes   33
   The perception of continuous speech   40
   Lexical access   45
   Recommended reading   59

4. *From Words to Meaning: Lexical Semantics*   61
   The problems of meaning   61
   Psychological semantics   64
   The organization of semantic memory   72
   Meaning, context and reference   81
   Conclusion   88
   Recommended reading   89

5. *The Sentence 1: Syntax and Semantics*   90
   The primacy of syntax? Chomskyan psycholinguistics   91
   Sentence processing   102
   The production of utterances   110
   The semantic representation   117
   Conclusion   122
   Recommended reading   123

6. *The Sentence 2: Pragmatics*   125
   The pragmatics of language   125
   Speech and the situation: 'Deixis' and reference   129
   Speech and speakers: Taking responsibility   134
   Putting information into perspective: Presupposition and
   topicalization   141
   Conclusion   149
   Recommended reading   152

7. *Discourse*   153
   The organization of discourse   153
   Discourse cohesion   161
   The orientation of discourse   165
   Conclusion   167
   Recommended reading   168

8. *The Position and Perspectives of Psycholinguistics*   170
   Language processing   171
   Psycholinguistics and linguistics   175
   Perspectives   177

Bibliography   180

Index   199

Foreword

It is only recently that psycholinguistics has emerged as a discipline; its existence stretches back scarcely forty years. During this relatively short time span, however, it has given rise to a considerable body of work, developed innovative techniques and raised questions of a radical nature, emerging as one of the liveliest branches of cognitive psychology.

The attempt to condense and present the current state of this research sector imposes a number of limitations and schematizations.

The current summary will restrict itself to experimental psycholinguistics conducted amongst adult subjects. Despite – or even because of – the wealth of interest they contain, we have had to exclude works concerning the acquisition and development of language from the scope of this study. Nor has it been possible to discuss the neurological and pathological aspects of language functioning, or the applications of psycholinguistics.

Even given these limitations, there can be no question of presenting here a complete review of the works and theoretical debates which have marked these three or four decades of research. We have chosen to focus on those problems and perspectives which seem to us to be currently of the greatest importance. The works cited are those which we consider to be the best illustrations of these perspectives, although the choice, arrived at with no little difficulty, has no doubt given rise to some injustices. Furthermore, the great theoretical debates have of necessity been schematized. However, we have tried to provide readers with sufficient bibliographical references to allow them – and, we hope, encourage them – to clarify and enrich the information we have given.

Finally, one of the difficulties encountered in writing an introduction to psycholinguistics lies in its interdisciplinary character. Its understanding requires some knowledge of the fields of linguistics, philosophy of language and artificial intelligence. Wherever necessary, we have provided a brief and, at the same time, as accurate as possible introduction to any indispensable concepts. Thus this book does not, for the most part, demand any prior knowledge of the reader. Here again, the bibliographical references will allow interested readers to pursue in-depth information.

At this point I am bound to thank numerous colleagues, both in France and elsewhere, with whom I have had the opportunity to discuss many of the problems dealt with in this book. I should also like to thank the students who have given me the chance to refine its contents during the course of many years of teaching. My thanks are also due to my wife, Josiane Caron-Pargue, whose attentive, critical reading has been indispensable to me. Finally, I should like to thank Professor Fraisse, who suggested to me that I should write the current work and has awaited its completion with benevolent patience.

This book has been substantially updated for the English edition in order to present as accurate a picture as possible of the current state of the discipline. I have also tried to adapt the bibliographical references to an English-speaking readership.

I should very much like to thank my colleagues who have assisted me with their comments on and criticisms of the first edition, and I am particularly grateful for the suggestions of an anonymous Harvester Wheatsheaf reviewer. I hope I have been able to take account of all these suggestions. However, I must, of course, take responsibility for any omissions or errors which are still to be discovered in the book. I should also like to thank Farrell Burnett, Senior Editor, for suggesting the current translation to me and for patiently bearing my long delays in the work of updating the text. Finally – last but not least – I should like to say how much I have appreciated the co-operation of my translator, Tim Pownall, and express my gratitude for his excellent work.

CHAPTER 1

The Objectives and Methods of Psycholinguistics

We can define psycholinguistics as the experimental study of the psychological processes through which a human subject acquires and implements the system of a natural language.

This apparently simple definition actually covers a whole range of problems. On the one hand, we need to define what a language is and formulate an objective description of it. On the other, we are faced with the necessity of defining what we mean by 'psychological processes' and the means we employ to study them. The response to these problems has had to be worked out over an extended period during which both linguistics and psychology have, independently of one another, been required to attain their status as scientific disciplines.

The birth and evolution of psycholinguistics

The activity of language, in its relationship to human thought, was an early focus for the attention of psychologists and, before them, of philosophers, whether they were attempting to account for the organization of languages on the basis of the supposedly universal laws of the human mind (the *Grammaire* of Port-Royal is a famous example of this) or whether, in contrast, they were trying to demonstrate the constraints and distortions which language imposes on thought. This long tradition of reflection and analysis has most certainly given rise to a body of work which, even today, can suggest useful avenues of research. However, it remains insufficient to constitute a truly scientific discipline. It was not until the beginning of the twentieth century that the conditions for such a study started to emerge.

1

Linguistic structuralism

Despite constituting a basis for a scientific study of languages, the works of nineteenth-century grammarians and philologists are mainly devoted to the problems of language development and interrelationship and adopt a historical, comparative perspective. Moreover, the explanations which they provide for linguistic phenomena are generally extrinsic in nature, being of a psychological, sociological or physiological order.

It was Saussure (whose *Course in General Linguistics*, held in Geneva from 1906 onwards, was to be published, after his death, in 1916) who first established explicitly the principles on which modern linguistics was to be founded. The distinction he introduced between language and speech (*langue* and *parole*) makes it possible to consider language as an object, independent of the individuals who use it. At the same time he contrasted the *diachronic* (historical) approach with a *synchronic* approach which views language as a simultaneous whole, a system which contains within itself the principle of its own intelligibility.

Language, according to Saussure, is a system of *signs* or double-sided units. Each sign associates a signifier (a 'sound image') and a signified (a 'concept'). However, the elements of the system are defined only in terms of their interrelationships. A sign acquires its value only through its difference from the other signs in the language (which makes it possible to understand its arbitrary nature).

This *structuralist* conception of language was later to be taken up by the Prague Literary Circle (Trubetzkoy, Jakobson), which was to lay the foundations of phonology (see Chapter 2).

Saussure's structuralism does not rule out recourse to mental representations ('sound image', 'concept'). A much more radical position was adopted in the United States by the *distributionalism* of Bloomfield which, despite being founded on ideas very similar to those of Saussure (the definition of language – the 'code' – as a synchronic system, the primacy of relationships over elements), forcefully refutes any 'mentalism'. According to this school of thought, it must be possible to analyze and describe the structure of a language without knowing anything about its meaning or conditions of use, without reference to the subjects who speak it, to their intentions or their thoughts.

The distributional method sets itself the task, first of identifying the different levels of units (phonemes, morphemes, etc.) which constitute a given corpus, and then of determining the way in which they can be associated with one another, through a study of the environments in which each element may occur (its distribution).

There is no doubt that structuralist thinking was fundamentally based on an abstraction which the later development of linguistics was to call into question. However, it played a decisive role in the implementation of a rigorous methodology and the establishment of linguistics as an autonomous science.

Scientific psychology

At the same time as linguistics was defining its object of study by ridding itself of psychologism, psychology was moving towards an analogous objectivation, metamorphosing from the science of the 'facts of consciousness' to become the science of behaviour.

Through a radical rejection of introspection in favour of what can be objectively observed, and by defining psychology as the study of stimulus–response (S–R) relationships, Watson pushed psychologists in the direction of a more rigorous methodology and a stricter conception of their discipline. Initially, however, this was to lead to a serious impoverishment of the problems addressed by the discipline. In particular, 'verbal behaviour' – when reduced to 'laryngeal responses' – was, in itself, hardly likely to arouse the interest of researchers. At the most, verbal material was seen to exhibit characteristics which were particularly suitable to the study of learning, and attempts were made to simplify it to the greatest possible extent. Works dealing with 'verbal learning' made use of lists or pairs of words or, preferably, meaningless syllables. Several decades were to pass before the conceptual apparatus had become sufficiently rich to be able to tackle the complexity of verbal behaviour.

The scientific approach is clearly reductionist. Watson's behaviourism no doubt contained an implicit – but effective – guiding idea: namely, that scientific knowledge of man is possible only if he is reduced, as far as possible, to a machine.

But the behaviourist 'machine' is too simplistic. The model it takes is that of the slot machine. A coin is inserted into the slot (stimulus) and something comes out (response). What happens between these two events? According to Watson, we neither know nor need to know. Despite this, his successors asked themselves what was going on inside the 'black box'. First Tolman and then Hull introduced the idea of 'intervening variables'; Osgood and Mowrer the notion of 'mediational responses'.

However, the decisive move forward was to come from a completely different field. Wiener's *cybernetics* proposes a general theory of machines, now conceived of not as simple apparatuses for the transmission of energy but as general systems of transformation. The same theory was also to popularize the notion of *information*, in connection with which Shannon was simultaneously developing a mathematical theory. From a mechanical model we progress to a more generalized informational model, and psychologists were swift to see the advantages they could draw from it.

Armed with the first fully elaborated theories which attempted to go beyond the S–R model – and, in particular, with the support of information theory – psychology in 1950 was ready to join forces with linguistics once more.

First stage: language as code

It was in 1951 that Cornell University hosted a first summer seminar which gathered together a number of psychologists and linguists who wished to define a common field of research. The results were promising enough for a second seminar to be held two years later at the University of Indiana. The following year (1954) a joint work, compiled under the direction of Osgood and Sebeok – a psychologist and a linguist – brought together the fruits of these interdisciplinary efforts. *Psycholinguistics: A survey of theory and research problems* defined a new discipline, gave it a name and proposed a vast research programme.

Three disciplines were brought together to form this movement. First of all, psychology, primarily represented by theories of learning (but which was already starting to shrug off the rigour of classical behaviourism and did not hesitate to refer to Gestalt theory or to evoke the concept of 'representations'). Secondly, structural linguistics, characterized by the distributionalist methods of Bloomfield and Harris (as well as the works of Jakobson). The final partner was the information theory which had developed from the works of Shannon. This theory introduced a large number of new concepts along with a mathematical apparatus borrowed from probability theory, and was to provide much of the theoretical background.

In effect, this was a theory of the transmission of information (Shannon was an engineer with the Bell telecommunications company) which was soon to prove inadequate but which, at the stage research had reached at that time, was valuable because it contributed a certain number of fundamental ideas.

First, the idea of *information*. This is defined as the selection of one event from a finite set of possible events. To take a simple example, the question 'Is it going to rain this morning?' may have two possible answers: 'yes' or 'no'. If we associate a signal with each event in the set, then the set of possible signals constitutes a *code* and a particular sequence of signals constitutes a *message*. The messages, coded in this way, are transmitted via a *channel* (telephone line, sound vibrations, etc.).

Information, defined in this way, can be quantified. If, for example, two equally probable outcomes exist (in the simplest case, the probability of a coin coming down heads or tails), then each is said to be equivalent to one unit of information, known as a *bit* (short for *binary digit*). In other words, a single question (requiring the answer 'yes' or 'no') is sufficient to obtain the required information. If four possible outcomes exist, two questions will suffice, so that each outcome has the value of two bits. More generally, for 2^n equally probable outcomes the selection of one of them has the value of n bits. Therefore, the quantity of information provided by a signal in a code containing n possible and equally likely signals is measured by the quantity $H = \log_2 n$.

It can be seen that information represents the uncertainty associated with an event. In most cases, however, the possible events are not all equally probable. To return to our original example, the answer to the question 'Is it going to rain?' will not be equally probable if the question is asked in the Sahara or in Scotland. In this case it can easily be shown that the average quantity of information transmitted by a signal is equal (if we designate the probability of signal i as p_i) to the quantity:

$$H = -\Sigma p_i \log_2 p_i$$

If all the p_i are equal, this quantity is equal to $\log_2 n$. In all other cases it is less than this value. In other words, a message will, on average, transmit less information than this and is said to contain *redundancy*. This redundancy is not useless. It serves to reduce the likelihood of an error in the reception of the message resulting from the loss of information during transmission on the channel. We should add that this redundancy can assume two forms, linked on the one hand to the unequal probability of each of the signals constituting the code (for example, in a text written in English the letter e will appear far more frequently than the letter z) and, on the other, to the variable probability of the appearance of the signal following the appearance of another signal (for example, after an m the appearance of an e is more probable than that of an r).

Another important concept is the idea of *channel capacity*. This refers to the maximum volume of information which can be transmitted in a given unit of time.

Information theory provides a theoretical framework which is well adapted to both the distributional analyses of linguists and to psychological theories of learning, and it is this framework which was responsible for the far-reaching consequences of this fusion of disciplines. Psycholinguistics, defined as dealing 'directly with the processes of encoding and decoding as they relate states of messages to states of communicators', proceeded to give rise to a vast body of work.[1] These studies focus principally on two themes: on the one hand, the psychological reality of the units identified by linguists (and, in particular, the perception of phonemes) and, on the other, the effects of the probabilistic structure of the linguistic code (frequency of units,

---

1. For an overview, see the reviews of Miller (1954), and Rubenstein and Aborn (1960). Hörmann's work (1971) provides a more detailed discussion of the question, and of the first works to be inspired by Chomsky.

redundancy, sequential dependence, etc.) on the performance of subjects in tasks of identification, recall and anticipation.

However, the limitations to this approach were soon to become apparent. Not that it is incorrect – the phenomena with which it deals are real enough – but it is inadequate. What was to take researchers beyond its restrictions was not the internal difficulties they encountered but the very superficial nature of the phenomena studied, together with the development of new theoretical models capable of embracing a broader set of facts and providing a more satisfactory explanation:

1. Languages clearly exhibit statistical properties (unequal frequency of units, differing probability of occurrence of units in a given environment, etc.). However, do these properties constitute primary phenomena, or do they result from regularities of a different character? As long as we limit ourselves to the description of a finite corpus (following the approach of the distributionalists), we can be content with a description of co-occurrences. But, as Chomsky (1957) emphasized, to speak a language is to be able to understand and produce an infinite number of sentences which we have never heard before. A 'finite-state' model,[2] such as the one which is assumed by the works published during this period, cannot account for this fact satisfactorily. We can imagine – as Chomsky was determined to demonstrate – more satisfactory theoretical models.

2. Shannon's theory is simply a theory of the *transmission* of information. However, the same period was to witness the spectacular development of machines which *process* information – that is to say, perform complex sets of operations on the information with which they are provided. Computers and the emergence of 'artificial intelligence' programs to run on them (especially with the work of Newell, Shaw and Simon from 1955 onwards) may provide a richer, more satisfactory model of human behaviour than the S–R model.

Second stage: language as grammar
Chomsky's work *Syntactic Structures* appeared in 1957. It was very soon to create considerable excitement in psycholinguistic circles, thanks mainly to G.A. Miller. Throughout the 1960s generative and transformational grammar was to constitute the almost exclusive basis of works in psycholinguistics.

According to Chomsky, the description of a language must consist of the formulation of a finite set of formal rules which make it possible to produce

---

2. A finite-state machine is a machine which can pass through a finite number of states, each of which is determined (with a certain probability) by the preceding state. The application of this model to language implies that a unit in the speech chain depends solely on the unit which immediately precedes it. This makes it difficult to deal with, for example, interrupted agreements or embedded clauses.

all the correct ('well-formed') sentences of the language, and only these. Such a set of rules constitutes a *generative grammar*.

These rules are of two types:

(a) phrase-structure rules which give rise to 'underlying phrase markers' via a series of 'rewritings'; they result in strings of symbols;
(b) transformational rules (some obligatory, some optional) which are applied to these strings to produce 'terminal strings'. The application of morphophonemic rules to these strings finally produces the sentence in the form in which it is spoken.

Let us take the example sentence 'The glass was broken by the boy'. The initial application of phrase-structure rules yields the phrase marker:

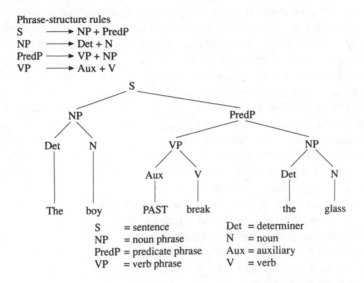

Phrase-structure rules

S ⟶ NP + PredP
NP ⟶ Det + N
PredP ⟶ VP + NP
VP ⟶ Aux + V

S = sentence	Det = determiner
NP = noun phrase	N = noun
PredP = predicate phrase	Aux = auxiliary
VP = verb phrase	V = verb

The terminal string would give the sentence 'The boy broke the glass'. An (optional) passive transformation would be performed in accordance with the rule: NP1 + Aux + V + NP2 → NP2 + Aux + be-en + V + by + NP1, which then yields: 'The glass was broken by the boy'.

Analogous transformations on *kernel sentences* make it possible to construct negative sentences, interrogative sentences, etc., as well as complex sentences (sentences composed of multiple clauses), nominalizations ('John refused to come' → 'John's refusal to come'), etc.

In *Aspects of the Theory of Syntax*, published in 1965, Chomsky provided a new version of his model (often known as the 'Standard Theory'). This included the following new principal elements:

- The syntactic component of language, which has just been described, is joined by a semantic component (which interprets the meaning of the sentence) and a phonological component (which translates the terminal string into sounds).
- The semantic component bears on the *deep structure* of the sentence – that is to say, on the structure obtained through the application of phrase-structure rules before the performance of transformations. This implies that the transformations have no effect on meaning (and also does away with the idea of 'optional transformations').
- The lexical elements are inserted at the deep-structure level.

Finally, Chomsky distinguishes between linguistic *competence* (the intuitive knowledge which all speakers possess of the rules of their language as they are described by the linguist) and *performance* (which concerns the processes linked to the production and comprehension of specific utterances).

Psycholinguistic research initially sought to prove the psychological validity of Chomsky's descriptions. Interpreting (incorrectly) the formal rules for the generation of utterances as the description of psychological operations, this research undertook many ingenious experiments in the attempt to demonstrate the reality of these operations.

One of the first fields – which we cannot discuss in depth in this volume – in which Chomsky exerted considerable influence was that of *language acquisition*. Thus a considerable body of work has been devoted to the establishment of the 'grammars' of children's language, the identification of the stages in their construction and the way in which they progressively come to resemble adult grammar.[3]

In effect, at the root of linguistic competence in human beings Chomsky was postulating the existence of an innate *language acquisition device* (LAD) which functions independently of cognitive development.[4] This LAD would allow children to proceed from an implicit knowledge of what the rules of a language must be in general to a progressive elaboration of the rules of their mother tongue on the basis of the utterances they hear.

Experimental work has principally focused on:

- the psychological reality of transformations (notably in the form of the 'derivational theory of complexity' which holds that the complexity of the processing of a sentence is a function of its transformational complexity);
- the role of deep structure in language processing.

---

3. For a summary of this work, see Brown (1973).
4. The opposition of Chomsky's theory of innateness and the constructivism of Piaget has given rise to an interesting debate between the two authors (Piattelli-Palmarini, 1979).

We shall have to turn our attention to these studies at a later stage (Chapter 5). For the moment we shall simply note that an assessment of them is essentially negative. It proved no more possible to establish the psychological reality of transformations than the idea of a *syntactic* deep structure.

The error of Chomskyan-inspired psycholinguistics (an error which can, of course, be established only with the benefit of hindsight!) was doubtless to understand a purely formal model of language description as a psychological model of processes. Nevertheless, we should not underestimate the positive aspects of this stage. In the first place, the anti-behaviourist reaction which Chomsky initiated now appears to be irreversible. Even if the mental operations postulated on the basis of generative grammar were not confirmed by experimental results, they have at least inspired psychologists with the idea that it is possible to attempt to construct models of the functioning of the human mind without necessarily lapsing into the illusions of introspection. Moreover, psycholinguistics has played an important role in the development of the cognitivist approach in psychology. Secondly, as we shall see, even the failures encountered by the Chomskyan perspective on the problems have brought to light aspects of language processing which would certainly not have been revealed otherwise.

Third stage: psycholinguistics today
From the 1970s onwards psycholinguistics started to react against its former domination by generative linguistics. This reaction took two forms:

- on the one hand, some psycholinguists still considered that the Chomskyan theory provided the most satisfactory description of the structure of language, but they focused on the study of the psychological procedures through which this structure is discovered and implemented; in other words, they emphasized *performance strategies*.
- on the other hand – and more radically – a number of researchers refused to consider any linguistic theory as definitive and looked instead to a variety of linguists (as well as philosophers of language) for heuristic suggestions with a view to establishing experimentally a psychological model of the language user.

Although the attempt to define the essential traits of contemporary events is a problematic one, we can nevertheless attempt the following characterization of modern-day psycholinguistics:

1. First of all, it is tending towards an increasing integration into the framework of cognitive psychology. Without doubt, a number of researchers, following Fodor (1983), continue to adhere to the theory of an autonomous language faculty, a 'module' possessing its own structure which is independent of the rest of the subject's mental life. For many other researchers, language processing is simply one of the aspects of the general functioning of the mind. As we shall see, the debate is not yet over. In both cases, however, the nature of the mechanisms to be identified is the same, and is expressed in the same terms. The approach in terms of information processing – which has continued to gain ground over the last twenty years, and has brought about psychology's definitive break with the behaviourist paradigm – now constitutes a common ground for all researchers. At the same time, the results of work investigating perception, memory, problem solving, etc., are becoming increasingly difficult to ignore in the study of language.

2. Secondly, the approach to language has widened. From the purely syntactic approach of the Chomskyan school (to speak is to construct or identify sentences formed in accordance with the rules of language) we have moved on through a study of the semantic aspects (to speak is to transmit meanings) to a study of the pragmatic aspects (to speak is to use language in a fashion which is adapted to the context, the listener and the objectives of the communication).

In the general theory of signs which he proposed in 1933, Morris distinguished between three types of approach: a *syntactic* approach which studies the relationships that signs have to one another; a *semantic* approach which focuses on the relationship between signs and the things designated by them; and finally, a *pragmatic* approach, the object of which is the relationship between signs and their users.

The first researchers into psycholinguistics concentrated primarily on the first of these aspects. It was not until quite late (towards the end of the 1960s) that research into the semantic aspects of language started to emerge (we shall turn our attention to this work in Chapters 4 and 5).

Researchers turned their attention to the pragmatic aspects a little later (in the mid 1970s). The principal themes are frequently borrowed from philosophers of language (Austin, Searle, Grice). From the linguistic point of view, interest has been focused on linguists such as Halliday (in English-speaking countries), Benveniste, Culioli and Ducrot (in French-speaking countries), who concentrate on the functional aspects of language and on the act of uttering as it is manifested in utterances (utterance-centred linguistics). We shall return to this topic in Chapter 6.

Awareness of such aspects, which are associated with the meaning and usage of language, does not simply provide psycholinguistics with new fields of research. It also necessitates a reformulation of the problems involved. If language is considered in terms of its syntactic aspects alone it is, in effect, conceived of as a formal object, isolated from the remainder of mental life. As soon as we try to account for its semantic aspects, however, it becomes difficult to ignore either the contextual and situational factors which determine its meaning, or the (extralinguistic) knowledge of the subject. And once we turn to the field of pragmatics, it becomes impossible to neglect these aspects. As we shall see, there are good reasons for asking whether these three levels – which we can, no doubt, distinguish between at an abstract level – are not really interdependent in the psychological processing of language. Thus from a *structural* approach to language, which characterizes psycholinguistics as inspired by Chomsky, we have proceeded to a *functional* perspective.

This widening of scope finds its expression in researchers' concern not to remain bound to the level of processing of individual sentences, but to start to tackle larger units within the framework of discourse. Although the theoretical apparatus is less well established here, such research is currently seeing some promising developments (which we shall examine in Chapter 7).

In this brief summary of the directions and stages of development of psycholinguistics we should not forget the (sometimes indirect, but today increasingly important) role played by research into the automatic processing of language in artificial intelligence. Largely developed over the course of the last ten to fifteen years, this research, while not necessarily providing plausible psychological models, has at least provided the psychologist with interesting suggestions and the example of rigorously defined theories. The exchange of ideas between artificial intelligence and cognitive psychology – within the framework of a 'cognitive science' which has been developing for a number of years – is certain to play an important role in the development of psycholinguistics, and of psychology in general.

The first attempts at machine translation ended in failure in the early 1960s. Following a decade of research of more limited scope, it was in about 1972 that the understanding of language by computers saw a significant improvement. Studies by Winograd, Schank, Rumelhart, Lindsay and Norman were published, independently of one another, in the same year. In 1973 Anderson and Bower, in *Human Associative Memory*, proposed a general model of memory functioning which is inspired by information technology and covers certain aspects of language. Anderson (1976, 1984) continued to enhance this model. In Chapter 4 we shall encounter a number of these theories which attempt both to account for psychological functioning and to simulate it on a computer.

After a happy childhood within the solid family tradition of behaviourism, psycholinguistics has experienced a long and difficult adolescence. It has undergone an identity crisis (with the fascination exerted by the Chomskyan model) and a juvenile crisis of originality (which has caused it to remain at the margins of other movements in psychology). Has it now matured into an adult? Only the future can tell.

The methods

Experimental procedures

The processes which the human mind employs to deal with language cannot, for the most part, be adequately explained in terms of introspection. They can be approached only by indirect methods. To this end, psycholinguistics has developed a large number of experimental techniques, many of them highly ingenious, and we can give only a brief overview of them here.[5]

In the main, works in this field have focused on *comprehension*. In general, we can distinguish between three types of method, depending on whether they are designed to determine the conditions of identification of the verbal stimulus, reveal the processing procedures as they are implemented, or subsequently characterize the product of this processing.

1. The first type comprises methods based on the controlled manipulation of the physical character of the stimuli – whether these are artificial stimuli, used predominantly in the study of the perception of words (see Chapter 3) or recorded words which can be distorted in various ways (masking by another sound, filtering out of certain frequencies, excisions, etc.). These methods enable researchers to determine both the nature of the information used by the listener and the role of contextual data in the reconstruction of missing information.

2. A second type of method – highly developed nowadays – aims to analyze the processing procedures while they are operative (researchers speak of 'real-time' or 'on-line' methods). These methods are generally based on very precise chronometrical measurements. For example, researchers measure the time a subject takes to decide whether the presented stimulus is a word or not (lexical decision), whether a sentence is true or false, etc. While the subject is listening to a verbal message it is also possible to measure the time taken to detect a specified sound, phoneme, word, etc. In the technique of *shadowing*, subjects have to repeat a message as they listen to it. The time interval between the message and its reproduction provides interesting information about the nature and complexity of processing.

---

5. For a critical presentation of the main methods, see, for example, Olson and Clark (1976) or Levelt (1978).

Alongside these chronometric methods, researchers also make use of physiological measurements such as ocular fixation time, electrodermal response, etc. Electroencephalographic measurements (evoked potentials) have also been producing interesting results for a number of years.

3. Finally, the most classical methods aim to explore the product of processing, whether this remains present in short-term memory (for example, when the subject is asked to locate a short noise – a 'click' – in a sentence which has just been heard) or whether, in the majority of cases, it is retained in long-term memory. To this end, experimenters can use the habitual recall procedures: free recall, cued recall, recognition. The subject can also be confronted with a variety of tasks: completing or paraphrasing an utterance, producing judgements about its acceptability or similarity to other utterances, etc.

Researchers studying the processes at work in the *production* of speech have fewer possibilities at their disposal. Experimentation in this field is difficult and the majority of the available data are based on observation: the analysis of errors, the study of the temporal organization of spontaneous language (rhythm, pauses, hesitations, etc.) as well as the study of aphasic speech.

The difficulties experienced in conducting experiments on the production of language mean, on the one hand, that there is only a small body of work in this field and, on the other, that the theoretical models are highly conjectural. It is to be hoped that research in this field will develop over the coming years. Two avenues of investigation appear to be promising:

- first, research into artificial intelligence;[6]
- second, the study of verbal production in well-defined situations. In such situations it is also possible to analyze and control the mental procedures implemented by the subject (here we are thinking primarily of situations of problem solving).[7]

General methodological problems

To conclude, let us indicate two problems of a very general nature which an experimental approach to the activity of language encounters:

1. So far we have spoken only of language. In fact, there is a considerable *multiplicity of languages* (between three and four thousand

6. Steedman and Johnson-Laird (1980) provide a number of stimulating ideas on this subject.
7. The analysis of verbal protocols plays an important role in the study of the processes of problem solving. The method proposed by Ericsson and Simon (1980) is based on a somewhat simplistic model of production, but there is no reason why it should not be refined.

languages are currently spoken in the world). What validity, then, can we attribute to results observed within one specific language? Certainly, we can hope that the mechanisms we reveal are based on general characteristics of the human race. However, we must make sure that this is really the case and undertake a sufficient number of cross-linguistic studies. This type of research started some ten years ago and can no doubt be expected to increase considerably over the coming years.[8]

2. A second problem (and one which is not limited to psycholinguistics) concerns the 'artificial' nature of *experimental situations*. Is it possible to generalize the results obtained in the laboratory, often using isolated sentences, out of context, deprived of any communicative function, and expect them to apply to the 'natural' use of language?

This question can be asked equally well of any other field of research in experimental psychology. It is, of course, possible to reply that scientific development is based on the assumption that the complex can be explained in terms of the simple. However, we still have to make certain:

1. That the simplicity of the studied phenomena is genuine. We shall see that there are times when this simplicity is misleading. Subjects bring to experimental situations all their implicit knowledge about language and its conditions of use. The result is that, *for the subjects*, the material can contain far more than the experimenter thinks they have put there.

2. That the experimental situation does not make use of *specific procedures* different to those which are encountered in everyday life. Such procedures can take two forms:

- the experimental conditions can *impose* on the subject operations which do not occur in habitual situations (for example, the comprehension of an isolated sentence such as 'The television has been repaired' presupposes, under experimental conditions, an inference, 'It was broken', whereas in normal communication the inference does not have to be made, since the listener is already aware of this fact);
- in contrast, the experimental conditions may *prohibit* certain operations which are required in the normal use of language (the procedures for identifying a referent, for example: if I am told 'The neighbour has had an accident', I have to identify which neighbour has been affected, whereas in the experimental situation such a sentence refers to nothing).

These difficulties in no way imply that we should give up experimenting. In fact experimentation is the only way of validating interpretations and

8. For a discussion, see Kail (1983).

establishing our knowledge on a scientific basis. The real problem of experimentation – in psycholinguistics as elsewhere – is not its 'artificial' nature but the relevance of the variables which are manipulated. In this book we shall see precisely how psycholinguistics has gradually discovered increasingly relevant variables, how it has enriched the scope of the problems with which it deals in order to move ever closer to the 'natural' reality of language. As Bachelard said, 'Science moves towards the real. It does not start from it.'

Recommended reading

As far as I know, there is no detailed historical study of psycholinguistics (or of the psychology of language). The works of the 'forerunners' (and Wundt in particular) are presented in Blumenthal (1970). Rieber (1980) also brings together a number of historical studies. Information on the recent origins of the discipline (but only within the framework of the USA) may be found in Cofer (1978).

From time to time *The Annual Review of Psychology* publishes a review of the current state of psycholinguistic research. The first of these (under the title 'Communication') was by G. Miller (1954). The title 'Psycholinguistics' first appeared with the article by Rubenstein and Aborn (1960). Further reviews followed from Ervin-Tripp and Slobin (1966), Fillenbaum (1970), Johnson-Laird (1974), Danks and Glucksberg (1980) and Foss (1988). The evolution of the themes and problems in the field can be traced through these reviews.

A number of important journals have been wholly or largely devoted to psycholinguistic research. The oldest (first published in 1962) is the *Journal of Verbal Learning and Verbal Behaviour* (which became the *Journal of Memory and Language* in 1985); more recent titles are the *Journal of Psycholinguistic Research* (since 1972) and *Language and Cognitive Processes* (since 1985). A number of important works appear in *Cognition, Cognitive Psychology* and (in an interdisciplinary perspective largely dominated by artificial intelligence) *Cognitive Science* as well as, of course, in the more general journals of experimental psychology (*Journal of Experimental Psychology, Memory and Cognition, Psychological Review*, etc.). As far as research into language acquisition (which I shall not deal with in this book) is concerned, the most representative journal is the *Journal of Child Language*.

CHAPTER 2

The Levels of Analysis

Before embarking on a detailed investigation of studies in psycholinguistics, it will be useful to look at one very simple example. On the one hand, this will give us an overall view of the various levels at which an utterance can be analyzed, thus allowing us to define a number of fundamental linguistic concepts. On the other, it will provide us with a context for the principal problems of psychology posed by the comprehension and production of an utterance.

Comprehension of the verbal message

I am having dinner with some friends, and one of them asks: 'Can you pass me the salt?' I pass the saltcellar. Like any other English-speaker, I have understood what was said to me. But what does that mean?

I have associated a sequence of sounds with a certain mental representation – a meaning. In order for this transition from sound to meaning to occur, complex processing has had to be carried out. We shall be analyzing the different aspects of this processing.

Identification of the units

e first problem is that of recognizing a sequence of linguistic units in a ntinuous stream of sounds. What are these units?

ie phonological level
we leave aside the purely sensory aspects of the auditory mechanism hich are not directly relevant to psycholinguistics, the listener's first task is identify, within the soundstream, a succession of units belonging to the nguage system: the *phonemes*. In our example the acoustic impression is

interpreted as a realization of the sequence /kənjupasmiðəsɒlt/.

The phoneme is not a sound but a class of sounds. The same phoneme can, in effect, be realized as different sounds: for example, the tone or intensity of the voice may vary, but the same phoneme will be perceived. What is more, quite dissimilar sounds can correspond to a single phoneme: thus in English the phoneme /r/ can be rendered in different ways depending on how it is pronounced: in Standard English or with a Scottish accent, for example.

In order to determine whether two sounds are realizations of the same phoneme, we can substitute one for the other in the same context (linguists call this *commutation*). For example, an English-speaker will recognize the word 'row' as being the same even if the /r/ is pronounced in different accents. In contrast, if the /r/ is replaced by an /l/ the word 'low' is obtained, and this will be identified as a different word.

Thus each language has its own set of phonemes (between 20 and 30 depending on the language). Clearly this set will vary from one language to another. For example, the German *ch*, the Spanish *j* and the French *u* do not exist in English; the phoneme /k/ can be realized in English by the tongue touching the front of the palate (as in 'key') or the back of the palate (as in 'cow'): these two sounds, which English-speakers do not generally distinguish between, can correspond to two distinct phonemes in other languages (for example, Arabic). In contrast, the sounds [o] (as in 'dough') and [u] (as in 'do'), which correspond to two distinct phonemes in English, are not differentiated in Arabic.[1]

A phoneme is thus characterized by its difference from other phonemes in the language system. The phonemes /b/ and /p/ differ by virtue of the former being voiced (accompanied by vibration of the vocal cords) and the latter unvoiced (no vibration of the vocal cords). This same opposition occurs between /d/ and /t/, /g/ and /k/, /v/ and /f/, etc. A list of *distinctive features* can thus be devised to represent the elementary units from which languages are constituted. Jakobson proposes such a list of twelve binary features[2] which can be used to describe the phonemic systems of all known languages. Since twelve features allow $2^{12} = 4,096$ possible combinations, it can be seen that each language uses only a small proportion of these combinations. In fact certain oppositions are generally associated with each other, a redundancy which adds to the efficiency of the system. For example, /b/ and /p/ differ not only in the voiced/unvoiced feature but also in the lax/tense feature.

1. *Phonology* is the study of the speech sounds of a language from the point of view of their function within the linguistic system. *Phonetics* is the study of the sounds themselves, independent of their function. Phonetic representations (sounds) are conventionally written between square brackets; phonological representations are written between slashes.
2. This list may be found in, for example, Jakobson (1963, ch. 6). Certain linguists, like Martinet, disagree with Jakobson's binary system and admit ternary, quaternary, etc., features. (See Martinet, 1967, ch. 3.)

Finally, it can be noted that all languages possess phonological rules which permit or prohibit certain sequences of phonemes. For example, any English-speaking reader will immediately be able to pick out the three English words in the following list, even if he or she has never encountered these words before (Halle, 1978): ptak, thole, hlad, plast, sram, mgla, flitch, dnom, rtut.

Thus one of the first problems faced by the psycholinguist is to determine what psychological processes the listener employs to identify the phonemes of his language from the available acoustic data. In the next chapter we shall see that this is by no means a simple problem.

Besides organization into phonemes, the soundstream contains a second type of linguistic information related to the *prosodic* aspects of an utterance: intonation, stress. In our example we can note that certain words are accentuated ('pass', 'salt') while others are not ('me', 'the'), and that the rising intonation at the end of the sentence underlines its interrogative character.[3] These prosodic features play a definite role in the comprehension of an utterance – although, as we shall see, the psycholinguistic study of them is not as yet very far developed.

The lexical level

Having identified the sequence /kənjupasmiðəsɒlt/ in our example sentence, the next stage is to break it down into meaningful elements – that is to say, to recognize it as the English words 'can', 'you', 'pass', 'me', 'the' and 'salt'. Unlike phonemes, these units are *signs*; in other words, they are composed of both signifier (a phoneme string) and signified (its meaning).

In fact the simplest meaningful unit is not the word but the *morpheme*. Some words comprise only a single morpheme (this is the case for the words in our example), whereas others can be broken down into several units. For example, 'passing', 'passed', 'passes' contain the affixes '-ing', '-ed' or '-es' to indicate tense or person, as well as the morpheme 'pass'. (It could be argued that the word 'pass' in our example contains a zero morpheme in addition to its verb root.) The same applies to compound words such as 'bypass' or 'overpass'.

Two distinct categories of morphemes can be identified. One comprises those morphemes – sometimes called lexical morphemes – which designate objects, qualities, states, etc. (simple nouns or adjectives, verb roots), and constitutes an open list – new ones can always be created. The second type (affixes, articles, pronouns, prepositions, etc.) are much more restricted in number, but more frequently used, and constitute a closed list. These are sometimes called grammatical morphemes, but their function goes beyond

3. In French, for example, this intonation may be the only mark distinguishing an interrogative from a simple statement ('Tu peux me passer le sel?').

the simple encoding of grammatical information. They express diverse, sometimes complex, relationships between the elements of an utterance, and we shall analyze some of them in Chapters 4 and 7).

To know a language and to be capable of speaking and understanding it, a subject must have learned its lexicon. In other words, everyone who speaks it has what can be termed an *internal lexicon*. This raises two important problems, with which we shall be dealing in the next two chapters:

- How is this internal lexicon represented and organized in the memory?
- What processes are used to access the lexicon?

Introspective observation offers no more help here than it does in the previous case: the identification of words appears to be a virtually instantaneous process whose results alone are accessible to observation. Only through precise and subtle experimental methods can these questions be answered.

Organization of the units

Identifying the words is only an initial stage. These words form a sentence – that is to say, they are organized in accordance with certain relationships and are assigned different functions. Recognizing these functions is an indispensable step towards understanding the sentence.

Within the perspective of Chomskyan generative grammar, we can propose the following, somewhat simplified analysis.

The deep structure of the sentence can be represented by means of the following phrase marker:

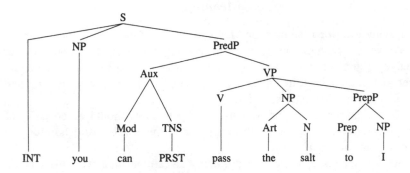

(where S = sentence; INT = interrogative; NP = noun phrase; Aux = auxiliary; VP = verb phrase; Mod = modal; TNS = tense; PrepP = prepositional phrase; V = verb; N = noun; Art = article; Prep = preposition).

A series of transformations is then performed on the terminal sequence which has been obtained in this way. First, the interrogative marker causes the subject ('you') to be moved behind the auxiliary ('Can you . . . '). The complement pronoun is then moved between the verb and its object, and the preposition is deleted. Morphological rules also come into play to provide the specific form of the verb and pronouns ('Can you pass me . . . '). Finally, we obtain the surface structure of the sentence on the basis of which the listener has to recover the deep structure which will be used in making a semantic interpretation.

The problem is to know how, and to what extent, the listener carries out this syntactic analysis. The cues the listener might rely on fall into three categories:

(a) the grammatical categories of the words in the sentence (verb, noun, pronoun, article, etc.);
(b) word order (in English the noun phrase generally precedes the main verb when it is the subject and follows the verb when it is the object; the subject is placed after the auxiliary if the sentence is interrogative);
(c) morphological features ('me' can only be a complement; 'pass' can be an infinitive form, etc.).

Of course, in addition to the above there are the semantic and situational cues which can affect syntactic analysis, or indeed be a substitute for it.

We still have to define exactly how this analysis is carried out. The spontaneous (and unconscious) procedures implemented by the listener are not necessarily identical to the reasoned analysis of the linguist as we have just described it.

Meaning

I. Having identified the units and recognized their function, the next stage is to derive a meaning from them. We need not linger for the moment over analyzing this notion of 'meaning'. Suffice it to say that it refers to a certain mental reality (Saussure speaks of 'concept') which is attached to and evoked by the linguistic signifier.

Two important problems are thus posed here: How should we conceive of this mental representation of the meaning of the words? And how do we access that meaning?

As we shall see, these two problems are still a long way from being satisfactorily resolved. One of the principal difficulties arises from the *polysemy* of natural languages – that is to say, from the fact that one word can have a multiplicity of meanings.

Each of the words in the sentence 'Can you pass me the salt?' without doubt evokes a well-defined meaning. In other contexts, however, these words could give rise to very different interpretations. For example, we can think of the sense of the verb 'to pass' in 'to pass an exam', 'to pass a red light', 'to pass the time', etc. In the same way, 'can' can express a material or moral capacity, as well as permission ('John can leave'), or an eventuality ('He can tell awful lies'). And the word 'salt' can have quite another meaning if it is uttered, for example, during a chemistry experiment.

Context clearly entails a selection from the possible meanings. But how?

II. Let us now turn our attention from the sense of the individual words to that of the sentence. The relationships we have indicated between the words are grammatical relationships; but these (since they, too, are linguistic signs) refer to the semantic relationships.

Considered from a purely grammatical point of view, the verb 'to pass', for example (in its transitive form, as here), requires a subject and complements. But from a semantic point of view, it signifies an action through which several objects are related: one carrying out the action (the Agent), one to which the action is done (Object), and one where the action ends (Beneficiary). The verb 'to pass' (and similarly 'to give', 'to sell', 'to entrust', etc.) can therefore be represented in the form of a relation consisting of three terms – or, as the logician would have it, a predicate with three arguments:

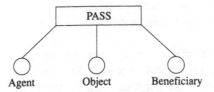

The three empty 'places' are filled by 'you', 'the salt' and 'me' respectively. The meaning of the sentence is thus defined on the basis of the verb, by determining the 'roles' attributed to the different elements specified in it.

These diverse semantic 'roles' may be likened to 'cases' in languages which have case declensions. Thus the role of 'object' corresponds to the accusative case, the role of 'beneficiary' to the dative, etc.

Fillmore (1968) proposed a generalization of this notion of case, making it the basis of grammar. Instead of the (purely syntactic) 'deep structures' of Chomsky, he proposed representing the base structure of a sentence in the form of a clause comprising a verb to which a set of noun phrases is attached by labelled relations. These relations correspond to a list of possible cases (agent, instrument, object, etc.). Grammatical rules then permit the derivation of different possible utterances. For example, the base structure of BREAK (Agent: the child; Object: the window; Instrument: a stone) permits: 'The child broke the window with a stone', 'The window was broken by the child', 'The window has been broken', 'A stone broke the window', etc.

As we shall see, Fillmore's ideas have had some considerable influence on studies which concentrate on semantic memory, as well as on research into artificial intelligence focusing on the automatic comprehension of language.

Reference and utterance landmarks

At this point the meaning of our example sentence may appear to be sufficiently well established. It could be paraphrased as follows: 'Person A asks person B if B can pass the salt to A'. Can we leave it at that?

In fact, the utterance as we have analyzed it remains an abstract entity – a textbook example. In order for it to be a real utterance, it needs something else: an anchorage in a real-life situation – a reference.

There are two sides to this problem:

I. 'The salt' refers to a concept (that of a defined substance with specific properties). For the listener, it is a question not only of evoking this concept but of identifying a particular instance of it – here, in the physical environment – and only that instance of it (the particular object intended by the speaker).

This supposes, on the one hand, that the meaning of words entails a specification of the procedures necessary to search for the objects (or the properties, processes, etc.) corresponding to them and, on the other, that there is a tacit co-operation between speaker and listener (the latter presuming that the former has produced the utterance in such a way that its referents can be identified unequivocally).

II. The two terms 'you' and 'me' refer not to concepts but to the particular event in which the utterance is produced. Their meaning concerns not the utterance but the *act of uttering*. 'I' ('me') designates the person who is speaking and 'you' the person who is being addressed.

All natural languages contain a collection of terms whose function is to 'point' to elements or aspects of the situation or act of uttering. These are generally called 'deictics' (from the Greek *deixis*, which means the act of showing, of designating). This category can include:

• markers of person: reference to the person who is speaking (first person)

or being addressed (second person); the third person being used for persons or things who are not participants in the utterance act;
- markers of time, which indicate the relationship between what is being uttered and the moment at which it is uttered (verb tenses, some adverbs: 'now', 'tomorrow', etc.);
- markers of place, which locate what is being uttered in relation to the place of utterance (demonstratives: 'this', 'that'; adverbs like 'here', 'there', etc.).

Some authors (for example Levinson, 1983) also propose the notion of 'social deixis', which encodes certain social relationships between the participants (for example, in French the distinction between 'tu' and 'vous' depends on the degree of familiarity or the hierarchical relationship between the interlocutors). We shall return to the problems of deixis in Chapter 6.

The existence of these 'utterance locations' (*repérages énonciatifs*) plays a central role in the linguistic movement of 'utterance-centred theories' which originated with Benveniste. Besides those we have just cited, this author (Benveniste, 1970) also includes among the 'traces of the act of uttering' (*marques de l'énonciation dans l'énoncé*) modal terms ('I think that . . . ', 'it is certain that . . . ', 'perhaps', etc.) by means of which speakers qualify their 'endorsement' (*prise en charge*) for the accuracy of what is said, as well as the linguistic procedures by which the particular type of speech act (statement, order, question, etc.) effected by the utterance is defined. We shall investigate this latter aspect in the next paragraph.

The speaker's intention

The utterance we are analyzing in our example raises one last problem.

As we have seen, this is an interrogative utterance. This being the case, it does not have only a meaning (that is to say, a mental representation to be constructed by the listener); it also has a communicative function: it solicits a response from the listener. The speaker is not only producing an utterance – that is to say, encoding a representation linguistically – but also *effecting an action* with the help of language.

Under the title *How to Do Things with Words*, Austin (1962) introduced this important idea of '*speech acts*'. This notion is clearly apparent in the analysis of what he calls 'performative verbs'. For example, to say 'I promise to come tomorrow' is not only informing someone of a promise, it is also the act of promising itself; to say 'I order you to leave' is actually giving an order, etc. In all these cases (listed at great length by Austin) the act is effected by the very utterance which expresses it.

However, this analysis can be generalized. All utterance is an act creating some new relationship between the speaker, the listener and the contents of the utterance. A question or an order instructs the interlocuter to respond or obey, and this can always be paraphrased by a performative verb: 'I ask you to ... ', 'I order you to ... '. Even a simple declarative utterance can be paraphrased by 'I declare that ... ', indicating that the speaker guarantees the accuracy of what is being stated.

Nevertheless, there are several ways of understanding that all utterance is an act. Austin distinguishes three:

- it is a *locutionary* act in the sense that the production of the utterance requires some mental activity (choosing the words, constructing a sentence) and physical activity (articulation of the utterance);
- it is a *perlocutionary* act in the sense that some consequence will follow from the fact that something has been said – this consequence might be desired or unforeseeable: I can reassure or disappoint my listener, or I can improve or impair my listener's estimation of me, etc.;
- finally (and most importantly) it is an *illocutionary* act in that, within my utterance itself, the rules of the language define a certain type of act and present it as such.

This notion of *illocutionary force*, attached to an utterance and defining its function in communication, has given rise to great developments in linguistics and in the philosophy of language (see, for example, Ducrot, 1972; Searle, 1969). As we shall see, it has begun to arouse interest among psycholinguists.

However, we have not quite finished with our example. If 'Can you pass me the salt?' is really an interrogative, the response should simply be 'yes' or 'no'. Evidently, this is not the case. If the listener interprets the sentence not as a question but as a request, then the literal interpretation is discarded in favour of an indirect interpretation. The listener refers to the situational context and, postulating that the utterance is relevant, infers the *speaker's intention*.

Grice (1975) sought to base this type of inference on what he calls a 'conversational logic'. According to Grice, verbal communication rests on a general principle, namely the *co-operative principle*: any contribution to the conversational exchange is presumed to correspond to what is demanded of the speaker by the objective of this exchange. This means that the speaker is supposed (a) to provide as much information as required, and no more (maxim of quantity); (b) to affirm only what the speaker believes to be true, or has proof of (maxim of quality); (c) to say only what is relevant (maxim of relation); (d) to be clear – that is to say, to avoid ambiguity, obscurity, verbosity, disorder (maxim of manner).

All conversation supposes a tacit acceptance of these rules, and it is on them that the listener's interpretation is based. If one of these rules is openly flouted, it is because the speaker has some reason X for not applying it, and knows that the listener is in a position to identify X as the reason for this infraction: it is, therefore, an indirect way of saying X. Grice calls this type of inference *conversational implicature*. Thus, in our example, the question posed infringes the maxim of relevance: the speaker clearly has no reason for wishing to be informed of the listener's physical ability to move the saltcellar. The utterance should therefore be interpreted as an indirect means of 'formulating a request (and, at the same time, of expressing that, for reasons of politeness, the speaker does not wish to give an order).[4]

Evidently, comprehension of the utterance consists, in the end, of grasping what can be called the *speaker's intention*. But this term should not be misunderstood: it is absolutely not a question of the listener showing any psychological penetration, 'intuition' or 'empathy', but of decoding the message according to the *rules* and use of language. Let us clarify this with a final remark about our example sentence: this concerns the distinction between *presupposition* and *implication*.

By asking 'Can you pass me the salt?', the speaker, in choosing to use the definite article, presupposes that there is salt in the immediate environment, and that the listener is not unaware of this. The existence of the salt is not affirmed directly, but is part of the actual meaning of the utterance (this would not be the case had the utterance simply used 'some salt').

The phenomenon of presupposition was first pointed out by logicians. 'The present King of France is bald' is a statement which cannot be qualified as true (at the moment) or as false (because then its negation would be true). Thus it can have a truth value only if there is a King of France: presupposition, then, is defined as the condition for a proposition being able to have a truth value.

Linguists have brought to light other means of introducing presuppositions: certain verbs such as 'to know' and 'realize' ('Peter knows that Jane has left' presupposes Jane's departure), 'to stop' ('My neighbour has stopped beating his wife' presupposes that he was beating her), etc.; certain relative clauses ('It was he who assassinated the president' presupposes that the president has been assassinated); certain adverbs ('Arthur was there too' presupposes that other people were there), etc. A convenient criterion is that of the negative, or interrogative, transformation which leaves the presuppositions intact (cf.: 'Peter does not know that Jane has left').

---

4. In order for a request (A asks B to do action X) to be properly formulated, certain conditions must be fulfilled: B would have to be in a position to carry out X, and be disposed to do so; A would have to want X; X would have to be not done already, etc. All forms of indirect request consist of asking if (or affirming that) one of these conditions is fulfilled ('Can you pass me the salt?', 'Would you like to pass me the salt?', 'I would like some salt', 'I haven't any salt'). See Gordon and Lakoff's analysis (1971).

Unlike presupposition, which forms part of the meaning of the utterance and is determined by purely linguistic considerations, implication supposes that the listener has recourse to extralinguistic knowledge in order to grasp the intention behind what is being said. In this way the request for salt could imply that the meal has been poorly prepared, or that the speaker wishes to change the subject of conversation, or feels neglected, etc. It is clear that at this point we are leaving the domain of linguistics and psycholinguistics.

From sentence to discourse

Our example was limited to a single sentence. In the everyday use of language it is generally a case not of isolated utterances but of sequences of utterances – that is to say, of *discourse*.[5] There are new problems here: understanding discourse is not just understanding each sentence separately, it is also grasping the *coherence* and discerning the *intention* of the speech. And in this case, the distinction between linguistic and extralinguistic is much more fluid. Let us return (one last time!) to our example, this time inserting it into some possible contexts.

I. Let us suppose that, in the same situation as before, the speaker had said: 'The salt is next to your plate. Can you pass it to me?' Comprehension of the second sentence would require an additional operation: that of identifying the antecedent of the (anaphoric) pronoun 'it'. The processing of anaphora (that is to say, terms which refer to another term introduced elsewhere in the discourse) gives rise to some interesting psychological problems. Identification of the antecedent can be reliant on various types of cues: morphological cues (gender and number) can sometimes be enough; certain syntactic constraints can also help (for example 'he' can be the co-referent of 'John' in the sentence 'When he entered, John smiled', but not in the sentence 'He entered when John smiled'); finally, plausibility or coherence may often also play a role. How are these different sources of information used? We shall see that the interpretation of anaphora has given rise to a number of studies which have considered it to be a very suitable method for analyzing the processes of language.

Moreover, the relevance of the first sentence remains problematic until the second sentence has been uttered. Even if it is semantically self-sufficient (it forms a true and verifiable statement), the listener knows – intuitively – that its meaning has not yet been completed: the intention to which it corresponds has not yet been identified.

---

5. *Discourse* is understood as any sequence of utterances, oral or written, produced by one or more locutors.

Finally, since the relation 'next to' is symmetrical, the speaker could also have said 'Your plate is next to the salt. . . .' This utterance would be logically equivalent to the first, but its function (and its influence on the discourse) would be quite different. The first utterance provides information regarding the salt; the second is about the plate. It might be said that 'the salt' is in the *topic* in the first sentence, and in the *comment* in the second. We shall return to this important functional distinction later.

II. Another situation: we are in the country, getting ready for a picnic. My friend, who is preparing a dish, says to me: 'The food is in the hamper. Can you pass me the salt?' This time, in order to connect the two successive utterances, it is necessary to make an inference: 'the salt' is included in 'the food', and if this is in the hamper, then the salt is too. That this inference is necessary for comprehension of the request and of the link between the two sentences must be acknowledged. But are we still in the domain of language, or are we now in that of general knowledge about the world?

From this example, it can be seen that difficulties may arise when, passing from utterance to discourse, we attempt to draw a distinct line between what is linguistic and what is not. We shall return to this question in the final chapter of this book. For the time being, let us note that it scarcely seems possible to confine any study of the psychological processing of language to isolated utterances.

Levels of processing and interactions

The analysis we have just performed on a very simple utterance enables us to realize that between the auditory perception of a sound sequence and the comprehension of a linguistic message lies a complex set of operations, among which a whole hierarchy of processing levels can be distinguished.

Nevertheless, we still have to ask ourselves how far the psychological procedures implemented by the speaker are adequately described by the above analysis. The analyses – and, indeed, the formal expressions – of linguists are certainly valuable in so far as they provide a precise and rigorous description of the system of language, bring to light important problems, and suggest hypotheses. But while they assist psychological investigation by allowing problems to be posed correctly, they cannot be a substitute for it.

We are now in a position to raise three very general questions which we shall encounter many times during the course of this book:

I. Do the various levels of analysis we have distinguished correspond psychologically to distinct components of processing? In other words, is there any case for supposing that a hierarchy of specialized 'processors' exists in the speaker, of which the first would have the function of identifying the phonemes in the speech chain, the second of recognizing the words, the third of analyzing the syntax, another of progressing to a 'computation' of the meanings, and another of applying the pragmatic rules? Or should the subdivision of tasks be envisaged in some other way?

II. A second question concerns not the nature but the functioning of these processing units.

We can think of these units functioning serially – that is to say, in a sequential manner, the product of one processing component being dispatched to the next, which duly processes it and sends it to the next, and so on. In such a scenario, the phonological component would recognize the phonemes, which would then enter the lexical processor, where they would be identified as words before being transmitted to the syntactic processor, etc. Each component is then conceived of as autonomous, receiving information only from the level immediately below it, and passing information on only to the level immediately above it. In artificial intelligence and cognitive psychology, this type of procedure has been designated by the term *bottom–up*.

Alternatively, we can envisage the different components functioning *in parallel*: as soon as a sentence is started, the phonological, lexical, syntactic, semantic and pragmatic analyses all commence simultaneously. Each of the components (or 'processors') communicates its results to all the others as they become available – either directly, or through the medium of a central processor. Unlike the former case, at least part of the processing is performed in *top–down* mode: that is to say, the semantic analysis, for example, can influence the syntactic or phonological analysis, etc.[6]

Even though intuitive good sense inclines us towards the second of these hypotheses, this is not enough. The phenomena we are considering happen very quickly and are not accessible to introspection. This therefore calls for experimentation – not only to select the most probable of the two hypotheses, but also to identify what information is used in the process of comprehension and, if there is an interaction, how exactly this interaction is effected.

Another question, partly connected with this problem, bears on the *automatic* or *controlled* nature of the processes concerned. The essential features of an automatic process would be that it begins, as soon as it is

6. This distinction between 'bottom–up' and 'top–down' processing (also called *data-driven* and *concept-* or *knowledge-driven*) plays an important role in other fields of information processing: notably in pattern recognition (see Lindsay and Norman, 1977, ch. 7).

supplied with data, to work through its functions without stopping, that it is usually very fast, that it is not conscious (only the results of the processing being accessible to the conscious mind), and that it does not demand the allocation of cognitive resources. A controlled process would be slower and subject to fairly narrow limits (in particular, it would be dependent on working memory) but, on the other hand, more flexible: in particular, it could be interrupted or modified at any time. We should note that a controlled process is not necessarily conscious.

III. There is one final question which bears on the autonomy of linguistic data processing in relation to other cognitive processes: are psycholinguistic procedures merely a particular instance of general procedures (which might be found in pattern recognition, knowledge retrieval, problem solving, etc.) or are they specific mechanisms requiring specialized apparatus? This problem has been introduced by Chomsky, whose arguments in favour of an innate *language acquisition device* (LAD) incline towards the autonomy of the linguistic in relation to the cognitive. More precisely, we shall have to ask ourselves whether the perception of phonemes, for example, requires specialized 'receptors', or if this is only a particular instance of the process of pattern recognition; whether the syntactic processing of utterances depends on a specific 'grammatical competence' or is based on general 'cognitive strategies'; whether the lexical meanings stored in memory are distinct from or form part of the knowledge set available to the subject (in other words, whether the semantic memory is comparable to a language dictionary or to an encyclopaedia) and so on.

Verbal production

So far we have discussed only comprehension. Clearly the analysis of verbal production can be approached within the same framework – this time inverting the same levels of analysis.

All the same, two important aspects must be taken into account in an analysis of speech production:

1. In the first place, it requires some *planning* activity. First, at a pre-linguistic level: the speaker must determine (depending on the aims of the communication, the situation, the speaker's representation of the listener, etc.) the contents of the message, its segmentation, the order in which to present it, etc. A truly linguistic level follows: the chaining of utterances, their syntactic organization, the production of articulatory movements, which all require planning at different levels. How these diverse planning levels are

constructed, how they interact, what their constituent units are: these are some of the questions which a study of verbal production should address.

2. The speaker has to choose not only what to say, but *how* to say it. The translation of a definite mental 'content' into an articulated utterance entails at least three kinds of choice:

- An initial problem is that of *choosing the words*. A single object, for example, may have a number of different names. The choice of one particular name is not arbitrary. It must simultaneously allow the listener to identify the object, highlight those aspects of the object which are relevant to the discourse, and permit the most economical expression possible.
- A second choice relates to the *order of utterance*: which element should be in initial position (the position of the 'topic')? The same event can, for example, be described using the same words in a number of different ways. Both the focus of attention and the expectations of the listener will vary depending on which element is 'topicalized'.
- Finally, given a particular propositional content, the speaker has to decide which kind of utterance act to use: choice of illocutionary act (statement, interrogation, order, promise, threat, etc.); equally, choice of attitude to be shown towards this content (doubt, certainty, hypothesis, etc.). This 'endorsement' of the utterance constitutes an indispensable part of it.

Conclusion

The analysis we have just given of the processes of comprehension and production provides some insight into the diversity of the problems facing the psycholinguist and the complexity of the operations at work in the manipulation of language.

The reader will have noticed that the greater part of these operations take place completely unconsciously and in a very short time span. They can therefore be investigated only indirectly, by using the various techniques described in the preceding chapter. Even those which are accessible to introspection are only vaguely and partially so.

The aim of the psycholinguist is to construct and validate a model of the human locutor. As we have just seen, this model should in fact be a double model: a model of comprehension and a model of production.[7] While these two models probably do not coincide, it is to be expected that they should have some elements in common. First of all, for the obvious reason that they would both have recourse to the same knowledge base (syntactic, lexical and

7. In this book we shall not be dealing with the problems posed by the model of acquisition.

semantic). But also for a more fundamental reason: the production of an utterance is performed in accordance with the processes of comprehension implemented by the listener; on the other hand, comprehension consists of identifying the 'speaker's intention' and reconstituting (at least partially) the operations through which the utterance was produced. The two systems of operation are thus intimately linked. In the following chapters, therefore, we shall study them in parallel, adhering to the same order we have adopted in describing the levels of analysis above. For reasons we have already stated, most of the data we shall cite concern the processes of comprehension, but they do also permit, at least in part, a clarification of the processes of production.

Recommended reading

In this chapter, I have sought to provide the minimum of linguistic information necessary for an understanding of the following chapters. A number of excellent works are available for a more detailed introduction to linguistic analysis, for example Akmajian *et al.* (1990). Crystal's dictionary (1991) will provide a definition of the exact meaning of the linguistic terms used.

In the following chapters I assume that the reader is familiar with the key ideas of cognitive psychology (and the 'information-processing' approach). There are some excellent introductions to this subject: for example, the works of Lindsay and Norman (1977), Lachman *et al.* (1979), Anderson (1990). The 'cognitive science' approach is excellently presented by Johnson-Laird (1988).

Finally, Chapters 6 and 7 of Herbert and Eve Clark (1977) provide an excellent account of the problems of speech production.

CHAPTER 3

The Perception of Speech

General problems

Speech presents itself as a continuous stream of sound. The listener's first task is to segment this stream into discrete units and to identify these units. That this task is by no means simple is demonstrated by the difficulties which still hinder research into the automatic machine recognition of speech or, at a simpler level, the difficulties we experience in following speech in an insufficiently mastered foreign language.

We can tackle this problem at an elementary level by attempting to determine the nature of the acoustic cues on which listeners base their identification of phonemes. Experimental phonetics has collected a large volume of data relating to this subject, and we shall attempt to summarize the most important elements here.

However, these data, which relate to the identification of isolated phonemes (or syllables), are insufficient to account for the perception of continuous speech, which displays a certain number of characteristics that suggest the involvement of more complex processes:

(a) The first is the *speed* of continuous speech, which generally proceeds at a rate of some 200 words per minute. This requires the listener to identify between 12 and 15 phonemes per second. In fact, the phoneme recognition capacity of the average listener is higher still, with perception becoming seriously impaired only at approximately 300 words per minute.

(b) To this we must add the great *variability* of the acoustic data. A single sentence, which we have no difficulty in recognizing, corresponds to a number of very different acoustic realizations depending on the age, sex and origin of the speaker, whether it is spoken loudly or softly, with the mouth full, etc.

(c) Finally, we can note the *incomplete* character of speech. A large number of words (and phonemes) are pronounced imperfectly, or even not at all, but this does not impede comprehension in the slightest.

An experiment conducted by Pollack and Pickett (1969) provides a striking illustration of this. They asked their subjects to listen to isolated words taken from a recording of spontaneous conversation. Only 47 per cent of the words could be identified correctly. Even when articulation was better controlled (a text read at normal speed), the level of correct recognition did not rise above 55 per cent.

We may conclude that even if the perception of speech is clearly based on acoustic data, it is most certainly not limited to this. To the *bottom–up* analysis of the signal we can add *top–down* processes in which listeners anticipate what they will hear. They then perform only a partial analysis of the acoustic data in order either to confirm or to correct these anticipations.

We are therefore entitled to ask ourselves if the basic unit of perception is not, in fact, the phoneme but rather the word itself – that is to say, the minimum significant unit. For this reason we shall devote part of this chapter to the problems of *lexical access*.

The perception of phonemes

From sound to phoneme

It seems clear, when we hear a word being spoken, that the sounds we perceive constitute a succession of distinct phonemes – or, at least, of distinct phones (that is to say, qualitatively different realizations of the phonemes of the language). Thus we might think that an appropriate segmentation of the word 'doom', for example, would yield three distinct sounds corresponding to the phonemes /d/, /uː/ and /m/.

In fact, things are quite different. Doubtless we are able to isolate a fragment which corresponds to the syllable /du/. If we progressively shorten the recording we shall continue to hear /du/ until, at the moment when the vowel disappears, the remaining sound, a rapid, deepening hiss, has nothing to do with any sound in the language. It is impossible to isolate a sound corresponding to /d/. A still better illustration is to perform the same operation with the syllable /di/. In this case, when the vowel has been eliminated, what remains is again a hiss, but this time a rising one (see Liberman *et al.*, 1967). In other words, what is perceived clearly as one and the same phoneme (here a dental, voiced, non-nasalized consonant) actually corresponds to very different stimuli.

In contrast (cf. Liberman *et al.*, *ibid.*), the same physical stimulus can provoke the perception of different phonemes. The insertion of a burst of noise at a frequency of 1,440 Hz before the vowel /a/ results in the perception of the syllable /pa/, whereas the same sound, followed by a /u/, is perceived as /ku/.

In short, we can say that there is no one-to-one correspondence between the objective acoustic data and the phonetic units we perceive. In fact, the physical basis of speech is a complex acoustic vibration which can be analyzed in the form of a spectrogram (Figure 3.1) on which time is represented along the x-axis, frequency along the y-axis, and the intensity of the recording corresponds to the distribution of acoustic intensities at the different frequencies.

We can see that the areas of greatest intensity are concentrated around certain frequency bands which vary with time. This concentration around specific frequency bands (known as *formants*) defines the vowels. For example, the first three formants of the sound /æ/ in English (as in 'cat') are located at approximately 700, 1,600 and 2,460 Hz.

Moreover, the first two formants are sufficient to define a vowel. The consonants, for their part, are defined by *transitions* – that is to say, by the rapid changes in the frequency of the formants of the vowel. In particular, the second formant's direction of transition determines the consonant's point of articulation (bilabial: *p*, *b*, *m*; dental: *t*, *d*, *n*; velar: *k*, *g*), while the moment at which the first formant appears gives the consonant its voiced (if it appears at the same time as the others) or unvoiced (if it appears only 30 to 40 milliseconds (ms) later) quality. Nasalization (*m*, *n*) corresponds to a vibration at certain frequencies accompanying the transition, etc.

When conducting experimental studies it is therefore possible to produce

Figure 3.1 Spectogram of the sentence: 'Personne n'a applaudi ce beau discours' ('Nobody applauded this fine speech') (*Source: C.R.I.N. et Institut de Phonétique de Nancy*)

artificial stimuli whose characteristics can be systematically varied.[1] Figure 3.2 gives an example of the stimuli used by Liberman and colleagues. In this figure we may note how the position of the formant differs depending on the vowel used. We further recognize that the transition of the second formant starts from the same (virtual) position: at about 1,800 Hz (this is the *locus* of the consonant – a locus situated at approximately 700 Hz gives a bilabial consonant; one located at around 3,000 Hz results in a velar). Finally, we can observe that the simultaneous nature of the transition of the two formants permits the perception of a voiced consonant (a slight shift in the appearance of the first formant would give a *t*).

Distinctive features and the detector hypothesis

As we have just seen, acoustic analysis does not allow us to think of a particular phoneme (at least as far as consonants are concerned) as corresponding to a defined physical object. What it does is to bring to light a set of characteristics (time of appearance of the first formant, transition locus of the second formant, etc.) which, taken together, *differentiate* one phoneme from another. Here we encounter the concept of *distinctive features* proposed by linguists. This allows us to understand the identification of a phoneme in terms of the observation of the presence or absence of one or other of these features.

An experiment carried out by Miller and Nicely (1955) provides support for this hypothesis. By presenting the sixteen principal consonants of the English language in a random order and under different masking conditions, and asking subjects to identify them, these authors were able to analyze the types of confusion which arose. The results led them to postulate five distinct 'channels' which are involved in the perception of consonants and correspond to the following features: voicing (voiced *versus* voiceless

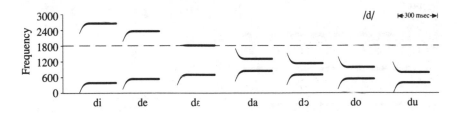

Figure 3.2 Examples of artificial stimuli giving the sound /d/ in front of different vowels (based on Liberman *et al.*, 1967)

1. For an idea of the first works of this type to be performed, see Cooper *et al.* (1952).

consonants), nasality (which contrasts *m* and *n* to the other consonants), stridency (*f*, *s*, *z*, etc., in contrast to the occlusives), duration and place of articulation. These results suggested that the identification of phonemes could be the result of a set of specialized 'detectors' which function in parallel and each of which is responsible for the detection of a particular feature.

A collection of data which points in the same direction concerns the *categorical* nature of phoneme perception. In one of the first experiments to investigate this question (Liberman *et al.*, 1957) subjects were presented with artificial stimuli corresponding to simple syllables (consonant + vowel) in which the transition of the second formant was systematically varied – this allowed the initial consonant to be identified as *b*, *d* or *g*. This experiment yielded two important results:

- First, almost all the stimuli were identified unambiguously by all the subjects. The switch from one phoneme to another happens abruptly (see Figure 3.3). In other words, continuous variation of the stimulus prompts discontinuous perception.
- Second, discrimination between two neighbouring stimuli was accomplished far more successfully when these were situated close to a 'phoneme boundary' than when both were perceived as realizations of the same phoneme (irrespective of the fact that the physical difference between the two stimuli remained the same). Similar results have been observed in numerous other cases: notably, delaying the appearance of the first formant (*voice onset time* or VOT) by regularly increasing amounts results in an abrupt transition from, for example, /ba/ to /pa/.

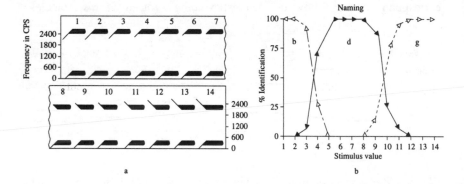

Figure 3.3 Naming of artificial stimuli: *a:* stimuli used; *b:* namings obtained (based on Liberman, Harris, Hoffman and Griffith, 1957, p. 359, 361)

The specialized detector hypothesis is further supported by the phenomenon of *selective adaptation*. In effect, repeated presentation of the same stimulus reduces the sensitivity of the corresponding detector. We can therefore expect that in a subject who has listened many times to the same syllable (for example, /ba/), the corresponding detector will become less sensitive, and the 'boundary' between *b* and *p* will be shifted. This is exactly what Eimas and Corbit (1973) observed. Moreover, this repetition of /ba/ results in an equivalent shift of the 'boundary' between *d* and *t*, suggesting that the detectors are specialized not for a single phoneme but for a phonemic feature (voicing in this example).

Lastly, we should note that the same phenomena of categorical perception have been observed by Eimas and colleagues amongst infants a few weeks old.[2] This invites us to consider these phonetic 'detectors' as part of an innate mechanism which is specific to the human perception of language.

In fact, this hypothesis soon proved difficult to support. First, categorical perception phenomena are not specific to language sounds, as was originally believed, and their existence has been demonstrated in connection with other, non-linguistic, stimuli. Equally, the existence of such phenomena in connection with linguistic stimuli has been demonstrated in mammals other than humans (such as chinchillas). We can therefore hardly retain the idea that this is a question of a pre-adapted language-processing mechanism. Moreover, it has been shown that categorical perception and selective adaptation can be explained in terms of the psychophysical properties of the acoustic signal. In this case they would derive from the general properties of the auditory system itself, not from any specialized apparatus.[3] The detector hypothesis has finally been abandoned. As we shall see, it was too simple a hypothesis to account for the complexity of the phenomena involved in speech perception.

Perceptual integration and context

In fact, as some of the observations cited above have suggested, phonetic features are not identified on the basis of a single acoustic cue whose presence or absence would be a necessary condition for identification. Rather, a *multiplicity of cues* are taken into account.

For example, the voicing feature for an occlusive consonant depends not only on the voice onset time but also on the duration of the transitions, the initial frequency of the first formant, the duration of the following vowel, etc. Furthermore, these cues are mutually substitutable, the presence of one

2. This work is reviewed and discussed in Eimas (1982).
3. For a detailed discussion of all these points, see Diehl (1981). For the perception of speech in infants, see also Eimas (1982); Jusczyk (1982).

compensating for the absence of another in such a way that the resulting perception remains unaffected. These substitution effects have been frequently observed (Repp, 1982).

Moreover, the way these cues are interpreted is context-dependent. The immediate context allows the same sound to be perceived as a different consonant depending on the vowel which follows it (for example, as /p/ or /k/ depending on whether it is followed by /i/ or /a/) or the syllable which precedes it (the same syllable, perceived as /ga/ after /al/, is perceived as /da/ after /ar/). More generally, there is a process of 'normalization' which depends on the voice, deep or high-pitched, of the speaker, together with the speed of delivery, and results in identical physical characteristics giving rise to the perception of different phonemes. In contrast, the same phoneme can give rise to very different phonetic realizations depending not simply on the speaker (as we have already noted) but also on context: for example, depending on its position in the word, and whether the word is stressed or not. For example, in English the /t/ in 'Tom' is not pronounced in the same way as the /t/ in 'hit', and there is a similar difference between the two instances of /d/ in 'did'. These 'allophonic variations' can provide important information about the acoustic signal's segmentation into words (Church, 1987).

Finally, these cues need not be solely acoustic. An interesting experiment conducted by McDonald and McGurk (1978) shows that visual information also has a role to play. These authors asked their subjects to listen to a variety of syllables (/ba/, /da/, /ga/, etc.) while at the same time presenting them with a screen display of the face of a person pronouncing different syllables. The unexpected result of this experiment is that most of the time what is perceived is neither the auditorily presented syllable nor the syllable corresponding to the visual information, but the product of integrating these two sources of information. For example, when the auditory information provided was /ga/ and the visual information corresponded to the production of /ba/, what the subjects heard was /da/.

To summarize: what these different observations demonstrate is that the perception of speech sounds is based on a highly diversified set of data. The physical data provide us not with phonemes but with a collection of cues which constitute the basis for the work of interpretation whose final product alone is available to consciousness. How should we think of this work?

Theoretical interpretations

The impossibility of constructing any one-to-one correspondence between the segments of the soundstream and phonemes soon caused problems for researchers working in the field of automatic speech recognition. The solution proposed in 1962 by Halle and Stevens was an *analysis-by-synthesis* model. In this model, speech is identified on the basis of an active production process. Listeners, who start from a provisional and partial analysis of the acoustic signal, produce (internally) a sequence of phonemes which they compare with the received message. As they do so, they form hypotheses on the basis of their own rules for verbal production, and test these against the acoustic data they receive until a satisfactory match has been achieved.

An interesting aspect of this type of model is that it emphasizes the similarity between the processes of speech perception and speech production. It also makes it possible to go beyond the level of the simple perception of phonemes to tackle the more complex issues which arise in the perception of continuous speech. The rules of production which listeners use to construct the hypotheses which they test against the acoustic data are not necessarily limited to articulatory rules and may well involve higher levels – lexical, syntactic, semantic – as we shall see later.

However, such a system is computationally highly complex and constitutes a process for producing and verifying hypotheses which is difficult to conceive of within the functioning of real-time speech perception which is, as we have seen, extremely fast. For this reason, researchers have attempted to seek the explanation of such functioning in automatic processes.

I. A tempting explanation is offered by the *motor theory* of speech perception proposed by Liberman (see Liberman *et al.*, 1967). According to this theory, what is evoked in listeners when they perceive an utterance are the articulatory movements which they would have to effect in order to produce the same utterance. In effect, the same mechanism would then be involved in speech production (which starts from a phonological representation, which is translated into motor commands, which produce the sounds) and perception (which follows the reverse path). Across a wide diversity of acoustic phenomena (for example, the different realizations of the phoneme /d/ depending on the following vowel), what the listener perceives is an articulatory invariant (the brief occlusion of the sound channel by the tip of the tongue at the base of the teeth, accompanied by vibration of the vocal cords). Categorical perception can also be understood in these terms. For example, three distinct articulatory movements correspond to the sound continuum /b, d, g/.

Presented in this form, the motor theory raises serious difficulties. First of all, the supposition that phonemes correspond to articulatory invariants is at odds with observations (see Howell and Harvey, 1983). The variability in realizations of a particular phoneme is as great at the articulatory level as it is at the acoustic level. Furthermore, the theory implies that we are able to identify only those sounds which we are also able to produce, and this is not the case. Young children are able to differentiate between sounds which they are not able to produce distinctly. Moreover, certain people who are congenitally incapable of speaking are still able to understand what is said to them. Therefore Liberman suggests that we should think of the articulatory invariants associated with the perception of phonemes as being situated at a higher, more abstract level than the level of the effector mechanisms.[4] This makes the theory difficult to verify.

The most recent version of the theory (Liberman and Mattingly, 1985) suggests attributing this mode of perception to an innate, specialized, automatically functioning 'module'. The functioning of this module would be comparable to that of our visual system, which translates a set of sensory cues into a representation of objects in three-dimensional space. In the current theory, an equally complex set of acoustic cues is automatically translated into an abstract articulatory pattern.

It is difficult to envisage an experimental verification of this theory. Moreover, we may note that in contrast to the analysis-by-synthesis model, which presumed an essentially 'top–down' control of the processes of perception by the higher processing levels, the perception 'module' functions here in a purely 'bottom–up' fashion which takes no account of contextual cues.

II. From a completely different viewpoint – one which goes back to the idea of an interaction between the different levels of processing – we can think of this process in terms of a system of excitations and inhibitions which occur automatically, in a predominantly parallel way, within a network whose nodes constitute the detectors which function at different levels (acoustic features, phonemes, words). These *connectionist models* currently suggest interesting avenues of research. We shall return later (see p.57) to the model proposed by Ellman and McClelland (1986).

The perception of continuous speech

The role of context

In a now old experiment, Miller and Isard (1963) demonstrated the role of linguistic organization in speech perception. Their procedure consisted of

---

4. Motor control is clearly not exerted on each muscle separately, but on co-ordinated systems which are adjusted automatically, a single motor command being able to give rise to different movements, depending on context. For an analysis of this concept of the mechanisms of verbal production, see Fowler *et al.* (1980). For discussion of work on the relationships between speech perception and production, see Howell and Harvey (1983).

asking subjects to listen to sequences of words accompanied by a masking sound of varying intensity, and then asking them to repeat what they had heard. The material presented was divided into four types:

(1) grammatically correct and semantically acceptable sentences: 'Gallant gentlemen save distressed damsels';
(2) grammatically correct but semantically unacceptable sentences: 'Lighted gentlemen dissolve furious appraisals';
(3) sequences obtained by distorting the word order of the type (1) sentences: 'Gentlemen gallant damsels distressed save';
(4) finally, sequences obtained by distorting the word order of the type (2) sentences: 'Gentlemen appraisals dissolve lighted furious'.

The type (1) sentences were the easiest to identify; the type (4) sentences gave rise to the highest number of errors. Finally, the type (2) and (3) sequences yielded intermediate results. We can see that both syntactic structure, on the one hand, and semantic coherence, on the other, both play a facilitating role and allow the listener to reconstruct the phonetic information masked by the sound.

That there is no consciousness of this reconstruction is demonstrated by Warren's research into *phonemic restoration*. Subjects were asked (Warren and Obusek, 1971) to listen to a sentence in which one word on the recording was partially distorted through the erasure of a phoneme or syllable and its replacement by a cough. For example, in the sentence:

The state governors met with their respective legislatures convening in the capital city.

the word 'legislatures' becomes 'legi*latures' or 'le*latures'. Even when they were warned of this, almost all the subjects claimed to have heard the complete word. The cough is perceived as being superimposed on the word, and its location is generally identified inaccurately. Moreover, the same stimulus is perceived differently according to context. Thus in the sentence 'It was found that the *eel was on the axle', subjects distinctly hear 'wheel'. However, if 'axle' is replaced by 'orange', the subjects hear 'peel', and if the replacement word is 'table', they hear 'meal', etc. (Warren and Warren, 1970).

A similar phenomenon may be observed in connection with *mispronunciations*. Cole and Jakimik (1978) asked their subjects to listen to stories in which certain phonemes had been replaced by others, and to identify these errors. The results (level of error detection and reaction time) differed greatly depending on whether the replaced phoneme was located at the beginning or end of a word, was situated in a stressed syllable, in a word which was more or less predictable in the context, etc. In broad terms, the more predictable the distorted phoneme, the more likely it is that the distortion will pass unnoticed. If it is detected, however, it will be detected more rapidly.

These different observations point to an interaction – which varies according to the experimental conditions – between two types of processing: a 'bottom–up' analysis of the acoustic data and context-related 'top–down' anticipations. They also raise a problem: is the identification of phonemes the primary, simple and elementary phenomenon on which the higher-level operations are based? In other words, even though there is no doubt that the phoneme possesses the status of a *linguistic* unit, does it also possess a *psychological* reality?

What is the basic perceptual unit?

While there is no doubt that we are able to recognize a phoneme and, for example, to detect the common element in the words 'bat' and 'bow', we must ask whether this is a basic perceptual ability. We should note that observations of children do not reveal any clear aptitude for phonemic segmentation before the age of 6–7 – that is to say, the age at which written language is learned (see Nesdale *et al.*, 1984). In fact, the identification of phonemes might be no more than the result of learning and of a higher-level analysis of the perceptual data.

In support of this idea, we can cite the results obtained in *phoneme detection* tasks. This experimental paradigm was introduced by Foss in order to explore the real-time procedures of sentence processing. While listening to a sentence, the subjects had to push a button as soon as they heard, for example, a word starting with a /b/. As processing capacity is limited, we can expect identification of the phoneme to be delayed (and thus the response time to be longer) if the part of the utterance which immediately precedes the phoneme gives rise to more complex processing.

However, it soon became apparent that this detection task was less simple than had been thought. Savin and Bever (1970) compared the time taken to detect either a particular syllable or the initial phoneme of this syllable in a list of syllables, and made the surprising observation that syllables are detected *faster* than phonemes. From this they concluded that the phoneme has no perceptual reality, that the perceptual unit is the *syllable*, and that phonemes are identified only on the basis of an analysis of this unit.

The work of Mehler and Segui also suggests that the first level of segmentation of the acoustic signal operates at the syllable level. For example (Segui, 1984), French subjects detect the same combination of phonemes more or less quickly depending on whether or not they constitute a syllable: thus /ba/ is detected more quickly in 'balance' than in 'balcon', whereas the reverse is true for /bal/.[5]

For some years this hypothesis of a syllabic representation has been the object of a considerable body of work. Two avenues of research appear particularly interesting:

- First, research into the *structure* of the syllable: this is not a simple sequence of phonemes but instead possesses a hierarchical organization. For example, the syllable 'stick' is composed of two parts, the 'onset' /st/ and the 'rhyme' /ik/. This latter section is itself subdivided into a 'peak' /i/ and a 'coda' /k/. It has been possible to demonstrate the psychological reality of this hierarchical organization experimentally (Treiman, 1986) and, interestingly, the same psychological reality has been found in the processing of written language (Treiman and Chafetz, 1987).
- Second, interest in the syllable has led to a closer study of *prosody*. In speech, syllables differ in stress, pitch and duration, and it is clear that this prosodic organization plays a role in the segmentation of utterances, in word identification, and in the higher-level syntactic and semantic analysis of sentences (Grosjean and Gee, 1987).

Other observations, however, suggest that we should consider the *word* itself as the basic perceptual unit. Foss and Swinney (1973), working with lists of disyllabic words, found that while detection time is shorter for the initial syllable than for the initial phoneme, it is shorter still for the word itself! This effect becomes more marked (Morton and Long, 1976) the more predictable the word is in context. Furthermore, Marslen-Wilson (1984) has observed that response times shorten as the phoneme is moved from the first to the second and then to the third syllable of the word.

It is even possible that the perceptual units on which processing is performed are sometimes larger than the word. Grosjean and Gee (1987) have suggested that analysis is performed on the *prosodic units* which are organized around stressed syllables and generally include one or more function words connected with the central word (for example, the sentence 'John / has been avidly / reading / the latest / news / from home' contains six of these units).

However, phonemes are also detected in pseudo-words (which cannot, by definition, be present in memory). What all these observations finally suggest is, rather, the idea of *parallel processing* taking place at different levels. Either of these levels (depending on the conditions of the task, the strategies of the subject, the structure of the language, etc.) then provides the information necessary for detection.

5. This effect, however, is not observed amongst English subjects (Cutler, Mehler, Norris and Segui, 1986). The authors attribute this fact to the different syllable structure of French and English, and suggest that a number of segmentation strategies may be applied in parallel.

Conclusion

The issue of speech perception poses many other unresolved problems. We can think of it as mobilizing at least three processing levels:

1. A first analysis of the acoustic signal is performed at the purely *auditory* level – that is to say, independently of linguistic knowledge. The sensory cues on which this analysis is based are manifold, partially redundant or mutually substitutable, and vary considerably depending on context. The details of this processing clearly do not fall into the domain of the psycholinguist, and we have already seen that the hypothesis of specialized detectors, pre-adapted to language perception, has had to be abandoned. However, research in this field is significant in determining the exact nature of the *output* – that is to say, of the phonetic representation which is the task of the other, specifically psycholinguistic, levels of processing.

2. A second level of processing then interprets the pattern of phonetic features which results from the first processing level in the form of a pre-lexical *phonological* representation. It is at this level that the phonological constraints of the language would have a role to play.[6] This representation is generally thought of as a sequence of phonemes, but, as we have seen, the hypothesis of a syllable-based representation may be closer to the truth.

3. Finally, the third level is that of the identification of the word – that is to say, the level of lexical access, to which we shall turn in the next section.

These three processing levels seem to function in parallel and (in the case of the last two, at least) interactively.[7] In the next section (pp. 54–56) we shall see that this interaction also appears in connection with higher-level processing.

To conclude: can we think of speech perception as a specific mode of perception which functions by means of its own, specific mechanisms? It is possible that the human brain contains specialized equipment for the analysis of the acoustic signal, specific to language functioning and forming part of the genetic heritage of the species. However, as we have seen, this hypothesis remains problematic. The uniqueness of verbal perception derives

---

6. This is clearest in the case of permissible or impermissible sequences. Thus if the sequence /bænkɛt/ is presented to one ear and the sequence /lænkɛt/ to the other, then (English-speaking) subjects hear 'blanket', not 'lbanket', the word-initial sequence /lb/ being prohibited in English. This is true even if the /l/ is heard 0.15 seconds before the /b/. In contrast, if the words 'tass' and 'tack' are presented, subjects are equally likely to hear 'task' or 'tacks', since both the sequences /sk/ and /ks/ are permitted in word-final position (Cutting, 1976).

7. We should also note that the fact that the acoustico-phonetic cues can be used at different levels contradicts a purely 'modular' conception of the processing levels. For example, in English an aspirated occlusive [t^H] is interpreted, at the phonological level, as the phoneme /t/, while the information concerning the aspiration is retained to indicate, at the lexical processing level, that the phoneme is in word-initial position.

more from its complexity than from its nature. It is characterized on the one hand by its multiple processing levels and, on the other, by the importance of processes of the 'top–down' variety. Having said that, there is currently no justification for claiming that language mobilizes any cognitive processes which cannot be found in other fields of activity.

Lexical access

The internal lexicon

The ability to recognize or produce a word presupposes that it has been recorded in memory. In other words, each speaker of the language possesses an *internal lexicon*, a set of representations corresponding to the meaningful units of the language. As a first approximation we can think of this lexicon in terms of a dictionary – that is to say, as an ordered list of 'lexical entries' each of which contains the set of information necessary to identify, understand and use the associated unit.

Each lexical entry must be characterized by at least three types of information:

(i)   the phonological form of the word (the acoustic, articulatory and possibly the written form);
(ii) its syntactic and morphological properties: category (noun, verb, adjective, etc.), gender, number, etc., which define the way in which it can be used in a sentence;
(iii) its meaning and possibly its situation-dependent conditions of use (familiar, vulgar, etc.).

The numerous works which have focused on the study of the internal lexicon over the last fifteen years have approached the issue in two different ways. Some have been primarily interested in lexical access – that is to say, in the mechanisms involved in the retrieval of words from memory for their recognition or production. Others have been concerned with the mental representation of the *meanings* (psychological semantics) and their organization in memory (semantic memory). Although the two questions are clearly linked, the work associated with them has developed relatively independently. We shall delay our study of the second body of work until the next chapter. Here we shall consider only the first aspect, which is more directly concerned with the problems of speech perception.

The study of lexical access must answer two types of question:

(a) The first concerns the *nature* of the internal lexicon: What units are represented in it? How are they classified and how are they interrelated?

(b) The second bears on the *processes* involved in accessing the lexicon: should we consider them as passive (automatic activation of a representation in memory) or active (search of the lexicon, systematic or otherwise)? Further, are we dealing with an independent mechanism which proceeds autonomously, or is it in a state of interdependence with other processes which are progressing simultaneously at different levels?

Introspection is of no help in tackling these problems. Lexical access is a very rapid process which progresses unconsciously.[8] Researchers have therefore turned to 'real-time' ('on-line') techniques aimed at observing these processes as they occur.

One frequently used method is the *lexical decision* task. In such tasks, subjects must quickly decide whether the presented stimulus (a sequence of letters) constitutes a word or not. Researchers may also ask for an *identification* of the word, either in order to measure the time taken to repeat the presented word (which presupposes access to its phonological representation in memory) or in order to study the errors made when the stimulus is presented rapidly (using a tachistoscope) or partially masked (by a sound or a visual mask). The technique of 'shadowing' primarily allows researchers to observe the effects of context on this identification. Finally, a third type of task requires the *detection* either of a previously specified phoneme or word, or of a certain word property (for example, subjects are asked to press a button as soon as they hear a word which rhymes with another given word or belongs to a certain category, etc.). In contrast to what was previously believed, these different techniques are not equivalent. In particular, it has been possible to show (for example, Jakimik, Cole and Rudnicki, 1985) that lexical decision involves processes at a later stage (that is to say, appearing *after* lexical access) than is the case with naming tasks.

The two basic phenomena

Ever since the first work on lexical access was undertaken, it has been possible to demonstrate the existence of two very general phenomena: the frequency effect and the priming effect.

I. The *frequency* of use of the different words of the language is clearly extremely unequal. The first works to appear in the field of psycholinguistics – which were inspired by information theory and therefore focused on the

8. Except in certain cases such as the 'tip of the tongue' phenomenon, the study of which has provided some interesting clues about the way words are represented in memory (Brown and McNeill, 1966).

statistical properties of language – concentrated on this fact, and revealed a certain number of phenomena associated with word frequency.

We should not, of course, forget that this frequency of use can be defined only very approximately. It is heavily dependent on the social, cultural and professional environment of the subjects, their habitual type of conversation or reading, etc.[9] However, it is possible to determine in general terms a certain, average hierarchy of verbal frequencies for the speakers of a given language. Current American studies mostly use the Kucera and Francis list, published in 1967, which was compiled on the basis of a corpus of slightly more than a million words.

Frequency observations based on sufficiently large, homogeneous corpora have revealed a number of remarkable similarities. For example, Zipf's Law states that if words are classified in order of decreasing frequency, the product $f \times r$ obtained by multiplying the frequency of a word by its rank in the classification is approximately constant, which corresponds to an optimum organization of code (maximum information at the least average cost). We can also note that the most frequent words also tend to be the shortest, etc.

However, the most interesting phenomenon from the psycholinguistic point of view links the frequency of a word to the speed with which it is accessed. As early as 1951, Howes and Solomon observed that the identification threshold of a word at a tachistoscope falls as its frequency increases (in accordance with a law of the form $t = -k \log f$, k being a constant). The same effect has since been encountered in a wide variety of tasks such as the identification of noise-masked words, lexical decision, detection, naming tasks, etc. The phenomenon has been frequently proved: the more frequent a word is, the faster lexical access to it is performed.

II. The second main phenomenon is that of *semantic priming*. Access to a word is easier (and therefore faster) if the word is preceded by another word which is semantically associated with it. Clearly, this effect is maximized in cases of repetition (that is to say, when the word is preceded by itself). For example, Meyer and Schvaneveldt (1971) observed that the word 'doctor' is identified more quickly in a lexical decision task if it is preceded by the word 'nurse' than the word 'bread'. In contrast, the word 'bread' itself facilitates identification of the word 'butter'.

The priming phenomenon should not be confused with anticipation effects which cause a word to be identified more quickly in a sentence or text, the more likely its occurrence is in the context. In fact, the material used in the cited experiments generally consists of simple lists of words, and

9. Fraisse (1963) has found that speed of access correlates more highly with *familiarity* (judged by the subjects themselves) than with frequency.

we are therefore dealing with an automatic phenomenon which simply involves the between-word relations in the lexicon. Like the frequency effect, the priming effect has been observed in a great variety of experimental tasks.

Although these two phenomena are well attested, their theoretical interpretation can give rise, as we shall see, to very different conceptions.

What does the lexicon contain?

A considerable body of work has been devoted to investigating the *contents* of the internal lexicon.[10] At first sight, the question appears simple: the lexicon contains the words of the language. But what is a word? This concept raises a number of problems.

I. First of all, from a linguistic point of view, the elementary unit of meaning is not the word but the *morpheme*. Does our internal lexicon contain all the words in the language or simply the morphemes which form them and can be combined in many different ways (in accordance with rules learned along with the lexicon)? Thus, are all the forms of a verb stored in memory, or only the root of the verb together with the endings which can be used with a large number of other verbs? The same problem arises in connection with prefixes, suffixes, compound words, etc.

Some of the data suggest that there is indeed a deconstruction into morphemes prior to lexical access. Thus the various (regular) forms of a verb exert the same effect of mutual facilitation that occurs when the same form is repeated (Stanners *et al.*, 1979). This suggests that all the forms are recorded and recognized as one and the same word. An ingenious experiment conducted by Taft and Forster (1975) provides analogous results in connection with words containing prefixes.

If we take, for example, the words 'rejuvenate' and 'repertoire', we see that the first word is formed using the prefix 're', whereas the second is not. Now, if in a task of lexical decision we present subjects with real roots ('juvenate') and pseudo-roots ('pertoire'), decision is faster in the second case than in the first. This is because the first morpheme ('juvenate') figures in the internal lexicon, and when subjects find it they then have to check whether or not it can be used on its own. In the case of 'pertoire', which is not present in the lexicon, the decision is quicker.

This effect disappears, however, if the list of presented words, instead of containing only compound words (or pseudo-compounds), consists mainly of simple words (Rubin *et al.*, 1979). Depending on the conditions of the task,

10. We can give only a brief summary here. For a more detailed review, see Butterworth (1983*b*).

subjects can either deconstruct the word into its constituent morphemes or access the compound word directly. The internal lexicon would thus appear to contain *both* compound words *and* morphemes.

To summarize: the experimental data, far from enabling us to choose one of the two hypotheses, invite us to retain both. This doubtless impairs economy of storage and the elegance of the system, but has the advantage of improving its effectiveness.

II. A second problem is that of *polysemic words*. Does a word like 'bank' possess two lexical entries (bank$_1$ = financial institution, and bank$_2$ = riverside), access to which is determined by context (or, if context is inconclusive, by frequency of use)? Or do we hold a single word in memory, whose meaning is selected *after* lexical access has occurred? The experimental data seem to support the latter hypothesis.

Amongst others, an experiment performed by Swinney (1979) provides proof of this. Subjects were asked to listen to a sentence containing an ambiguous word the interpretation of which was imposed by the context. At the same time they were visually presented with a word stimulus which was semantically associated with one or other of the two possible meanings of the ambiguous word in a lexical decision task. If the stimulus was presented at exactly the same time as the ambiguous word, the same facilitation (priming) effect was noticed for both meanings – and that irrespective of the fact that the context authorized only one of those meanings. If the stimulus was presented a little later (1.5 s), only the meaning corresponding to the context was primed. The polysemic word would thus appear to have only one entry in the internal lexicon. Initially all its possible meanings seem to be activated, and it is only later that the meaning which corresponds to the context is selected.

We should point out, however, that Swinney's results (often cited in support of the modular conception of lexical access) have not always been replicated. We shall return to this point later (p. 58).

III. Finally, *idiomatic expressions* ('kick the bucket', 'pull someone's leg', etc.) seem to be recorded directly in the lexicon (Swinney and Cutler, 1979). They thus constitute units which are stored in the same way as words.

One or more lexicons?

So far we have spoken of *the* internal lexicon. But should we think in terms of one lexicon, or more than one?

1. First, we should ask ourselves whether *function words* (articles, pronouns, prepositions, conjunctions, etc.) are recorded in the same way, and

in the same lexicon, as 'semantic' words (or 'content words' such as nouns, verbs or adjectives). In fact, function words possess particular properties. First, their lexical access does not seem to conform to the frequency effect (Bradley, quoted in Butterworth, 1983b). Second, in certain cases of aphasia, they can result in a selective deficiency (Morton, 1982). This problem is interesting but has, as yet, been little studied. Moreover, the notion of 'function word' covers a very heterogeneous set of items.

2. Should we think in terms of a common lexicon used in both spoken and *written language*? Doubtless, during the process of learning to read, identification of a written word passes through a stage of phonological 'recoding'. However, skilled readers are able to identify the written form of a word directly. There would thus seem to be a second internal lexicon, or at least a second access code for the lexicon, in which the lexical entries are presented in their written form. Numerous studies concerning this subject[11] suggest that we should consider the idea of dual access (visual and phonological). Here the two processes would operate in parallel, with phonological recoding playing a role either during the period of storage in working memory (in particular when the material requires more extended processing) or when the material is difficult or unfamiliar.

3. Finally, we can think (like Morton, 1982) of *production* and *comprehension* as making use of two distinct lexical systems. This hypothesis is primarily founded on the classic distinction between expressive (or Broca's) and receptive (or Wernicke's) aphasias. However, the clinical description of these aphasias is complex and involves processes other than lexical access. Furthermore, the available experimental data are very meagre in this regard.

The mechanisms of lexical access

We now have to consider the *processes* by means of which lexical access is performed – that is to say, the processes which enable us to proceed from a visual or auditory stimulus and find a word in memory together with the information associated with it.

We can think of these processes in two ways. The first consists in considering access to the lexicon in terms of the dictionary consultation model where, to look up a word, we thumb through the volume, find the page which probably contains the word, and then run through the list of terms until we have found the required word. This active sequential search process largely corresponds to the model proposed by Forster. A different hypothesis holds that there is no search, but that the information gathered by

11. For a detailed review of this work, see McCusker *et al.* (1981). See also a recent criticism of these works by Van Orden *et al.* (1990).

the system automatically activates words (or, more precisely, word-producing mechanisms or 'logogens'). In this hypothesis, as soon as a certain activation threshold has been reached, the 'logogen' becomes active and the word is produced or identified, rather as a glass starts to resonate when a musical instrument in its vicinity produces a particular note at a particular pitch. This process of passive activation is the one suggested in Morton's model; it may also be found (in slightly different forms) in Marslen-Wilson and in Ellman and McClelland's connectionist model. We shall now examine these different models in greater detail.

Forster's model: sequential search

For Forster (1976) the internal lexicon can be represented as a system of 'files' (Figure 3.4): a master file containing the set of information (syntactic, semantic, morphological) relating to each word, and three peripheral files containing 'pointers' to the master file. The first of these peripheral files contains the 'entries' corresponding to the written form of words (and is used in written language processing), the second contains the phonological form (and is used in speech perception); while the third is organized along syntactico-semantic lines (and is used in speech production).

How are these peripheral files organized? The answer is as distinct 'bins' in which the words are classified in accordance with their frequency. Listeners use sensory information (acoustic, for example) to limit their search to a particular 'bin' which they work through until they have found the word corresponding to what they have perceived. A pointer is then used to access the master file which contains information concerning the word, its association with other words, etc. At this point the search is completed. However, if the stimulus does not correspond to any word contained in the

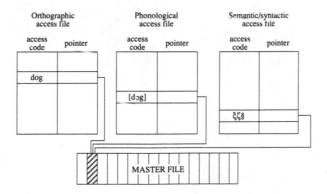

Figure 3.4 The organization of the internal lexicon (based on Forster, 1976, p. 268)

file, the search has to be continued right through to the end of the bin before this fact becomes known. All this explains, on the one hand, the effect of frequency on access time (the most frequent words are found at the very start of the search) and, on the other, the longer response times observed for non-words than for words (since the whole list must be searched before a response is possible).

The subdivision of the peripheral files into 'bins' clearly has the role of obviating the need to search through the entire lexicon each time a word is encountered. But on what basis is this subdivision effected? Certain experimental results (Taft and Forster, 1976) suggest that access is performed on the basis of the initial syllable of the word.

Forster's model is supported by some weighty experimental data and enables us to account for a large number of observations. However, it does not easily allow for the integration of the phenomenon of semantic priming, which is not easily accounted for in terms of a simple ordered search process. Moreover, the model implies a *modular* conception of language processing, with lexical processing being thought of as independent of the other levels (syntactic and semantic). In effect, Forster considers that the 'linguistic processor' consists of a series of autonomous processors, each of which receives the product of the preceding processor, deals with it and transfers the results to the next processor (Forster, 1979: see Figure 3.5).

The lexical processor receives the results of the phonological analysis, identifies the words in its file and transfers the result to the syntactic processor. As soon as this has an adequate number of words at its disposal, it elaborates a structure for the sentence and transfers it to the message

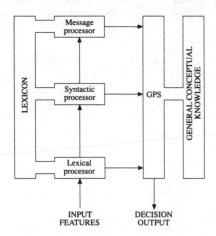

Figure 3.5 Model of language processing (based on Forster, 1979, p. 34)

processor which works out the meaning of the sentence. At the same time, each of these three processors also transmits the results of its operations to a 'general problem-solver' (GPS) which uses the general knowledge stored in memory to decide on the final (conscious) result of the interpretation, but cannot intervene in the functioning of the specialized processors. The specialized processors function automatically, with only the GPS functioning in a controlled way.

In this model, the effects of context can intervene only at the level of controlled processes (that is to say, in the 'general problem-solver'). We shall return to this issue later.

Morton's model: logogen activation

The model proposed by Morton (1979, 1982) differs substantially from the model described above.[12] It postulates a system of *logogens*, mechanisms whose effect is to produce the conscious representation of a word. For every word in the lexicon there is a corresponding logogen.

The logogens are activated by the information provided by the system. This information can be not only auditory or visual but also linked to the linguistic context, the situation or the subject's general knowledge. All this information is supplied simultaneously and the logogen is triggered when it reaches a certain level of activation and the word becomes available (see Figure 3.6). Following this, the logogen returns to its initial state only gradually, remaining partially activated for a while. This makes it possible to explain both the frequency effect (a frequently used logogen is never fully

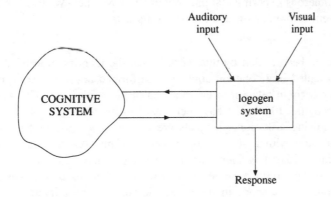

Figure 3.6 Morton's model (first version) (based on Morton, 1983, p. 479)

12. Morton's model has developed considerably since its original formulation. The 1982 article traces this development in detail.

deactivated and is therefore triggered more quickly) and the priming effect (the activation of a logogen entails the partial activation of others which are 'close' to it).

We can see that the model proposed by Morton, in contrast to Forster's, implies a continuous interaction between all the information sources and all the processing levels. Moreover, the activation of the logogens is thought of as a passive process.

The model presented in Figure 3.6 is merely a highly simplified outline. In fact, Morton has gradually increased its complexity and has distinguished between different logogen systems for words presented orally or in writing, for reception and production. It is also necessary to postulate a direct translation (without logogen mediation) between phonemes and graphemes, and between acoustic data and articulatory responses in order to account for the possibility of reproducing non-words. Figure 3.7 gives an idea of this model.

One interesting aspect of this model is that it allows us to account for the various language difficulties which are associated with cerebral lesions in terms of a functional disruption of one or other of the pathways which are envisaged by the model (Morton, 1982).

The work of Marslen-Wilson and the cohort model

The importance of contextual effects and the interactive character of the processes mobilized during lexical access have recently been brought to light by the work of Marslen-Wilson and colleagues (Marslen-Wilson and Tyler, 1980; Marslen-Wilson, 1984).

Of the numerous experimental data obtained by Marslen-Wilson, we shall simply present a number of significant results here.

I. One point to be revealed by this work is that the identification of a word which is presented in a coherent context is performed not only very quickly but also *very early* in relation to the duration of the word itself. The word is generally recognized before it has been heard in its entirety.

In a shadowing task, some subjects are able to repeat the text to which they are listening with a shift of only some 250 ms. A comparable mean response time (275 ms) is found when the subjects have to detect a word (previously specified) in a sentence which is spoken to them. Now, the average duration of a word in these experiments is approximately 370 to 400 ms. This means that when subjects make their response they can have heard only the first two or three phonemes.

II. This word identification depends on the syntactic and semantic context. Systematic variation of the syntactic and/or semantic information available

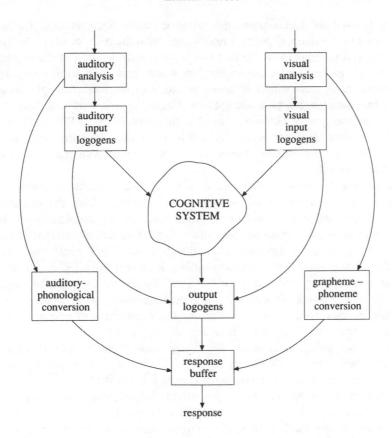

Figure 3.7 Elaborated form of Morton's model (based on Morton, 1983, p. 480)

to the subject leads to a consequent variability in the time required for identification.

If, instead of presenting the word in a normal sentence, the researcher presents subjects with disordered word sequences, the mean response time rises from 275 to 360 ms. In meaningless but syntactically correct sentences, however, the mean response time is only 336 ms. Moreover, the facilitation effect (both in normal sentences and, to a lesser extent, in sentences which are grammatical only) increases regularly as the target word is moved towards the end of the sentence. This facilitation effect also occurs at the beginning of a sentence if this sentence is preceded by another which provides it with a coherent context.

III. Finally, the recognition of a word is linked to the composition of the lexicon itself. The word is identified as soon as the subject has gathered enough information to be able to distinguish it from other possible words.

Marslen-Wilson demonstrates this using a lexical decision task. Let us take an English example, the two non-words 'sthoidik and 'trenker'. In the first case, it is possible to decide that this is not a word as soon as the second phoneme is reached (there are no English words beginning with 'sth-'). In the second case, however, it is necessary to wait until the fifth phoneme before this decision can be made (several English words start with 'tren-'). By varying the type of non-words used in this way, Marslen-Wilson shows that the response time remains the same if it is measured from the moment at which there are no further words in the lexicon corresponding to the available information.

To account for these results, Marslen-Wilson – in contrast to Forster – proposes an *interactive* model of language processing. From the moment when the perception of a sentence commences, all the processing levels (phonological, lexical, syntactic, semantic) start to function in parallel. These diverse levels of processing interact – that is to say, each level (with the probable exception of the acoustico-phonetic level) is affected by the information arriving, not just from the immediately lower level, but also from the higher levels. This allows optimum functioning of the system. The message is interpreted as soon as the available information (whatever its source) permits this to be done in safety.

As far as lexical access is concerned (this time in contrast to Morton's model), words are identified not by the selective activation of a single logogen but by a process of progressive *elimination*. At the start of a word, a 'cohort' of words compatible with the available information (acoustic as well as contextual) is evoked. As the volume of available information increases, the number of possible 'candidates' is reduced until only one possible word is left (as we have seen, this can happen very quickly). This is the word selected.

In a more recent version of his theory, Marslen-Wilson (1987) has decided to modify this conception slightly to take account of a variety of objections. First of all, activation is no longer an all-or-nothing process but is instead in a state of continual evolution. This makes it possible to account for the frequency effect and the identification of mispronounced words (otherwise, for example, 'cigarette' pronounced as 'shigarette' would have to be eliminated from the cohort at the very outset). Second, the context effect should not lead to the recognition of words which are absent or prevent the identification of unexpected or inappropriate words. It thus appears correct to accord priority to the bottom–up processes, which alone can lead to the activation of words, and an initial selection of possible candidates. The context effects would then apply only to the results of these processes and would conclude selection and ensure semantic integration.

The TRACE model

The TRACE model proposed by Ellman and McClelland (1986) was inspired directly by the Marslen-Wilson model. It is viewed, however, from a connectionist perspective. The functioning of this model is completely interactive – that is to say, all the processing levels (phonetic, phonological, lexical) are in a state of constant interaction. Each level is represented by a network of nodes which function as detectors[13] (of phonetic features, phonemes and words). The internodal connections are inhibitory within a level and excitatory between levels, and bidirectional in both cases. Thus the nodes corresponding to the phonemes /k/ and /æ/ activate the node corresponding to 'cat' which, in its turn, excites the nodes for the phonemes /k/, /æ/ and /t/. At the same time, activation of the /æ/ node inhibits the /ʌ/ node and thus impairs activation of 'cut'. Excitations and inhibitions develop across time in a massively parallel way. What is interesting about this model is its ability to account for word identification even in the case of a distorted or incomplete input. It accounts elegantly for the majority of the data concerning speech perception.

Automatic processes and controlled processes

Active search or automatic activation; modular or interactive processing – we do not necessarily have to choose between these alternatives. In fact, there is a body of experimental data which suggests that two different types of process are involved in lexical access (as is the case, more generally, in all cognitive activity): *automatic* processes on the one hand, and *controlled* processes on the other (see above, p. 28).

An experiment conducted by Neely (1977) successfully demonstrates the existence of these two types of process in a lexical decision task in which he systematically compares the effects of two factors: semantic priming, on the one hand, and the subject's conscious expectations, on the other. The subjects are told that when they are presented with the word 'bird', the target word which accompanies it will generally be the name of a bird. However, if they are presented with 'body', the target word will designate a part of a building (for example, 'door'), and if they are presented with 'building', the target word will refer to a part of the body ('arm', for example). In one-third of the cases the target word does not correspond to the subjects' expectations. Moreover, the time separating the prime word from the target word can vary between 250 and 700 ms. The results are very clear. With delays at their shortest (250 ms), only the semantic priming effect is observed. From 400 ms onwards, however, a progressive facilitation appears for the words which correspond to the subjects' expectations, whereas the

---

13. In so far as they can result from a learning process, these 'detectors' do not fall under the criticisms to innate detectors, which have been developed above.

response time lengthens for those which are semantically primed but do not correspond to expectations. Neely concludes from this that two processes exist: an automatic activation when the word is presented and a controlled attentional process which can enhance or inhibit this activation and is performed more slowly.

Swinney's (1979) experiment, cited above, supports this conclusion. The different meanings of an ambiguous word are activated automatically, but the meanings which do not correspond to the context are suppressed at a second stage by a controlled process. This latter effect appears after approximately 200 ms (Tanenhaus *et al.*, 1979).

Thus contextual effects would derive from a slower, controlled processing which would occur after lexical access. As for lexical access, this would be performed automatically as a function of the sensory data alone.

The existence of certain experimental data, however, suggests that this distinction is not so clear-cut as we have just described it. These data relate primarily to the activation of the meaning of an ambiguous word. Although it is clear that Swinney's results have been substantiated by a large number of researchers, others have succeeded in showing that a strongly biased context leads to the selective activation of only one of the two possible meanings at the time when the word appears (Tabossi, 1988; Simpson and Krueger, 1991). Moreover, electroencephalographic recordings have shown that the two meanings of the word give rise to different profiles (Van Petten and Kutas, 1987).[14]

In conclusion, even if lexical access is essentially the result of automatic processes and is directly activated by the sensory input, the data available to us do not justify the claim that this automation is totally unresponsive to some kind of top–down influences.

Conclusion

Despite the large volume of work directed at the problem of lexical access over the past fifteen years, we are still far from being in a position to give a simple, decisive answer to the questions it raises.

It appears that we should be wary of constructing too simple an idea of the internal lexicon: one of a rationally and economically organized system, comparable to a well-ordered dictionary or to the lexical 'knowledge base' of an information system. First, because the internal lexicon is the product of individual history and a succession of individual acquisitions resulting from the vagaries of experience. Second, because the system appears to be founded not on a principle of economy but rather on one of effectiveness,

14. For a critical review of studies of this problem, see Simpson (1984); for a number of more recent references, see Simpson and Krueger (1991).

with redundancies and multiple access pathways which assure flexible adaptation and functional reliability. We shall encounter this problem of the organization of the lexicon at another level (that of meaning) in the next chapter.

As far as the procedures for access are concerned, we are currently unable to decide conclusively between the various models which have been proposed. There is general agreement that much of the processing of the verbal message is based on procedures of the 'top–down' type. However, the problem is to decide the point at which they become operative. As we have seen, there is a large number of arguments in favour of a modular conception of the 'lexical component'. This perspective views access to the lexicon as an autonomous process which is activated by the sensory data alone, with post-access procedures being invoked later to perform a context-dependent selection. However, it is impossible to ignore the body of data which seems to point to the early effect of contextual influences. No doubt it would be possible to defend the modular theory by claiming that we are still dealing with post-access procedures which simply act more quickly than was originally believed. However, adopting this position makes it difficult to resolve this debate empirically.

For the moment it would seem prudent to conclude that lexical processing is only partially autonomous, and not to exclude the possibility that a top–down control may intervene under certain circumstances (which still largely remain to be defined). The connectionist models (McClelland, 1987) will probably provide some interesting ideas here.

However this may be, the accessing of a word cannot be thought of independently of the accessing of its *meaning*. Whether at the level of contextual effects or at that (possibly more elementary) of priming phenomena, the verbal signal cannot be thought of as a simple visual or auditory 'pattern' which is first identified as such in order to be interpreted at a later stage. Its meaning is an integral part of it. It is to this subject that we shall turn next.

Recommended reading

Further information on the phonetic problems approached at the beginning of this chapter may be found in the (already cited) work by Akmajian *et al.* (1990).

Besides the articles cited in this chapter, a special edition of *Cognition* entitled 'Spoken word recognition' (Tyler and Frauenfelder, 1987) contains a collection of articles which give a good idea of the current state of problems and theories.

An exhaustive theoretical examination of the questions of lexical access may be found in Forster (1976), Morton (1982) and Marslen-Wilson (1987; see also Marslen-Wilson and Tyler, 1980). The collective work edited by Marslen-Wilson (1989) offers a broad panorama of current research.

CHAPTER 4

From Words to Meaning: Lexical Semantics

The word is a single entity with a double face: a signifying face (a certain combination of phonemes or letters) and a signified face (the meaning). The studies of lexical access we have just discussed were concerned with approaching the internal lexicon through the first of these faces, by identifying a perceptual 'pattern' as a signifying unit. We shall now take a look at the other approach, examining studies (relatively independent of the above) which concentrate on meaning.

Two principal questions can be raised here:

(a) What is the *nature* of lexical meanings? In other words, how is the sense of a word represented in the mind? This is a problem of *psychological semantics*.
(b) How are these meanings organized in memory? This is the question which studies of *semantic memory* attempt to resolve.

These studies are relatively recent (they began to develop in the early 1970s). Before investigating them, we shall be better placed to understand their theoretical background if we first examine what we understand by 'the meaning of a word'.

The problems of meaning

First, let us distinguish between *meaning* and *reference*. A word can refer to (that is to say, designate) an object, but we cannot conflate its meaning with that object or with its relation to that object. This is because, on the one hand, while retaining the same meaning it can refer to innumerable other objects; and, on the other, because two different expressions can both refer to the same object while they nevertheless have different meanings. A famous example of this is given by Frege: 'morning star' and 'evening star' both refer to the planet Venus, while they clearly have different meanings.[1] And what might words like 'because' or 'after' refer to? The meaning of a word thus appears to be an abstract reality, different in nature from the particular objects to which it can be applied. How should we define it?

I. As Saussure (1916) points out, a linguistic sign can take on its value only in relation to the other signs of the language. A language's set of signs forms a system in which differences between signifiers correspond to differences between the signified. The 'concept' which represents the signified correspondent of a word can be defined only in terms of its *difference* from the other possible signified objects. A classic example of this is that the English word 'blue' can designate a particular colour only by virtue of the existence of the words 'violet', 'green', etc. Other languages may divide the colour spectrum differently.

We may, therefore, think of defining the meaning of a word as the set of features which distinguish it from the meanings of the other words in the language. This idea forms the basis for the *componential* theory of meaning.

This conception (introduced by Hjelmslev and developed by linguists like Katz and Fodor, Weinreich, Bierwisch, etc.) has been influenced by an approach which was successfully employed in the field of phonology. As we have already seen (p. 17), a phoneme can be defined as the set of 'phonetic features' through which it differs from the other phonemes of the system. In the same way, the pair 'man'/'woman' is differentiated by the feature [± male]; similarly with the pair 'boy'/'girl'. These two pairs then differ from each other by the feature [± adult], etc. We can thus envisage the possibility of defining the meanings of all the words of the language in terms of a finite number of elementary 'semantic features' (or 'semes').

This linguistic approach coincides with the idea advanced by some philosophers (Locke, Leibnitz, etc.) that all the concepts of human thought can be defined in terms of a combination of elementary and irreducible ideas.

II. This approach, however, presupposes a system of clearly defined and precisely delimited concepts. In reality this is the case only for scientific or technical concepts, while the concepts of natural thought are far from

1. 'The evening star is the same star as the morning star' does not mean the same as 'the evening star is the same star as the evening star'.

possessing this degree of rigour. They are 'vague' notions whose limits are often ill-defined and which correspond more or less precisely to real objects.

The limits of a natural category are not clearly defined (for example, a table or a dresser are articles of furniture, but what about a bedside lamp or a television?). Furthermore, the inclusion of an object in a category is not a clear-cut, all-or-nothing affair (a trout is 'more' a fish than a seahorse is, and 'to a certain extent' a whale can be regarded as a fish). Thus certain examples are more *typical* than others. According to Eleanor Rosch (1976), who has devoted a considerable volume of work to this aspect of natural thought, the mental representation of a concept is that of a privileged representative, the *prototype*, and inclusion in a category is determined by the degree of resemblance to this prototype.

III. A word evokes not only a concept but also the whole set of knowledge associated with that concept. Thus, for example, the word 'star' might bring to mind a whole range of knowledge (which, obviously, varies according to the individual) which could be astronomical, historical, literary, mythological and even anecdotal. We might, therefore, regard the meaning of a word as reflecting the set of *knowledge* associated with it.

The meaning of a word can thus be represented formally as a list of implications: if x is a man, then x is male, x is adult, etc. This is what the logician Carnap calls 'meaning postulates'. This approach has a twofold advantage over the componential conception of meaning. First, the list is not necessarily limited (this obviates the necessity of enumerating a set of properties which are not only necessary but also sufficient to define the concept). Secondly, the properties ('male', 'adult') do not have to be considered as irreducible units of meaning (and this obviates the thorny problem of having to decide which are the primitive 'concepts').

However, this also assumes that the meaning of a word forms an open, undefined set whose content varies between different individuals and different times. This is no longer a 'dictionary definition' but an encyclopaedia article (moreover, this encyclopaedia is in a state of permanent revision; every copy is different).

Moreover, a word also evokes – by virtue of the knowledge set associated with it – a set of representations, emotions, attitudes, which are not conceptual in nature. We are talking here of *connotations*, which can be purely individual but can also be common to a group of individuals, however large or small. Political, advertising and poetic discourse make much use of this. To what extent should the psycholinguistics of meaning take this phenomenon into account?

IV. Finally, let us consider whether the idea that there is a fixed meaning attached to a word may be only an illusion. The same word can be used in a variety of contexts, for diverse ends, and be endowed with very different values. So could it be that the meaning of a word is simply what it is used for, the *use* to which it is put in a specific context?

In this connection, Wittgenstein (1951) suggests that language is not a representation of reality but a tool for communication which is realized in a diversity of 'language-games' governed by tacit rules. If this is true, then the meaning of a word is relative to the 'language-game' in which it is used. *The meaning of a word is its use*, just as the 'meaning' of a playing card depends on the game – bridge, poker, rummy – being played at the time.

This notion of 'meaning as use' is the inspiration for the *procedural* conception of meaning, which regards the meaning of a word not as a mental 'content' evoked by the word but as a set of procedures which, depending on the context in which they are applied, can give rise to different 'meaning effects'.

In conclusion, we can see that while it may be easy to say that we do or do not know the meaning of a word, it is much less easy to state exactly what we understand by that. Are we talking about a set of semantic features? A prototypical representation? A network of knowledge? Or a set of procedures? As we shall see, psychological research has been engaged in exploring each one of these approaches.

Psychological semantics

Componential semantics

The first major studies in psychological semantics began to develop when linguistic theories of meaning were sufficiently elaborated to be able to provide them with a theoretical framework. It is the componential theory which has exerted the greatest, as well as the earliest, influence on psycholinguists.

H. Clark (1970) proposed a reinterpretation of the classic data concerning *word associations* in the light of the componential hypothesis: if the semantic structure of a word is conceived of as a set of 'features', the production of an association can be interpreted as an operation consisting of changing, adding, or deleting one or more of these features, the most simple case being the simple inversion of a feature (for example 'man' → 'woman', where the single feature [± male] is changed). This would explain the high frequency of contrastive associations.

Similarly, the *semantic distance* between two words can be defined in terms of the number of semantic features which differentiate them. Thus Miller (1969) shows that in a task of classifying a collection of words, the words are perceived as being closer (that is to say, are most frequently grouped in the same class) the more semantic features they have in common, in so far as linguistic analysis makes it possible to define such features. A similar method was used by Fillenbaum and Rapoport (1971) in the analysis of various semantic fields.

Although these first observations are in agreement with the componential theory, they do not constitute direct proof of it. A number of later studies attempted to establish more directly the psychological reality of semantic features.

I. In a series of experiments, H. Clark and colleagues (see Clark, 1974, for a complete presentation) sought to demonstrate that the *semantic complexity* of a word (that is to say, the number of features it possesses) has an effect on the comprehension time for a sentence in which it appears.

These studies are concerned mainly with antonymous pairs such as 'long'/'short'. One of these terms is 'marked' – that is to say, in relation to the other term it has an additional (negative) feature. The 'unmarked' term designates the whole of the dimension: we can say 'How long is it?' but not 'How short is it?', and the 'marked' term ('short' in this example) therefore carries the additional specification that it refers only to the lower end of the dimension. It was observed that 'short' required a slightly longer comprehension time than 'long' (in a reasoning task, for example).

Nevertheless, we must point out that the tasks used by Clark generally involved more complex processes than simple comprehension (sentence verification, reasoning, etc.). The differences observed might therefore concern not the structure of meaning, but its utilization. In tasks bearing more directly on comprehension, Kintsch (1974) found that semantic complexity had no effect on the length of time required to produce or complete a sentence on the basis of a word of varying complexity, to detect a phoneme following a word of greater or lesser complexity, or to recall sentences containing words of varying complexity. Most of the later studies (for a review, see Cutler, 1983) have also failed to find evidence of a semantic complexity effect either on lexical access or on the comprehension of sentences.

II. A second group of observations put forward to support the componential theory bears on children's *acquisition* of lexical meanings. In an important article, Eve Clark (1973) proposed interpreting the development of meanings in children's vocabulary as the successive acquisition of the various semantic features attached to the word.

Three types of data can be interpreted in this way:

• First, the 'overextensions' which are frequently observed in young children: a word is applied to a category of objects which is much larger than adult usage would permit (for example, 'dog' might be used for all four-legged animals) because, for the child, it does not yet comprise all the semantic features which would restrict its usage.

- Second, children can be observed to confuse – often surprisingly – terms which differ by only a single feature, the best-known example being that of children 3–4 years old observed by Donaldson and Balfour (1968) to confuse 'more' and 'less'. According to Eve Clark, these two terms have the feature [+ quantity] in common and differ only by the feature [± polarity], the latter feature not being acquired until the child is older. Analogous observations have been made in connection with other word pairs: 'same'/'different', 'before'/'after', 'come'/'go', etc. In all cases, it is the specific differentiating feature which appears to be learned later than the feature common to both words.
- Finally, the order in which certain terms are learned can be interpreted in the same way. The pair 'big'/'small', for example, is learned at a younger age than 'high'/'low' or 'long'/'short', which have the additional feature [+ vertical] or [+ horizontal].

Nevertheless, here again later observations have failed to confirm Eve Clark's theory. It has been possible to demonstrate that these observed 'overextensions' – besides their limited character – do not affect comprehension (the child who calls all four-legged animals 'dog', for example, has no problem when asked to point to a dog in a group of animals). As regards the experiments concerning relational terms, it has been demonstrated (for a review, see Carey, 1982) that the results obtained were due to non-linguistic 'response biases'. It is generally accepted today that the componential hypothesis, at least in its strictest form, cannot account for semantic development.

III. Finally, tasks of learning and memory can be called upon to provide evidence that meaning is broken down into its simplest units. For example, on comparing the studying time required to learn lists of sentences, Le Ny and colleagues (Le Ny *et al.*, 1973) reveal that this depends on semantic complexity (measured by the number of semantic features contained in the words); and, moreover (Cordier and Le Ny, 1975), that a facilitation of learning (positive transfer) can be observed when the subjects have already learned sentences containing semantic features in common with those to be studied.

Another experiment by Johnson-Laird, Gibbs and de Mowbray (1978) also brings to light evidence of the psychological reality of semantic features. In a list of words, the subjects have to find those which belong to a certain category (for example, consumable solids). They are then asked to recall as many words as possible from the list. Words corresponding to the category (e.g. 'bread') are recalled best, while words which have a semantic feature in common with the category (e.g. consumable liquids like 'beer' or non-consumable solids like 'coal') are better recalled than those with no semantic feature in common (e.g. 'petrol').

However, it can be argued that the decomposition into features does not arise from the simple process of comprehension, but is induced by the particular task in question, and by the subject's strategies in accomplishing this task. In a simple recall test, Kintsch (1974) found no differences in subjects' recall of sentences of varying semantic complexity.

IV. In conclusion, while the componential hypothesis is attractive (and has at least provided the inspiration for the first works on meaning), the experimental data on which it rests have not, in the final analysis, been sufficiently probing. It has, without doubt, been possible to bring to light evidence, in certain cases, of a decomposition of meaning into its simplest units, but this decomposition appears to be linked more to the tasks used (verification procedures, learning strategies) than to the process of comprehension itself. There can be no doubt that the human mind is capable of performing the task of analyzing its representations, but there is no reason to believe that this analysis will already have been fully prepared in the form of a set of elementary units within the representation itself.

We should add that the componential analysis can be applied satisfactorily only in certain well-defined semantic domains. In many cases, it is difficult to define the elementary 'features' which distinguish the meaning of any one word from that of similar words: for example, if the feature [± male] differentiates between 'horse' and 'mare', what are the *semantic* features which differentiate 'horse' from 'donkey'? And are the features by which concrete nouns are defined the same in nature as those which constitute the meaning of function words (articles, conjunctions, etc.)?

The propositional conception

In order to avoid the difficulties of the componential approach, Kintsch (1974) proposes a psychological conception of meaning which renounces the idea of decomposition into elementary features and defines the meaning of a word as a list of properties.

The basic semantic unit is no longer regarded as a semantic feature (or elementary concept), but as a *proposition*. A proposition is a relation (or *predicate*) concerning one or more terms (or *arguments*) which can be notated P (a, b, c ...). The predicate can have a single argument:

the dog barks: BARK (dog)

or several:

Mother bakes a cake in the oven: BAKE (mother, cake, oven).

Moreover, propositions can serve as arguments for other propositions:

The stars are bright because of the clear night: BECAUSE (BRIGHT (stars),
CLEAR (night)).

The meaning of a word can thus be represented in the form of a list of
propositions, each term of which refers, in its turn, to a new list, and so on.
This list represents the complete set of knowledge associated with the word.
To recall a distinction made above, Kintsch thinks of the representation of
meaning in memory in terms of an encyclopaedic rather than a dictionary
model.

As can be seen, the same propositional format can be used to describe the
meanings of words and sentences. But equally, it allows us to account for
textual organization (we shall return to this in Chapter 7).

What particularly interested Kintsch were the problems of text
comprehension, and most of the experimental data he relied on were
intended to establish the psychological validity of the idea of propositions.
As a result his account of lexical meanings remains largely speculative,
based on a theoretical and, as we have seen, experimental critique of the
componential theory.

As we shall see, this type of approach has inspired many of the current
models of semantic memory. The principal criticism which can be levelled at
it is that it ignores the specifically *linguistic* aspects of meaning. By
identifying lexical organization with the organization of the subject's
'knowledge base', this approach sees the word as a label which is applied to
a certain conceptual content, and neglects the relations between the word and
other units of the language system.

Moreover, we shall see in the next chapter that the propositional
conception of meaning suffers from certain inadequacies at sentence (and
discourse) level.

The prototype approach

As we noted above, the 'concepts' referred to by the words of a natural
language do not have the precise and well-defined character of scientific
concepts. The categories they define are fuzzy, and the boundaries of
category membership are fluid.

A large body of experimental data has been amassed on this subject, thanks mainly to the efforts of Rosch.[2] These data suggest that the order and frequency with which the items in a given category are evoked makes it possible to identify relatively constant scales of typicality (for a given culture). In sentence verification tasks, response times are shorter when the sentence refers to an item which is typical of its category ('An apple is a fruit') than when it contains an atypical example ('A nut is a fruit'). The typical examples are more easily memorized, etc.

Although Rosch's theory extends well beyond the domain of language – and, in effect, concerns the nature of cognitive representation in general – it nevertheless has important implications for psychological semantics:

(a) It emphasizes the global character of the representations associated with words. Within this perspective, the meaning of the word 'bird', for example, would be not a set of characteristics defining what a bird is, but a specific non-analyzed representation of the typical 'bird'. Furthermore, this notion of typicality is not restricted to concrete objects: the idea of prototypical meaning can be extended to abstract terms and even to function words and grammatical categories (see Bates and McWhinney, 1982).

(b) Moreover, the prototype theory emphasizes the fact that the meanings of words cannot be reduced to precise and well-defined concepts but, rather, consist of a 'family resemblance' between otherwise different objects: two objects can have a prototype in common without being in the slightest bit similar.

If we wish to retain the preceding approaches, these observations oblige us to introduce a new degree of complexity: either by attributing a variable 'salience' to the semantic features in the componential approach; or by distinguishing 'defining' (or essential) features and 'characteristic' (or accidental) features (Smith, Shoben and Rips, 1974; see below, p.75) in the propositional approach. It nevertheless remains the case that, for the moment, the notions of typicality and prototype have only a descriptive value, and their exact psychological status is still to be determined.

Procedural semantics

To know the meaning of a word is to know how to use it. The procedural approach (particularly well illustrated in the work of Johnson-Laird and Miller – see Miller and Johnson-Laird, 1976; Johnson-Laird, 1977, 1982)

2. See Mervis and Rosch (1981) for a review of this work.

consists of defining a meaning by its usage – that is to say, in terms of the procedures it sets in motion.

The meaning of a sentence can thus be considered as analogous to a computer program – that is to say, a set of instructions which call up a series of procedures. The meaning of a word is to be regarded not as a static entity (set of features or list of propositions) but as a 'sub-routine' called up by the program which is running at the time.

Language functioning is conceived of here by analogy with programming languages. The aim of a programming language is to provide the computer with sequences of instructions which, once entered in the machine, are 'compiled' – that is to say, translated into machine language in the form of a series of elementary operations which the machine is able to perform. In an analogous way, we can regard comprehension of an utterance by a human subject as being the 'compilation' of a program in the form of elementary mental operations.

For example (Miller and Johnson-Laird, 1976, pp. 170ff.), the meaning of the utterance 'Did Lucy bring the dessert?' consists of a series of instructions which (in a certain context) can be expressed as:

- find in memory an episode where F (x, y);
- give F the value of 'bring', x the value 'Lucy' and y the value 'dessert';
- if the description is found, reply 'yes'; if nothing is found, reply 'I don't know'; if information contradictory to the description is found, reply 'no'.

From a lexical point of view, 'bring' calls up a 'sub-routine' consisting of:

- find in the considered domain an event e where COME (x);
- test whether: during e, HOLD (x, y).

The sub-routine 'hold' is then called up in its turn, and so on. Meanwhile, the words 'Lucy' and 'dessert' which were assigned to the 'pointers' x and y call up sub-routines to search the memory for 'Lucy' (this might depend on the conversational context, since the listener might know several people called Lucy, but the running 'program' will generally allow this name to be assigned to a single individual) and for 'dessert'.

We should note that this interpretation is valid when the interlocuters are talking about a past event, about which only one of them has direct information. In another context (for example, if the question is posed by one of a group of picnickers), the interpretation will be different. It all depends on the highest-level 'program' in which the sentence being considered is involved.

Compared with the preceding ideas, the procedural approach is much more flexible. It takes account not only of the effects of context and the various forms of language use (orders, questions, etc.) but also of the 'extensional' aspects of meaning (by means of procedures for naming or identifying). Furthermore, it offers – as we shall see again later – a way of approaching the meaning of 'function' terms (determiners, conjunctions, etc.), which have hardly been touched on before.

All the same, for the moment we must recognize that there is insufficient experimental data to support this approach, and that it relies mainly on theoretical arguments and computer simulations. Moreover, the propositions it puts forward (particularly on the effects of context) are still too vague to be operational. Nevertheless, it does appear to be an interesting direction for further research.

Conclusion

In the first experimental studies, it was the *componential* approach that stimulated the most interesting hypotheses. Unfortunately, it has not been possible to find convincing proof of these hypotheses. No decisive proof has been found of a decomposition of meaning during the processing of words. Meanwhile, the idea of a small number of semantic primitives which are sufficient and necessary for defining word meanings remains purely speculative. And although the term 'semantic feature' continues to be used frequently by psychologists, they generally use it in a very vague sense.

The other idea is that a word evokes a knowledge set which is stored in memory and associated with that word. It is this idea, also very vague, that is the basis for Kintsch's *propositional* theory. This constitutes more an *a priori* definition of meaning than an empirically based theory.[3]

As for the data on *typicality*, they do not provide the basis for any particular theory, but constitute a set of facts which any theory of meaning must take into account. As we shall see later, a theory of the propositional type is easily able to integrate these data.

What these different approaches have in common is that they regard the meaning of a word as an invariant mental content (which may be called a 'concept') associated with this word. As we shall see, it is this conception which largely prevails in the current models of semantic memory.

However, this approach is not without a certain number of difficulties – to which I shall turn later – which relate primarily to the great variability in the meaning of words depending on the context in which they appear. The *procedural* conception of meaning seems to be best able to take account of

---

3. In fact, this notion amounts to representing the psychological significance of a word along the lines of a dictionary definition. In fact, Kintsch (1972, p. 264) proposes the transcription of an encyclopaedia article for the representation of the lexical entry 'nebula'.

these problems and provide the foundations for a plausible psychological theory.

The organization of semantic memory

The problem of the nature of meaning leads naturally to the question of how meanings are organized in memory, and by what processes they are evoked. In other words, what is the organization and functioning of the *semantic memory*?

This notion, first introduced by Quillian in 1966, has since been used with a variety of connotations. In principle, it designates a set of knowledge concerning the meanings of words – that is to say, a sort of internal dictionary. But even Quillian regarded these meanings as covering an 'encyclopaedic' knowledge set – that is to say, everything a human subject can know about the world. It is in this sense that Tulving (1972) contrasts semantic memory with 'episodic' memory, which bears on particular events and dates in an autobiographical manner. This latter distinction is now itself being abandoned; as a result, the term 'semantic memory' is being used to cover the entire contents of the long-term memory.

We shall examine first the models which are primarily concerned with the lexical aspect of meaning, and second the larger, more ambitious models which bear on the more general problem of the representation of knowledge.

Lexical meanings

How are word meanings stored in memory? This can be thought of in two ways:

- in the form of a set of relations which one word has with other words;
- or in the form of a list of properties (or 'features') stored with the word.

Collins and Quillian's model

The first model of semantic memory, proposed in 1966 by Quillian (see Quillian, 1967), who then refined and developed it in collaboration with Collins, employs the first type of representation: that of a *network*.

The model is that of a dictionary: the definition of a word is given by a configuration of other words which are interrelated in a variety of ways. These words, in their turn, refer to their own definitions, which bring other words into play and so on. For example, the word 'plant' (which is defined as 'PLANT$_1$: Living structure which is not an animal, frequently with leaves, getting its food from air, water or earth') refers to the words 'structure', 'living', 'animal', 'food', etc. This can be represented as (see Figure 4.1):

- a *type node* (here 'plant'), constituting the lexical entry for the word;
- a set of *token nodes*, representing the words figuring in the description; these, in their turn, also refer to type nodes (the definitions of these words);
- different types of *associative links* which link these nodes to each other.

In this way, words (or concepts) are defined in terms of other words, without the need for primitive concepts. Moreover, Collins and Quillian advance an important principle, that of *economy of storage*. Each piece of information appears only once in the network. For example, the fact that a canary, a sparrow, a robin, etc., have feathers is attached not to the corresponding node for each bird but to a superordinate node, namely 'bird'. Similarly, the fact that they eat, move, etc., is attached to the 'animal' node.

In order to establish the psychological validity of their model, Collins and Quillian turned to an experimental paradigm which has dominated most research into semantic memory, that of *sentence verification*. By measuring the time taken to answer 'true' or 'false' to a sentence of the type 'an A is a

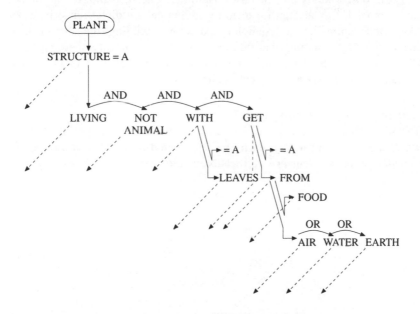

Figure 4.1 Representation of the meaning of the word 'plant' ('Living structure which is not an animal, frequently with leaves, getting its food from air, water or earth') (based on Quillian, 1967)

B' (membership of a category) or 'an A is B' (possession of a property), the length of the path through the network from one concept to another can be evaluated, and in this way the adequacy of the model can be tested.

In the simplified network in Figure 4.2, we see that the sentences 'A canary is yellow', 'A canary has feathers' and 'A canary eats' follow network paths of differing lengths, and therefore that the time required to verify the sentences also varies.

The first results to be obtained by Collins and Quillian accorded very well with their hypotheses. But it was not long before other authors (for example, Rips, Shoben and Smith, 1973) obtained results which did not support their theory. First, the effect of typicality became apparent: 'A penguin is a bird' requires a longer verification time than 'A robin is a bird'. Furthermore, certain results contradicted the model: thus the 'mammal' node should be an intermediate node between 'dog' and 'animal', but results showed a shorter verification time for 'A dog is an animal' than for 'A dog is a mammal'.

Finally, it has been demonstrated (Conrad, 1972) that the postulated economy of storage was not always verified. Certain properties, common to one category, could also be directly attached to various examples in that category (for example, 'has wings' is directly attached to 'swallow', 'sparrow', etc., and not just to the 'bird' node).

These observations do not raise insurmountable difficulties. The model can be amended to account for them by adding certain direct links (between 'dog' and 'animal', for example) and short-circuiting the intermediate concepts, or by assuming that different links have unequal weightings, etc. Glass and Holyoak (1975) have thus proposed a reorganized model which accounts for the experimental data quite satisfactorily.

Network model or features model?

The same data can be explained in a different way, by supposing that the words are stored separately, each one represented by a list of attributes (or semantic features). Sentence verification would then no longer be a case of

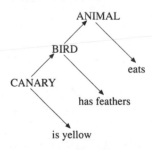

Figure 4.2

tracing through a network, but of a comparison between two sets of features. A model of this kind was proposed by Smith, Shoben and Rips (1974), and is supported by a large amount of experimental data.

In this model, each word comprises a set of features which vary in the extent to which they define category membership. For example, the feature 'has feathers' is essential to the concept 'bird', while other features (for example, size, the ability to fly) are less essential. Verification of category membership thus takes place in two stages. First, a global comparison, leading to a rapid decision if the similarity goes beyond a certain criterial threshold ('A robin is a bird') or, conversely, fails to reach a minimal criterion ('A robin is a stone'). In cases that fall between these two values, a second process of comparison comes into play, involving only the defining attributes. Evidently the first of these stages of comparison, the global stage, is in fact a return to the idea of evaluating the 'typicality' of the object.

The main difference between these two types of model lies in the relative importance they attribute to prior *storage* of information in memory, and to the *computation* of information not stored in memory. In this way, the category relations ('A canary is a bird') are pre-recorded for Collins and Quillian, whereas for Smith *et al.* these relations are constructed following a process of comparison. For certain attributes ('A canary has a beak') the reverse is true. In fact, it is evident that, psychologically speaking, certain information is never recorded and has to be inferred ('Louis XIV had lungs'), and that information is stored as a function of what the subject has learned, not as a result of its logical status (for example, as Collins and Loftus point out (1975), 'A whale is a mammal' is very likely to be learned information, not the product of a comparison between the characteristics of a whale and those which define mammals).

Thus the problem of 'storage or computation' is case-specific, and the answer will vary according to the individual and the information concerned. The two types of model, therefore, really differ only in their formulation. Formally, however, they are equivalent, as Hollan (1973) has demonstrated. Collins and Loftus (1975) have proposed a model which represents a synthesis of these two approaches.

Collins and Loftus retain Quillian's network representation (a concept is a node which is linked to other concepts), while from Smith *et al.* they take the idea of an unequal 'criteriality' of the different links attached to a concept. Moreover, the principle of economy of storage is rejected. Instead, all the information acquired in connection with a concept is directly linked to that concept.

When a node is activated, its activation is propagated along the arcs of the network. The 'criteriality' of the items of information encountered determines whether they are summated, and the process continues until the decision threshold is reached.

Besides the conceptual network (organized on the basis of semantic similarity) Collins and Loftus also postulate the existence of a separate lexical network (consisting of words, organized according to phonetic or orthographic similarity) which undergoes an analogous activation process and is connected to the semantic network.

All things considered, the experimental data which are currently available are far from providing decisive answers to a number of problems which still remain to be solved:

- To what extent is the information in memory accessed by an automatic 'activation' or by an active search?
- Does the representation of concepts in memory take the form of global units or sets of elementary features?
- Are there grounds for distinguishing between 'lexicon' and 'encyclo-paedia'?

Currently, the way in which different authors respond to these questions appears to be based more on theoretical preference than on experimental arguments.

Finally, we may question whether the very limited experimental paradigm – verification of single sentences – on which the majority of research has been based for over ten years is truly relevant to the exploration of the organization and functioning of the semantic memory. This is the question raised by Kintsch in a review of these studies (1980). He argues that the only well-established phenomenon – the effect of semantic similarity on verification time[4] – doubtless has more to do with the general decision-making processes than with the structure and functioning of the internal lexicon. Finally, Kintsch suggests that we should turn our attention to a higher level of investigation than that of the word.

Semantic networks

We shall now turn our attention to models which are far more general, extensive and ambitious in scope. They are concerned with the *representation of knowledge*, and their relation to psycholinguistics is sometimes tenuous – apart from the fact that the knowledge in question is generally

---

4. Semantic similarity reduces the verification time for a true sentence, and increases it for a false sentence. This phenomenon, however, is not specific to language. It is also found, as Kintsch notes, in tasks of perceptual judgement or pattern recognition.

learned (and can be formulated) in verbal form. While these models provide only a limited explanation of the actual processes of language comprehension, they are particularly concerned with representing what form the results of these processes take in memory. For this reason, therefore, the psycholinguist cannot neglect them.

Moreover, the aim of these models is to account for the whole range of cognitive activities (reasoning, problem-solving, concept formation, etc.) as well as language comprehension. Their interest, therefore, lies in the way they situate language within the much more general framework of overall mental activity.

Rumelhart, Lindsay and Norman's model

By way of example, let us discuss the model proposed by Rumelhart, Lindsay and Norman (1972) and its subsequent elaboration (Norman and Rumelhart, 1975).

As in Kintsch's theory, the basic element is the *proposition*, represented as a link between a set of nodes. The basic 'meaning store' thus contains two kinds of element:

- *relations*: scenarios which have various roles (Fillmore's cases). Thus the verb 'fall' (Figure 4.3) is represented as a certain type of act ('move'), which affects a certain object (to be specified), according to a certain pathway (to be specified), under the influence of a certain instrument (gravity);
- *concepts*: constants which fill the empty places within the relations,

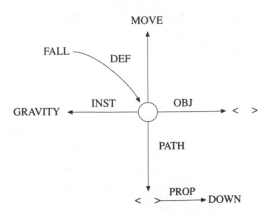

Figure 4.3 Representation of the verb 'to fall' (based on Rumelhart, Lindsay and Norman, 1972, p. 226)

whose meanings are themselves constituted in terms of relations with other concepts (membership: 'is a'; properties, localities, etc.). For example, Figure 4.4 illustrates the definition of 'mountain' (= 'natural object, situated on the surface of the earth, which rises abruptly to a high summit').

In the later version of the model, the meanings are themselves broken down into primitive elements (for example, 'give' is broken down as indicated in the diagram in Figure 4.5: 'X gives Y to Z' = 'X does something which causes a change from the state of X has Y to the state of Z has Y'). The scenario containing these various elements (actions, actors and objects) constitutes an *event*. The nodes which appear in it are, in fact, 'secondary' nodes which refer to the 'primary' nodes where their definitions appear (this distinction roughly corresponds to Quillian's 'token nodes' and 'type nodes'). Finally, a set of events, linked by temporal relations (succession: *then*; or simultaneity: *while*), constitutes an *episode*.

We can see that all the representations – relations, concepts, events, episodes – share the same format (that of the proposition, as in Kintsch's theory). This format, however, is not specific to language: procedures (a cooking recipe, a solution to a problem, etc.) are coded in memory in the same way. Finally, certain nodes of the network contain the necessary sensory and motor information to guarantee the 'interface' with the outside world.

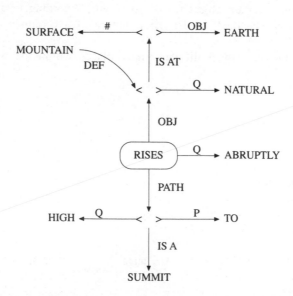

Figure 4.4 Representation of the word 'mountain' (based on Rumelhart, Lindsay and Norman, 1972, p. 226)

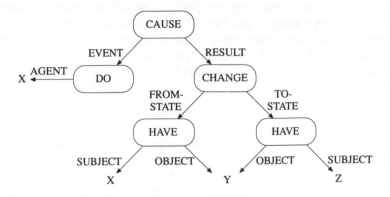

Figure 4.5 Representation of the verb 'to give' (based on Norman and Rumelhart, 1975)

Other models

Besides Rumelhart, Lindsay and Norman's model, other models of semantic memory have been proposed, which we can outline only briefly here.

We have already mentioned the Kintsch model (1972, 1974), which is not presented in the form of a network, but can easily be adapted to that kind of representation. Unlike the other models discussed here, it is not conceived of as a model for computer simulation but is aimed explicitly at accounting for the functioning of human memory. Its main purpose is for studying text comprehension, and for this reason we shall return to it in Chapter 7.

Schank (1972), on the other hand, is primarily interested in the automatic comprehension of language. He postulates a representation of knowledge in the form of networks of 'conceptual dependency', quite close in their conception to those of Rumelhart, Lindsay and Norman, but employing a slightly different typology of relations. The originality of Schank's work lies, on the one hand, in the effort to reduce the diverse types of actions and states to a small number of fundamental elements and, on the other, in the major role played in language comprehension by the processes of context-dependent anticipation. This latter idea led him to develop the notions of script, plan, and goal (Schank and Abelson, 1977): we shall return to this work in Chapter 7.

Anderson and Bower (1973) postulated a general model of memory (HAM = *human associative memory*), comprising a representation of knowledge in the form of a network. On the basis of this, Anderson (1976, 1984) has constructed a more ambitious and elaborate model, ACT (= *adaptive control of thought*), which aims to account for the entire range of human cognitive activity. This model comprises two parts: a 'declarative' part, in which knowledge is represented in the form of a propositional network (based on the subject–predicate schema) and a 'procedural' part, which interprets and uses this knowledge (in the form of 'production systems'). Most of the linguistic aspects (syntactic and semantic) of the model are related to this procedural component.

Discussion

At present, the representation of knowledge in the form of semantic networks is very widely accepted. However, the representation of these networks varies greatly from author to author – the differences, in fact, have more to do with personal preference than with empirical or theoretical reasons.

These differences relate essentially to two points:

(a) What is the relative importance of *declarative* knowledge (that is to say, the data recorded in memory) and *procedural* knowledge (that is to say the rules of use for these data)? In Rumelhart, Lindsay and Norman's model, everything is recorded in the declarative form; whereas in Anderson's model, a large part of the interpretation is attributed to the procedural component.

(b) What *types of relations* make up the network? Some models rely on the case relations proposed by Fillmore (with a greater or lesser degree of nuance or modification). Others are restricted to a limited number of much more general relations (for example, Anderson's 'subject' and 'predicate'). The choice, which varies according to author, ultimately appears to be an arbitrary one.

Given our current state of knowledge on this subject, it is impossible to provide a definite response to these different questions – even supposing that they can be answered empirically. In any case, the fact is that these different models contain a degree of generality which precludes their experimental validation.

We must also point out that, in fact, these diverse semantic network models are derived more from the field of artificial intelligence than from psychology. No doubt they all aim to have a psychological validity – or at least plausibility. However, it is difficult to assess the extent to which they are based on well-established experimental data, intuitive consideration, programming constraints, or simply personal preference.

More radically, we might also contest the very idea of a rigid and permanent organization of knowledge in memory. The work of Ehrlich (1979), for example, suggests that semantic memory can be regarded as a generative 'free-elements system' with a high degree of flexibility. Furthermore, the lack of isomorphism between conceptual organizations and verbal structures leads Ehrlich to draw a clear distinction between 'semantics' and linguistic units.

In the absence of any satisfactory explanation of the mechanisms for constructing and evoking meanings, can these models at least enable us to describe meanings correctly? This is the next question to which we must turn.

Meaning, context and reference

In the final analysis, the question of whether we represent the meaning of words in the form of semantic components, networks or meaning postulates is perhaps only a minor problem. These representations are, in effect, formally equivalent, and at the moment it is scarcely possible to see what kind of empirical data could enable us to decide between them. The real problem is to identify the facts for which these representations are unable to account.

Function words

First of all, there is a broad category of words which studies in psychological semantics have often regarded with only marginal interest, but which nevertheless play an important role in language. These are the function words – determiners, pronouns, prepositions, conjunctions, etc. Lacking a 'content', not referring to anything, not associated with any knowledge set, they remain largely ignored in models of semantic memory. Yet they are part of the lexicon – indeed, among the most frequently used elements – and it appears to be impossible for a natural language to exist without them.

One characteristic which most of these function words seem to have in common is their *polyfunctionality*. That is to say: on the one hand they are likely to take on a wide diversity of values depending on the context; on the other they simultaneously assume a set of functions in any particular occurrence.

We shall confine ourselves to two examples of this here.

Articles
Like many other languages, French has two categories of articles which function as determiners for the noun phrase: the definite article (*le*, *la*, *les* = 'the' in masculine, feminine and plural form) and the indefinite article (*un*, *une* = 'a/an' in masculine and feminine form, and *des* = 'some'). Despite

their apparent insignificance, these small words permit the performance of a great variety of functions.

In a remarkable study of how French-speaking children learn the system of articles, Karmiloff-Smith (1979) both identified the stages of acquisition of these different functions and simultaneously provided a detailed analysis of them.

The first form of the article to be used by children appears as a neutral sound (/ə/ = 'euh') and does not yet distinguish between definite and indefinite. It seems to have two functions: (1) to differentiate words designating things (nouns) from words designating actions (verbs); (2) to distinguish common nouns from proper nouns. Next stage: the two forms are distinguished, the indefinite being used for naming (*un chat* = 'a cat'), while the definite has a deictic function – that is to say it is used, often accompanied by a gesture, for pointing to the object of attention (*le chat* = 'the cat'). A third function which arrives with the appearance of inflections (*le/les*, *un/des*) is to mark the singular or plural aspect of the object. Then, at the fourth stage, *un* takes on a numeric function ('one'), while *le* gains an 'exophoric' function (designating an object which is the only one of its kind within the immediate environment). A fifth stage introduces class membership: *les* acquiring the meaning 'all' and *des* the meaning 'some'. At the next stage a new function appears: *un* alludes to a non-specific reference, while *le* takes on an anaphoric value, referring to an object previously mentioned in the discourse (*UNE voiture s'approchait sur la route. LA voiture roulait à vive allure* = 'A car came along the road. THE car was going at great speed'). A seventh and final stage arrives with the 'generic' use of articles (*L'aigle est un rapace diurne* = 'The eagle is a diurnal bird of prey'; *Un angle droit mesure 90°* = 'A right angle measures 90°').

It is easy to see that all these functions are present in the adult use of language – some can be superimposed, others are dictated by the context.

Connectives

Often simply considered to express a relation (logical, causal, temporal, etc.) between clauses, the connectives – *and*, *or*, *if*, *but*, *thus*, etc. – actually possess a broad range of functions in natural languages. We shall limit ourselves to some observations of the French conjunction *si* (= 'if'), which has been the most widely studied.[5]

The range of values which can be taken by *si* is well known – and is found in all languages. Its primary function is to indicate a relation between the two clauses it joins. This relation, however, can vary enormously according to context: implication is only one of a number of cases; the

---

5. See Caron (1983) for a more detailed study of the problems posed by the semantics of connectors.

relation can also be one of contrast, co-occurrence, complementarity, etc. It is difficult to accept that all these possible meanings could simply constitute a number of 'semantic features' all associated with *si*, which can be given greater or lesser emphasis depending on the context.

Second, the role of *si* is to neutralize the statement contained in the clause it is introducing. This neutralization, however, can itself take various forms: from simple hypothesis (*S'il pleut demain* . . . = 'If it rains tomorrow . . . ') to suggestion (*Si nous allions faire un tour?* = '(How about) If we go for a walk?') or to state a recognized fact that is considered inessential (*S'il a renversé ce piéton, ce n'est pas sa faute'* = 'If he did knock down that pedestrian, it wasn't his fault').

Finally, the second clause is presented as being conditional upon the first. But here again, this conditioning can assume a number of forms. It is not necessarily a question of truth value, since the *si* clause can be just as likely to introduce a question, an order or an exclamation (*Si c'est comme ça, zut!* = 'If it's like that, dash it all!'). What is being established (within the framework defined by the first clause) is the relevance of the second utterance. However, the nature of this relevance also depends on the conversational context. And furthermore, it is no longer concerned with the semantic content but with the very *act* of producing the utterance.[6]

Many of the other connectives can be analyzed in the same way.

Generally speaking, it does not seem possible to think of the meanings of these function terms as stable representations which are fixed in memory. Rather, they have to be thought of as the product of a construction generated at the moment of use and highly dependent on context: not only linguistic context, but also the context of the situation in which the utterance occurs.

Should we, then, think of function words as having their own specific character (as we saw above – p. 50 – they might perhaps be a subset of the lexicon endowed with a particular status)? We shall see that this context-dependent 'flexibility' of meaning can also be found in the case of content words.

Semantic flexibility

I. An initial, well-known problem is that of the *polysemy* (or lexical ambiguity) of certain words. A simple way of resolving this is to accept that an ambiguous word can, in fact, correspond to several distinct lexical units. For example, the word 'study' would correspond to the two units 'study$_1$' and 'study$_2$', which comprise two different meanings – 'reading room' and 'period of research'. An identical phonological – or written – form would

---

6. For a more detailed analysis of the meaning of *si*, as well as a collection of experimental data which support this analysis, see Caron (1987).

thus refer either to several nodes on the semantic network or to several lists of features.

The role of context would thus be to bring certain *selectional restrictions* to bear (Katz and Fodor, 1963) which enable the inappropriate meaning(s) to be eliminated. For example, in 'He interviewed them in his study' and 'He interviewed them during his study' the prepositions 'in' and 'during' respectively require a complement comprising the feature [location] or [process] and thus impose the selection of meaning 1 or meaning 2.

The problem this poses for psychologists is one of knowing whether these constraints come into play before or after lexical access – in other words, whether only the meaning which conforms to the context is activated, or all the possible meanings are activated and then give rise to a selection process. As we have seen (p. 49), experimental results seem to support the second hypothesis.

In fact, this theory raises a number of problems. First of all, the 'selectional restrictions' which supposedly determine the interpretation can always be violated. This is the case in the metaphorical use of language, to which we shall return later. For example, 'He meandered through his memories' is a perfectly acceptable sentence. More generally, however, everything can depend on the situation. Johnson-Laird (1983) notes, for example, that the sentence 'I saw the Azores flying the Atlantic' is, theoretically, ambiguous but is usually interpreted in only one way: the Azores have the [fixed object] feature and therefore cannot be the subject of the verb 'fly'. If the sentence appears in a narrative about the earth exploding, however, it can take on a quite different meaning.

Moreover, the ambiguity of words is often far from being as clear-cut as in the cases (like 'study') which have most often been used in experimental situations. Many words cover a wide range of meanings without there being a very clear-cut distinction between them.

Simply reading a fairly detailed dictionary is enough to make us realize this. Let us take the word 'sense' as an example. We can move without any clear distinction of meaning from 'sense of hearing', 'sense of smell', etc. to 'pleasures of the senses' on the one hand, and 'sense of balance', ' – of rhythm', or ' – of responsibility' on the other. There is little in common, however, between 'intoxication of the senses' and 'common sense'. We can follow a similarly unbroken path to arrive at, for example, 'taking leave of one's senses', which has very little in common with 'in the opposite sense' or 'it doesn't make sense', etc. We can proceed in much the same way with frequently used verbs such as 'take', 'give', 'fall', etc.

In the final analysis, polysemy can be seen as a phenomenon which, far from being exceptional, is without doubt extremely general and which, in most cases, consists not so much of a contrast between clearly distinct meanings as of a modulation of meaning according to context.

II. This *semantic flexibility* has been confirmed experimentally by Bransford and colleagues (Barclay *et al.*, 1974; Bransford *et al.*, 1976).

In order to demonstrate that the interpretation of a word varies with the context in which it is presented, these authors relied primarily on a task of cued recall. They presented their subjects with lists of sentences containing, for example, one of the following two:

(1) The man lifted the piano.
(2) The man tuned the piano.

They then asked their subjects to recall the final word of the sentence, giving them the cue of either 'something heavy' or 'something with a nice sound'. The first cue was of significant help in the recall of the word 'piano' for those subjects who had heard sentence (1), but not for those who had heard sentence (2); for the second cue this was reversed. Interpretation of the word 'piano' (in so far as it was recorded in memory) is, therefore, not the same in both sentences.

A similar effect was observed in the classic task of sentence verification (Barclay and Jahn, 1976): for example, the sentence 'Oranges are juicy' is verified more quickly if it is preceded by the sentence 'The girl squeezed the oranges' than by 'The girl picked the oranges'. These results could be interpreted as showing that the effect of context is to activate certain 'semantic features' (or certain links in the semantic network) to a greater or lesser extent. This explanation, however, does not accord well with other experimental results.

In the first place, context can not only emphasize certain properties of the word, it can also supply additional specifications. Thus recall of the sentence 'The fish attacked the swimmer' (Anderson *et al.*, 1976) is better if the cue provided is 'shark' than if it is 'fish'.

Moreover, as Bransford *et al.* (1976) point out, the sentences 'The girl bought some sweets' and 'The girl made some sweets' are recalled better if the cues given are, for the first sentence, 'in a shop', and for the second, 'in the kitchen'. It is difficult to imagine that 'shop' and 'kitchen' are included in the set of 'semantic features' recorded with the word 'sweet'.

Finally, in a series of ingenious experiments, Bransford and McCarrell (1974) have demonstrated that textual comprehension can vary considerably depending on the prior information available to the subjects – information which might be provided, for example, by a title or a picture. We shall return to these experiments in the next chapter, but for now let us note that they provide evidence of the fact that words take on their meaning only in relation to a particular field of reference.

The idea at which Bransford and colleagues (Bransford and McCarrell, 1974) finally arrived was that words (and, more generally, linguistic devices) are not in themselves carriers of meaning, but constitute the 'instructions' for constructing meaning. This accords with Johnson-Laird's suggestions, and with the proposals of 'procedural semantics' (see also Sanford and Garrod, 1982).

III. *Metaphor* can be considered as a particular case of semantic flexibility. The metaphorical use of language is extremely frequent and cannot be ignored by a theory of the psychology of meaning. Nevertheless, it has only recently begun to be of interest to psychologists.[7]

In principle, the comprehension of a metaphor should involve complex processing. If we take a sentence like 'Billboards are warts on the landscape', interpretation appears to require three stages: (1) literal interpretation of the expression; (2) awareness of the impossibility, or irrelevance, of this interpretation (a billboard cannot be a wart); (3) construction of an interpretation derived from a search for elements common to the two terms when these are put into relation (for example: ugly protrusions on a surface, etc.). In a cued recall test using sentences of this type, Verbrugge and McCarrell (1977) demonstrated that these common elements are effective cues for recall (which allies metaphor with the phenomenon of semantic flexibility).

However, does processing involve a prior computation of the literal meaning? If the three-stage schema presented above is correct, then comprehension of a metaphorical utterance should take longer than when the utterance is to be understood in its literal sense. This is indeed the case when subjects are processing isolated sentences, but this difference disappears when these sentences occur within a wider context. The metaphorical expressions are understood just as quickly as in cases where they can be interpreted literally. They even tend to be understood more quickly when they are commonly used expressions (such as 'Let the cat out of the bag') (Ortony, Schallert, Reynolds and Antos, 1978).

We shall see later that the same phenomenon is present in 'indirect requests' (of the type 'Can you pass me the salt?'). This has led some authors (Gibbs, 1984) seriously to contest the psychological validity of the distinction between 'literal meaning' and 'derived (or metaphorical) meaning'.

IV. All these phenomena – semantic flexibility, ambiguity, metaphor – are not easily reconciled with the hypothesis of an invariant lexical meaning attached to each word. Language is used to speak *about something* – that is to say, about a certain extralinguistic reality – perceptual or conceptual; and

---

7. See Ortony, Reynolds and Arter (1978) for a review of this research.

it is through their relation to this particular reality that words take on their meaning. Semantics cannot evade the issue of *reference*.

Meaning and reference

Let us return to the work of Bransford and colleagues. They suggest (see Bransford *et al.*, 1976) that meaning can be regarded in quite a different light from that of classical psycholinguistics. The latter is based on an *interpretative* conception: the meaning of a sentence is the result of a combination of the semantic representations attached to the words of which it is formed.[8] Bransford proposes replacing this with a *constructive* conception: meaning is a representation constructed as a function of the instructions provided by the words. The meaning of these words lies not in the mental representations they evoke but in the way in which they allow a particular extralinguistic field to be structured (or restructured).[9] This conception appears to attenuate – indeed, eliminate – the classic distinction between *meaning* and *reference*: the word or utterance is not conceived of as the bearer of meaning; rather, its meaning is the product of the organization it imposes on the particular (representative or perceptual) field to which it refers.

An analogous conception had already been proposed by Olson (1970), who, taking Wittgenstein's idea of 'meaning as use', developed the theory that the function of the word is not to represent or to symbolize an object or event, but to *differentiate* it from other possible objects or events within a given 'array' – that is to say, within a particular field of reference.

However, this field of reference itself is not an objective given. Even if we take the case of the simple perceived environment, this is organized as a function of the task to be accomplished and the goals of the act of communication. Nevertheless, it more often refers to the mental representation and results from a mutual adaptation of speaker and listener, defining a 'common ground' in relation to which meanings and references are constructed. This notion of 'common ground' has been studied by Clark in particular, and we shall return to his work in this field later (Chapter 6).

In conclusion, the various studies we have cited in this section suggest that we approach meaning from quite a different perspective from that adopted by most of the semantic theories we have described. Meaning appears to be not so much a mental *content* evoked by the word as a *form* imposed on an extralinguistic content to which the act of communication itself is then referred. Meaning and reference are thus inseparable. As for the

8. This conception, which is closely linked to the Chomskyan approach, has been developed by Katz and Fodor (1963), who have had considerable influence on studies in psychological semantics.
9. In his theory of 'mental models', Johnson-Laird (1983) develops ideas which are quite closely related to those of Bransford.

content itself, that is determined by the situation and the goals of the communication as the interlocuters envisage them. Semantics cannot be separated from pragmatics.

Conclusion

Research into psychological semantics began to develop when it became possible to borrow sufficiently elaborated theoretical models from other disciplines – namely, linguistics and artificial intelligence. However, these models, while giving rise to a rich collection of psycholinguistic research, have sometimes led to a dead end.

I. From a linguistic perspective, the *componential theory* of meaning has provided some fruitful working hypotheses. But this has doubtless led all too quickly to postulating the existence of isolable 'atoms of meaning', conceived of as constituting the elements of thought, grouped together in packets and covered by a verbal label.[10] In fact, as we have seen, the decomposition of meaning into simpler elements, while it is a perfectly legitimate operation for the linguist, does not necessarily constitute a permanent psychological reality. It can be performed, but only up to a certain point and under certain conditions. The real problem, from a psychological point of view, is to know *when* and *how* this deconstruction is performed.

Furthermore, we sometimes tend to forget that the 'semantic features' described by linguists are not elements of content, but *distinctive* features (as in the field of phonology, which provided the inspiration for the componential analysis). The meaning of a word, therefore, is to be found not so much in the representations it evokes as in the differential organization which it introduces into those representations.

II. Currently, the *semantic network* models proposed by artificial intelligence incontestably provide the most convenient representation of the storage of knowledge in memory. However, the problem of how this 'knowledge base' is related to the 'internal lexicon' remains. The simplest and most popular idea is to attach each word to a node on the network (that is to say, to a concept). However, the effects of context, semantic flexibility and metaphor suggest that the links between lexicon and conceptual memory are much more flexible – a single word can 'point', depending on the

---

10. The influence of British empiricism is evident here. In many studies of psychological semantics, Locke's 'simple ideas' are to be found, sometimes in conjunction with the 'mental chemistry' of John Stuart Mill.

conditions in which it is used, to different parts of the network.

While we can still use the term 'semantic memory' (even though it is not unambiguous) for the set of knowledge available to the subject, it appears to be essential to distinguish it from *lexical memory*, whose content would be quite different. Besides information regarding the form (phonological, articulatory, graphic) of words, it would also contain the semantic information which enables them to be used. This information, however, is no longer to be regarded as representative contents (which are stored in the 'semantic' memory) but as *procedures* for evoking and processing these contents. Defining these procedures, establishing their typology and their conditions of implementation, constitutes a vast field of future research for psycholinguists.

However, lexical semantics cannot be approached in isolation. The word can function only within a context. It is therefore to a higher level, that of the sentence, to which we shall now turn our attention.

Recommended reading

The problems of meaning have given rise to a vast body of literature in the fields of philosophy and logic: Kempson's work (1977) provides a good introduction to this subject. As for linguistic semantics, Lyons (1977) is a good reference. Readers who wish to learn more about these problems will find a number of major philosophical and linguistic texts in a collection edited by Steinberg and Jakobovicz (1971).

From a psychological viewpoint, Miller and Johnson-Laird (1976) provide a wealth of information regarding lexical semantics.

Smith (1978) and Kintsch (1980) present a review of the experimental works concerning semantic memory. For a clear presentation of the model proposed by Rumelhart *et al.*, see Lindsay and Norman (1977, chs 10 and 12). For the other models, see the references cited in the text of this chapter. For a discussion of semantic networks, see Johnson-Laird *et al.* (1984).

CHAPTER 5

The Sentence 1: Syntax and Semantics

There can be no doubt that one of the characteristics of human language is its ability to make possible a practically unlimited number of different messages through the combination of a finite number of words (which are themselves constructed from a few dozen phonemes). The systems of communication used by animals are restricted, as far as we can currently tell, to a very limited repertoire containing, at most, a few dozen distinct messages. Children of 18–20 months, who are also capable of producing twenty or so different 'single word utterances', are situated at a comparable level. It is at the moment when they start to combine words that we can consider them truly to have attained human language.

The elementary unit of communication is the sentence – that is to say, a combination of words obeying certain rules, expressing a specific meaning and implementing a particular act of communication between two or more partners. This immediately raises three types of problem:

1. In every language, the way words are combined to form sentences obeys a set of rules which constitute the *syntax* of the language. All speakers know (implicitly) the syntax of the language they speak. They are able to produce and understand sentences which conform to these rules, to recognize whether a sentence is well formed or not, etc. In other words, they possess a linguistic *competence*. Therefore one of the first tasks we must confront is determining the nature of this competence and deciding what lies at its roots. (Are we dealing with a set of arbitrary rules acquired through learning, with innate structures which form part of the genetic heritage of the human species, or with constraints motivated by the functional necessities of communication?) A second problem is to explain how these rules are implemented – that is to say, to account for linguistic *performance* (in both production and comprehension): through what procedures is the syntactic structure of a sentence constructed or revealed? Are these procedures the

90

product of an 'autonomous' component, or do they interact with procedures belonging to other levels?

2. The sentence possesses a meaning which cannot be reduced to the sum of the meanings of the words which compose it, but constitutes a specific mental organization. This gives rise to a second type of problem, this time *semantic* in nature. First, how is the meaning of a sentence constructed? And second, what does this meaning consist of, and how is it represented in thought?

3. Finally, a sentence is not simply the verbal encoding of a certain state of affairs. It is also an act of communication, addressed by someone to someone, in a certain situation, with a particular objective. As we shall see, we cannot neglect these *pragmatic* aspects of verbal activity if we are to account for the semantic and syntactic aspects. We shall consider this question further, therefore, in Chapter 6.

The primacy of syntax? Chomskyan psycholinguistics

Throughout the 1960s, psycholinguistic research focused predominantly on the question of syntax. The model proposed by Chomsky, which gives syntax a central role in linguistic theory, has enjoyed considerable prestige, and the key goal of the work of most psycholinguists seems to have been the simple psychological validation of generative and transformational grammar.

The interest of the Chomskyan model for psycholinguists was due, first of all, to the fact that it presented a complete, formal theory of the language system: complete in the sense that it attempted to enumerate the set of rules which were necessary and sufficient to produce all the possible sentences of a language (and only these); formal in that these rules are independent of the expressed content, the situation or the speakers' intentions. These rules thus constitute a system which contains within itself the basis of its intelligibility. In this way language is defined as an autonomous system which constitutes a specific field of study.

Furthermore, the model offered an alternative to the behaviourist approach (which was beginning to run out of steam) without losing any of its methodological rigour. The very precisely defined system of syntactic rules provided a possible model of the operations executed within the 'black box' between stimulus and response. It is possible to construct hypotheses about the functioning of thought (and submit these hypotheses to experimental validation) without falling into the traps of introspection. In this way, the Chomskyan theory constituted the first rigorous, systematic model for a psychological approach to information processing, and was to play a decisive role in the development of cognitivist thinking.

Finally, we should note that despite the postulation of innate mechanisms, the theory has been perceived as possessing certain affinities with Piagetian ideas. It shares the same structural, formal approach and sees the same primacy of operational structures over contents (see Sinclair de Zwart 1967, 1973).

To sum up: in emphasizing the organization of language and providing a rigorous description of the rules of this organization, the model of generative and transformational grammar made it possible to reintegrate into psychology a type of approach which – as has been variously illustrated by *Gestalttheorie*, the work of Piaget and the commencement of research into artificial intelligence – broke with the tradition of associationist atomism.

In essence, the Chomskyan model invited psychologists to investigate two matters:[1]

- First, it accounted for the construction of sentences through the application of a series of *transformations* of a 'deep structure': it was therefore possible to ask to what extent these transformations correspond to provable psychological operations.
- Second, it provided a *structural description* of each sentence: the question therefore arose whether the perception and representation of sentences is organized in a way which conforms to these descriptions.

Syntactic complexity and psychological complexity

There is no doubt that Chomsky is a linguist, not a psychologist. The model he proposes attempts to provide a formal description of language, not of the processes (of production or comprehension) by which it is implemented. However, this model, if it is correct, must describe the *competence* of subjects – that is to say, the knowledge (implicit, of course) which they have of their language. Their *performance*, or the set of psychological processes by means of which they produce or understand utterances, will depend on this competence.

We can think of the relationship between performance and competence in various ways. The simplest way – and the one which has been most generally adopted ever since the first studies of the question – is to consider the formal *linguistic* operations by means of which a sentence is 'derived' from its deep structure as *psychological* operations. So the production of a sentence becomes a series of transformations applied to the deep structure, which reflects the semantic relations to be expressed. These transformations

1. It is necessary to add a third: language acquisition, a subject we are unable to tackle within the framework of this book, but one which has motiviated a large number of studies. Chomskyan theory provides the means for producing a precise description of the 'grammars' of child language and their progressive construction. Moreover, the hypothesis of an innate 'language acquisition device' makes it possible to predict certain invariants in this acquisition.

finally yield the surface structure of the sentence. Understanding consists in following the same path in the opposite direction: undoing the transformations in order to reveal the deep structure, which then has to be interpreted semantically.

This prompts the idea that the psychological complexity of the processing of an utterance increases with the number of transformational rules involved in the derivation of that utterance. This is known as the *derivational theory of complexity* (DTC) and has been the inspiration for most of the work in the field of generative grammar.

IPN transformations

In the first version of the theory (Chomsky, 1957), phrase-structure rules were considered to generate a 'kernel sentence' on which various optional transformations can be performed to give rise to a family of sentences. Thus a single transformation of the kernel sentence (K) 'The secretary types the letter' permits the derivation of the sentences:

- negative (N): 'The secretary does not type the letter.'
- interrogative (I): 'Does the secretary type the letter?'
- passive (P): 'The letter is typed by the secretary.'

It is also possible to perform two transformations (IN, for example: 'Doesn't the secretary type the letter?') or three (IPN: 'Isn't the letter typed by the secretary?').

If we think of these transformations as corresponding to psychological operations, we should expect the associated processing time to increase with the number of transformations to be performed. The first experiments conducted in connection with this subject were carried out by Miller and colleagues (Miller, 1962), who attempted to test this hypothesis directly.

Miller simply measured the time taken by subjects to produce a sentence (belonging to the family K, P, N, PN) which they derived from another sentence. The results fully support the hypothesis. The sentences requiring two transformations take longer than those which need only one. The time required for a given transformation is fairly constant (whether in performing or 'undoing' a transformation) and, generally speaking, the times are additive.

It is possible, however, to criticize the artificial nature of this experiment. The subjects may perform transformations when they are asked to, but do they do so in their normal use of language?

To counter this problem, researchers turned their attention to more indirect verifications, basing their arguments on the evidence provided by memory. If the comprehension of a sentence presupposes the identification of the transformations which produced it and the kernel sentence from which it is derived, then the representation of this sentence in memory must contain this different information. In other words, we can think of what is 'coded' in memory as being (a) the kernel sentence, and (b) the identification of the transformations to be performed. This 'coding hypothesis', which was proposed by Mehler (1963), has resulted in a number of different experimental verifications.

Mehler noted that the majority of errors made in a sentence recall task consisted of the simplification of sentences through the omission of one or more transformations. Another experiment, conducted by Savin and Perchonock (1965), attempted to judge the space occupied in short-term memory by sentences of varying degrees of complexity (we know that working memory capacity is relatively constant). These researchers therefore presented subjects with sentences containing 0, 1, 2 or 3 transformations, followed by a list of words. The number of words the subjects were able to remember at the end of the sentence made it possible to estimate the space still available in memory after its memorization. It was observed that sentences containing a large number of transformations required correspondingly more space in short-term memory – a result which confirmed the 'coding hypothesis'.

But here again, we might question whether the procedures used by subjects in a task of rote learning are the same as those used in the *comprehension* of language. A large number of studies have therefore attempted to investigate the effects of transformations in tasks which demand comprehension – that is to say, in sentence verification tasks. In such tasks, subjects have to judge whether or not pictures presented to them correspond to a given sentence, and their response time is measured. In this case the results fit the predictions of the theory far less comfortably.

There is no doubt that, generally speaking, negative and passive sentences take longer to verify than affirmative or active sentences. However, there are a number of facts which complicate this picture.

1. First of all, there is an interaction between syntactic complexity and truth value. It takes slightly longer to decide that an affirmative sentence is false than to say that it is true. For negative sentences, however, it is the other way round (a false negative is responded to more quickly than a true negative) (Gough, 1965).

2. Most importantly, semantic and pragmatic factors are involved. Thus Slobin (1966) has shown that passive sentences are verified less quickly than active sentences only where the two terms (agent and patient) can be inverted ('reversible' passives), such as 'The cat is being chased by the dog'. In the case of 'non-reversible' passives, where the roles of agent and patient are imposed by the meaning of the words ('The flowers are being watered by the girl'), the verification time is no longer than it is for active sentences.

In the same way, Wason (1965) has shown that the difficulty in processing negative sentences disappears when these are used in a context which makes their use plausible – in the expression of exceptions, for example. When subjects are presented with a row of eight circles, seven of which are coloured blue and only one of which is coloured red (circle number 3, for example), they respond noticeably faster to the sentence 'Circle number 3 is not blue' than to the sentence 'Circle number 7 is not red'.

All in all, what is shown by the experiments in which subjects actually have to process sentences – that is to say, when they have to understand them – is that the complexity of processing depends more on the sentence's meaning and conditions of use than on its 'derivational history' (the syntactic transformations it involves).[2]

Other transformations
Experimental research into many of the other transformations described by the theory has generally produced negative results which have often completely contradicted the theoretical predictions.

We shall give only a single example, taken from Fodor and Garrett (1967). Let us take the sentence:

The shot the soldier the mosquito bit fired missed

If we now add adjectives, for example:

The first shot the tired soldier the mosquito bit fired missed

the sentence becomes far more complex. In fact, in deep structure each adjective corresponds to an embedded sentence (for example, 'the soldier is tired'), which has to undergo a first 'relativization' transformation ('the soldier who is tired'), a second 'deletion' transformation ('the soldier tired'), and a third permutation transformation in which adjective and noun are swapped ('the soldier tired' → 'the tired soldier'). Thus two adjectives require six additional transformations.

In a paraphrasing task, however, the authors observed that this increased syntactic complexity not only did not bother their subjects, but actually led to an improvement in their results!

To summarize: the idea – which *a priori* seems very attractive – that the

---

2. Furthermore, in the second version of his theory, Chomsky (1965) abandons the idea of optional transformations. Negative, interrogative sentences, etc., are no longer differentiated by the presence of transformations but involve different deep structures.

linguistic *operations* described by generative grammar correspond to psychological operations has had to be abandoned. It remains to be established whether or not the syntactic *structures* described by generative grammar have a psychological reality. This would provide a weaker version of the psychological validity of the linguistic model.

Syntactic structures

The Chomskyan theory proposes a dual structural description for any given sentence. On the one hand the sentence possesses a *surface structure* and on the other a *deep structure*, the former being derived from the latter by a series of transformations.

Surface structure may be described in terms of a hierarchical organization of *constituents*. Thus the simple sentence 'The postman delivers the mail' can be subdivided into two main constituents: 'The postman' (noun phrase) and 'delivers the mail' (verb phrase). Each of these can be further analyzed into lower-level constituents, etc. This yields a hierarchical structure which can be represented as a tree (see p. 7 above) or by nested brackets:

(((The) (postman)) ((delivers) ((the) (mail)))).

Deep structure may differ from surface structure to a greater or lesser extent (we shall look at some examples later), and it is on deep structure that semantic interpretation is based.

A large volume of study has been devoted to demonstrating the psychological reality of these two types of structure.

Surface structure
It has been observed that the syntactic structure of a sentence plays a role in its perception (Miller and Isard, 1963; see p. 40 above). Similarly, Epstein (1961) has shown that a list of meaningless syllables, such as:

The yig wur vum rix hum in jeg miv

is learned much more easily if it is provided with morphemes which give it the structure of a sentence:

The yigs wur vumly rixing hum in jeggest miv.

Moreover, numerous works have demonstrated the psychological relevance of the idea of constituents which form cohesive processing units. The best-known experimental method is that employed by Bever and MIT colleagues (see, for example, Fodor and Bever, 1965). While listening to a sentence, subjects also hear a brief sound (a 'click') whose position they are then asked to identify. As an example, let us take these sentences:

(1) As a direct result of their new invention's influence the company was given an award.
(2) The retiring chairman whose methods still greatly influence the company was given an award.

In (1) the constituent boundary is located after 'influence'; in (2) it is after 'company'. If the click is placed within 'company', subjects tend to move it towards the constituent boundary. This can be interpreted in terms of the 'pregnance' of the syntactic constituents (at least of the main constituents) which could be thought of as forming the perceptual units that would tend to displace intrusive elements to their boundaries.

Deep structure

Chomsky's key contribution, however, is the idea of 'deep structure'. This does not have to coincide with surface structure, and in such cases researchers have attempted to demonstrate that it is deep structure which determines the psychological organization of the sentence.

Thus (Walker, Gough and Wall, 1968), in the sentence:

The scouts the Indians saw killed a buffalo

the deep structure comprises two elements: 'The scouts killed a buffalo' and 'The Indians saw the scouts'. If subjects are presented with two words and asked to decide whether both are present in the sentence, it is observed that response latency depends on the distance between the two words in deep structure (not in surface structure). Thus the shortest response latency is observed for the pair 'scouts, killed', whereas the pairs 'scouts, saw' and 'Indians, saw' result in identical response latencies despite the fact that they are distributed differently in surface structure.

Similarly, in cued recall tests, words form more effective cues the more important their function in the sentence is. However, it is their function in deep structure rather than in surface structure that is decisive. For example (Blumenthal, 1967), in two sentences sharing an identical surface structure:

Gloves were made by tailors
Gloves were made by hand

'tailors' is a more effective cue for the first sentence than 'hand' is for the second (because in deep structure, 'tailors' is the subject of the first sentence). A word will therefore act as a better recall cue if it occurs more than once in deep structure (even if it appears only once in surface structure). Thus in the pair of sentences:

John is easy to please
John is eager to please

'John' appears only once in the deep structure of the first sentence (which can be paraphrased as 'It is easy for someone to please John'), but twice in the deep structure of the second sentence ('John is eager that John pleases someone'). 'John' is therefore a more effective cue for the recall of the second sentence than the first (Blumenthal and Boakes, 1967).

Finally, Bever, Lackner and Kirk (1969) used the 'click' method to show that when the constituent boundaries in deep structure do not coincide with the surface structure boundaries, displacement is performed towards the former.

These results demonstrate conclusively that the listener constructs an organized representation of the sentence. But are we sure that this is a *syntactic* organization? As Johnson-Laird (1974) has noted, these results can equally well be interpreted as indications of *semantic* processing. Furthermore, some data suggest a psychological organization which is relatively independent of syntax.

Thus Chapin, Smith and Abrahamson (1972) found that click displacement can be determined by both surface and deep structure. However, Carroll, Tanenhaus and Bever (1978) have shown that the organization of words into processing units may not correspond to either of these two structures but to 'functional units', more semantic than syntactic in nature, which are primarily determined by working-memory capacity. The work of Gee and Grosjean (1983), referred to below (p. 114), supports this idea.

In conclusion, there seems to be no more proof of the 'psychological reality' of a syntactic deep structure than there is of transformations.

The new Chomskyan theory

Chomsky's Standard Theory model has finally been seen to be irrelevant from the psycholinguistic perspective. However, it has also encountered serious difficulties in the field of linguistics itself, and this has led to a substantial reworking of the theory.

The current form of the theory, proposed by Chomsky (1981) under the name 'Government–Binding (GB) Theory', differs significantly from the Standard Theory. We shall limit ourselves to pointing out some of its key characteristics here:

1. The concepts of deep structure and surface structure are retained (under the names D-structure and S-structure), but the semantic interpretation (or, more exactly, the 'logical form' on which this interpretation is based) is constructed on the basis of the surface structure alone. Effectively, this surface structure contains 'traces' of transformations performed on deep structure.

2. The multiplicity of transformational rules is replaced by a single rule: 'move α' – any constituent of a sentence may be moved anywhere. However, the application of this rule is subject to a number of constraints, the description of which is the principal object of the syntactic theory. A small number of very general principles should suffice.

3. This set of principles constitutes the Universal Grammar: the various natural languages differ from one another only in the values they attribute to a set of parameters. At birth, children would possess the principles of the Universal Grammar, which would comprise a biologically determined knowledge set. All they would have to learn (apart, of course, from the lexicon) would be the particular value assumed by the different parameters in their language.[3]

Two aspects of GB Theory in particular have given rise to experimental research.

The processing of anaphora
One of the key aspects of the theory is the specification of the constraints upon the possible relationships between a pronoun and its antecedent. Simplifying greatly, it is possible to identify the following principles:

- A pronoun ('him', for example) may not have an antecedent within its domain (in general terms, the 'domain' can be equated with the clause).
- A reflexive ('himself', for example) must have an antecedent within its domain.

Moreover, the antecedent must be located higher up the phrase-structure tree than the pronoun. These syntactic constraints explain the different interpretation of the pronoun in:

(1a) John said he was tired
(1b) He said John was tired
(2a) John said Bill loved him
(2b) John said Bill loved himself

A number of researchers have attempted to discover whether the choice of antecedent obeys these syntactic constraints. The principle underlying these

---

3. A number of studies have attempted to bring this 'parameter setting' to light. For a review of this research, see Stevenson (1988).

experiments is to test (by means of a lexical decision task, for example) whether, at the moment when the pronoun is presented, the words corresponding to the syntactically possible antecedents are reactivated (a phenomenon which gives rise to shorter reaction times). For example, Nicol (quoted in Nicol and Swinney, 1989) presented sentences such as:

(3a) The boxer told the skier that the doctor for the team would blame himself for the recent injury

and noted that after 'himself' reactivation of the word 'doctor' is significant, whereas that of 'boxer' and 'skier' is not. In contrast, if 'him' is substituted for 'himself':

(3b) The boxer told the skier that the doctor for the team would blame him for the recent injury

the two words 'boxer' and 'skier' are activated, while 'doctor' is not.

A series of experiments of this type (for a review, see Nicol and Swinney, 1989) thus leads us to think that the activation of the possible antecedents is performed automatically on the basis of purely syntactic, rather than semantic, criteria. For example, in the sentence:

(4) Ellen aimed a pistol at Harriet but she did not pull the trigger

the antecedent of 'she' is obviously 'Ellen', for reasons which are purely pragmatic (that is to say, they derive from our knowledge of the world). Syntactically, either of the proper nouns could constitute the antecedent; indeed, in a verification task (Corbett and Chang, 1983) it has been shown that both names are activated equally on the appearance of the pronoun. This process would then be analogous to the one proposed by Swinney (1979) concerning lexical access to ambiguous words: an initial, automatic processing stage (here, syntactic in nature) would provide a set of possibilities, and only when this stage has been completed will a choice be made on the basis of semantic or pragmatic knowledge.

Empty categories
One special case of anaphora which is covered by Chomsky's theory is particularly interesting: empty categories. These are sentence components which are not realized phonologically, notably *traces* which correspond to a position which has been left empty by the movement of a component, as in:

(5) I wonder which of the books John has read (*t*) before class

where the wh-phrase 'which of the books' has been moved from its initial position after 'read' but has left an invisible trace.[4]

A number of experiments have been devoted to demonstrating the psychological reality of these empty categories.[5] Swinney *et al.* (1988), for example, have noted that in sentences such as:

(6) The policeman saw the boy that the crowd at the party accused (*t*) of the crime

the word 'boy' is reactivated after 'accused' (that is to say, at the position of the trace left by its movement), while 'policeman' and 'crowd' are not reactivated.

Other syntactic theories

Despite this renewal of interest in theories of Chomskyan inspiration, the current situation is far from that of the 1970s, when the Standard Theory was generally considered to be the definitive form of linguistic theory.

First of all, a number of linguists started to cast doubt on the autonomy of syntax as conceived by Chomsky, and suggested that sentences can be derived from a semantic deep structure. This is the direction taken by Fillmore (1968) with his theory of case grammar, to which we have already referred. Secondly, the supporters of *generative semantics* (Lakoff, Ross, McCawley, Postal) were to propose an even more radical theory in which semantic structure is involved at all stages of syntactic derivation.[6]

Although these attempts were later abandoned, other linguistic theories have been proposed which reject the idea of an autonomous syntax independent of the semantic aspect. These theories include Langacker's (1986) 'Cognitive Grammar' or, in France, Culioli's (1990) theory of utterance operations.

---

4. It is possible to identify certain phonological effects of these traces. Some contractions are possible only when traces are absent. For example, 'want to' can be contracted to 'wanna' in

Who does John want to speak to (*t*)?

but not in

Who does John want (*t*) to speak to the students?

5. For a detailed review, see Fodor (1989).
6. For a review of some of the essential ideas of generative semantics, see Lakoff (1970). Parisi and Antinucci's brief *Essentials of Grammar* (1976) presents the broad lines of a grammar inspired by this movement in a simplified form

Finally, other authors, while preserving the idea of syntactic autonomy, have attempted to construct grammars with a greater claim to psychological plausibility. This is the case, for example, with Gazdar *et al.* (1985) Generalized Phrase Structure Grammar or Bresnan's (1982) Lexical Functional Grammar (LFG), both of which reject the idea of transformation and, as a consequence, that of deep structure. Both grammars – and Bresnan's LFG in particular – accord considerable significance to lexical information.

This proliferation of linguistic models, between which it is difficult to distinguish empirically, has finally led many psycholinguists to distance themselves somewhat from such models, and even to change the fundamental terms of the question they are addressing. The question is no longer: How do subjects construct *the* syntactic structure of a sentence? but rather: What do subjects construct when they interpret a sentence, and how do they construct it?

Sentence processing

While the formal linguistic model of generative grammar was still considered to be a relevant psycholinguistic model, the interpretation of a sentence consisted of reconstructing its syntactic derivation – in other words, of reproducing the series of operations which had generated the sentence.

The simplest idea is clearly to apply the grammatical rules in reverse. Since all the rules are of the form $X \rightarrow Y$, it is sufficient to perform the reverse operations $Y \rightarrow X$. The problem is that this appears to be impracticable for transformational rules (how is it possible, for example, to reconstruct an element deleted by a transformation of the form $X \rightarrow \emptyset$).

Thus the most appropriate model appeared to be that of *analysis by synthesis*, which we have already mentioned in connection with speech perception. Faced with a sentence, subjects construct a set of possible syntactic derivations, compare the results with their perception, and terminate the search when they have found a satisfactory match. However, this model also rapidly becomes impracticable when it is confronted by a slightly complex sentence. In such a case, the number of hypotheses to be tested rapidly reaches astronomical proportions. The simple implementation of algorithms which calculate all the possibilities in a regulated fashion must at least be augmented, if not replaced, by *heuristics* – that is to say, procedures which *a priori* make it possible to select the most probable hypotheses.

Even while remaining faithful to the Chomskyan model, it thus became necessary to accept the importance of purely psychological procedures which did not form part of the operations described by linguists.

The 'perceptual strategies'

The difficulties underlying the analysis-by-synthesis model on the one hand, and the failure of the derivational theory of complexity on the other, led Fodor and Garrett to suggest, from 1967 onwards, that the essential task of psycholinguistics was the study of the *strategies* which enable listeners to collect and use the cues on the basis of which they are able to determine the relations obtaining between the elements of a sentence. In an important article, Bever (1970) developed this idea, listed a number of these strategies and identified the theoretical implications of this approach.

The strategies described by Bever – and justified by him on the basis of a set of experimental data – are founded on both the grammatical properties (nouns, verbs, adjectives, inflections, etc.) and the semantic properties of words. Examples of such strategies are:

- segmenting the sentence into sequences of elements which can be linked by relationships of the type 'actor–action–object';
- considering the first noun–verb–noun sequence as the main clause (unless there is an explicit marker of subordination), etc.

These strategies are based on general principles of perception (for example, it is impossible for an element to perform two functions simultaneously). This led Bever to suggest that it is in the constraints associated with cognitive procedures that the source of linguistic structures is to be sought. Linguistic competence thus depends on performance (not the other way round) and linguistic structures are based on constraints of a cognitive nature.

The strategies described by Bever were, as we have just seen, partly semantic in character. The studies which have followed have generally been conducted from a more purely syntactic perspective, with the aim of constructing plausible models of human 'parsing' (that is to say, the apparatus for syntactic analysis), which is frequently thought of as an autonomous processing module.

One of the most influential models is Frazier's (Frazier and Fodor, 1978; Frazier, 1987), which derives the parsing operations from two heuristic principles:

- the principle of Minimal Attachment: 'Do not postulate any potentially unnecessary nodes';
- the principle of Late Closure: 'If grammatically permissible, attach new items into the clause or phrase currently being processed.'

Since sentences are processed as they are perceived, the application of these principles can lead to a 'garden-path effect'. In other words, the deduced structure may prove inadequate, thus necessitating backtracking on the part of the subject. For example, in the sentence:

The girl knew the answer was correct

the initial analysis interprets 'the answer' as the object of 'knew'. When the sentence continues after 'answer', a reanalysis becomes necessary.

According to Frazier, these two strategies, which both derive from a general principle of economy of processing, are able to account for a large number of observations (for a review, see Frazier, 1987). We shall investigate the experimental data invoked in support of this model below.

The contribution of information technology: ATNs

At the same time as psychologists were starting to turn their attention to the procedures used by human subjects to analyze sentences, computer scientists were independently tackling the same problem. A widely used type of model for machine language processing is the ATN (*augmented transition network*).

An ATN consists of two elements: first, a set of 'transition networks' which constitute the grammar of the system; and second, a processor which performs the various operations commanded by the point of the network at which it is located. The simplified example given in Figure 5.1 illustrates the functioning of an ATN.

Let us take the sentence 'The old train left the station'. The processor starts at state S_0. This has a single arc leading from it carrying the instruction

Sentence Network:

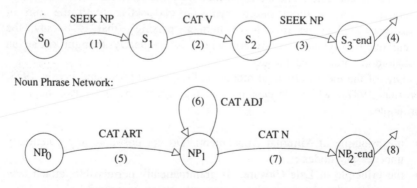

Noun Phrase Network:

Figure 5.1 An example of a simplified ATN (based on Wanner and Maratsos, 1978, p. 124)

to 'seek a noun phrase'. The processor notes the point at which it leaves the main network and transfers to the NP network. First arc: is the word being processed an article? The response is yes and the processor therefore records 'the' together with the label 'determiner' before moving to the next arc. Here, two arcs leave from the state NP_1: the first of these initiates a search for an adjective, and 'old' is found. This is recorded with the label 'modifier', and the same arc is followed again. However, since 'train' is not an adjective, it is necessary to pass on to the next arc. This time the test is positive: 'train' is a noun and is recorded with the label 'head'. The NP network terminates, and the processor assembles the noun phrase whose elements it has just identified and returns to the point where it exited from the main network. It notes that the first arc has been successfully traversed and assigns the label 'subject' to the noun phrase. It then passes on to the next arc, etc.

Of course, this model has been greatly simplified, but it does at least show how a grammar can be realized in the form of a network by processing a sentence 'from left to right' – that is to say, as the words are encountered (by a human subject), and without recourse to anything other than surface structure. One or more instructions correspond to each 'state' in the system. If more than one instruction is available, these are attempted one by one until one of them can be performed. Certain instructions may divert processing to another network (a 'sub-routine'). The important point is that the processor stores in memory (together with the results of its previous operations, of course): (a) the point at which it exited from one network to continue processing in another (multiple 'nestings' are also possible); (b) the point at which it has made a choice between a variety of possible instructions. This last point is important, since it enables the processor to return to an earlier point when an interpretation is contradicted by the continuation of the sentence.[7] Furthermore, in cases where a variety of interpretations are possible there is no reason why labelling should not be deferred until sufficient information has been gathered.

The interest of this type of model lies in the fact that since it represents grammatical knowledge in the form of a set of procedures, it naturally suggests itself as a model of psychological operations – one, moreover, which can be equally well applied to production or comprehension. Wanner and Maratsos (1978), in particular, have tried to establish experimentally the psychological validity of this type of model. To this end, they have used a variety of methods (phoneme detection, recall of a list of words presented at a point in a sentence) to measure the memory load imposed by the processing of a sentence. Their results accord well with predictions.

---

7. For example, the sentence 'The rich yield' might require reinterpretation depending on whether it continues 'little assistance' or 'from this year's harvest'.

However, although ATNs represent an attractive model, they nevertheless raise certain difficulties, the greatest of which is linked, paradoxically, to their power. An ATN can, in principle, process sentences of any degree of complexity. This, however, is clearly not the case for human subjects. In contrast, an ATN will have trouble interpreting a sentence which is ungrammatical ('Me not happy') or incomplete ('I'm going to box his . . . ') but would pose no problems for a human listener. Finally, in common with many of the models of artificial intelligence, ATNs are unsuited to accounting for the learning process.

Is syntactic processing autonomous?

From the perspective of Chomskyan psycholinguistics, the main problem to be resolved in understanding a sentence is the identification of its syntactic structure, as it is only on the basis of this identification that a semantic interpretation can be performed. This idea has been increasingly called into question: is it necessary to think of syntactic analysis as an automatic operation which takes place prior to any interpretation? And, ultimately, are there grounds for postulating any syntactic processing? The question of the autonomy of the syntactic 'component' has given rise to a great deal of debate but, as yet, no definitive resolution.

A number of the experimental arguments used to support the existence of an autonomous syntactic 'component' (that is to say, a stage in the processing of a sentence which has as its aim the identification of its structure through the analysis of syntactic cues only) were introduced by Forster and colleagues (Forster and Ryder, 1971; Forster and Olbrei, 1973; Forster, 1979). The procedure used consists either of deciding whether a visually presented sentence is correct or not (a task analogous to that of lexical decision) or of reproducing a sentence presented one word at a time at a very rapid speed (16 words per second). The sentences differ in their syntactic complexity and their semantic acceptability (normal, bizarre or anomalous sentences). The results show that the very clear influence of syntactic complexity on complexity of processing (measured in terms of response time or the number of correctly reproduced words) is independent of the semantic character of the sentence. In particular, the effect of the 'reversibility' – or lack of it – of passive sentences which has been illustrated by Slobin (1966) is absent here. According to Forster, these results prove the existence of autonomous syntactic processing.

More recent work has brought further evidence to light in support of this autonomy. For example, as we have seen above, this is the case with research into anaphora inspired by the current Chomskyan theory (see Nicol and Swinney, 1989). The syntactic strategies proposed by Frazier (1987) were also conceived of as independent of semantic processing, which would occur later and would possibly give rise to a reanalysis ('garden-path effect'). For example, in the sentences:

(1) The spy saw the cop with binoculars
(2) The spy saw the cop with the revolver

the principle of Minimal Attachment requires that the prepositional phrase (introduced by 'with') is attached to the verb. To interpret it as the complement of the noun phrase ('the cop') would in fact require the creation of an additional node in the phrase-structure tree. While there is no problem applying this strategy to sentence (1), it fails when it reaches the word 'revolver' in sentence (2). It is therefore necessary to modify the initial analysis. This is exactly what has been noted by Frazier and Rayner (1982), who observe that type (2) sentences require a longer reading time than type (1) sentences. Moreover, recordings of subjects' eye movements show that they backtrack when they reach the end of a type (2) sentence.

But are these effects really due to purely syntactic factors, or do they come from the reader's semantic expectations? This is the question posed by Taraban and McClelland (1988), who note that in the majority of the sentences used by Frazier and Rayner, the semantic content raises the expectation of a verb complement (the reader of the sentence 'The spy saw the cop' expects the instrument of observation to be defined). However, it is possible to construct sentences which cause the reader to expect a noun complement; for example:

(3) John ordered a pizza with pepperoni
(4) John ordered a pizza with enthusiasm

Taraban and McClelland therefore construct two lists of sentences corresponding to these two types of expectation. The reading times observed for the first list – which, in fact, reuses the material employed by Frazier and Rayner – confirm these authors' results. However, the results for the second list are the exact reverse: the reading time for type (4) sentences, which correspond to the principle of Minimal Attachment, is longer than for type (3) sentences.

The effects of context-dependent expectations have also been demonstrated by Tyler and Marslen-Wilson (1977), who asked their subjects to listen to sentences containing a syntactic ambiguity which could be resolved with the help of the prior context, for example:

(5) If you walk too near the runway, *landing planes. . .*
(6) If you've been trained as a pilot, *landing planes. . .*

Immediately after the last word ('planes') they presented the word 'is' or 'are' visually and asked their subjects to say it as quickly as possible. The response times were significantly lower when 'are' was coupled with sentence (5) and when 'is' followed sentence (6). The grammatical structure of the ambiguous phrase ('landing planes') is thus determined as soon as the phrase is heard on the basis of cues which cannot be syntactic but derive from the subjects' interpretation of the sentence.

A possible interpretation of these results would, of course, be to accept that the syntactic component does not construct a single structure but all the possible structures and that the observed contextual effects intervene immediately after computation to aid in the selection of the correct analysis. This, however, would be to make the modular theory of syntactic autonomy practically incapable of disproof.

Marslen-Wilson and Tyler (1980; 1987) suggest that we reject not only the idea of a 'syntactic component' but also, more generally, the notion of distinct 'processing levels': the subject's activity consists essentially of constructing an *interpretation* of the sentence; this interpretation commences at the beginning of the sentence and is simultaneously based on all the types of available information (lexical, syntactic, contextual).

The arguments, both syntactic and theoretical, presented by Marslen-Wilson and Tyler in support of this 'interactive' conception of language processing seem quite convincing. However, that the existence of automatic syntax processors which function unmonitored by the subject should not be rejected entirely is suggested, for example, by an experiment conducted by Florès d'Arçais (1982), who asked subjects to point out errors in the sentences they were given to read. Although the rate of identification of syntactic errors was generally very low (in contrast to typographical and semantic errors), they gave rise to longer and more frequent ocular fixations than the correct passages. There would thus appear to be an automatic syntactic processing whose results are not necessarily used consciously by the subject.

Syntax or semantics?

The idea of a purely syntactic processing level has also been seriously questioned by research inspired by artificial intelligence, the thrust of which is close to that of work undertaken by Marslen-Wilson. However, this time the criticism is based not on experimental arguments but on simple reasons of common sense. What do listeners try to do when they hear a sentence? To understand what has been said to them. What is essential is thus the job of semantic interpretation, and syntactic cues (word order, grammatical categories, morphological markers) serve only as clues helping in this interpretation. It is enough to use these clues as they arise to construct the meaning of the sentence and it is useless to construct a superfluous syntactic structure. In more colourful terms: 'If you can read the signposts, you don't need a map' (Johnson-Laird, 1977).

In an attempt to explain sentence processing, Johnson-Laird (1977) proposed bringing together the formalism of ATNs and the ideas of procedural semantics within what he termed STNs (*semantic transition networks*). These operate according to the same principles as ATNs, but with the crucial difference that what is constructed is not a syntactic structure but a direct semantic representation. The instructions which correspond to each arc of the network consist of calling up procedures associated with each word in order to identify a referent, attribute different roles (agent, patient, instrument, etc.), construct temporal and spatial relations, etc. The same function is equally applicable to both production and comprehension.

In the same vein, Riesbeck and Schank (1978) describe a language comprehension program which progressively constructs a 'conceptual' representation, in which the sentence is analyzed as it progresses as a function of the 'expectations' associated with previously analyzed elements, and general knowledge recorded in memory. If we take the example sentence:

John was given a book by Mary

'John' triggers a procedure which consists of constructing a representation ('a man named John') and storing it under the label TOPIC. This is followed by 'was': one of the procedures attached to 'be' consists of searching for a past participle. This arrives immediately with 'given'. The verb 'give' triggers the construction of a representation: (Agent) ATRANS (Object) (Recipient).[8] The procedures attached to 'be' place the TOPIC in the 'Recipient' slot and trigger a search for 'by', while the procedures attached to 'give' trigger the search for a noun with the feature 'material object', etc. Finally, the completed sentence gives rise to the representation:

A woman called Mary ATRANS a physical object used for reading to a man called John.

Once it has been interpreted in this way, the sentence is sent to the general 'understanding system' ready for integration with knowledge already present (concerning Mary, John, books and reading, etc.) and generation of the necessary inferences.

These ideas, which evidently turn their back on syntax and, more generally, linguistic analyses, are clearly of interest because they are,

---

8. ATRANS is a 'primitive action' which consists of transferring possession.

intuitively, quite plausible. Furthermore, they have given rise to computer simulations which, within certain limits, function reasonably well. As psychological models, however, they remain speculative, inhabiting the realms of armchair psychology and still lacking experimental validation. Nevertheless, to their credit we should note that in their general inspiration they agree fairly well with Marslen-Wilson's observations,

Furthermore, these models are able to account for both the comprehension and the production of language in terms of the same set of rules. Although this may be an advantage for a model of artificial intelligence, it is not necessarily so for a psychological model which may need to deal with two distinct types of processes. We must now turn our attention to the current state of knowledge concerning the production mechanisms.

The production of utterances

While the study of comprehension processes can help to shed light on the study of production processes,[9] there is clearly a set of problems which are specific to the latter. One important difference becomes clear immediately: listeners can content themselves with a partial analysis of utterances which they have to comprehend (semantic and situational cues frequently free them from the necessity, for example, of performing a complete syntactic analysis); when speakers produce utterances, however, they have to make explicit every aspect of what they say.

The activity of verbal production is characterized by two essential aspects:

- First, verbal production requires *planning*: in so far as any linguistic production constitutes an entity which is organized at various levels (discourse, sentence, phrase, word), each of these levels necessitates the elaboration of an overall plan for the realization of the production.
- Second, the implementation of these plans requires a series of *choices* amongst the variety of means made available by the language.

Planning utterances

Speech production is an activity which is performed with a view to a certain objective (to provide the listener with information, to persuade the listener to accept a particular representation or to act in a particular way, etc.).[10] At an

9. To some extent comprehension processes consist of reproducing the procedures used by the speaker to produce the utterance. This is, in fact, the essential idea of the 'analysis-by-synthesis' models.
10. This objective is itself part of more general short-term or long-term plans. Of course, on the one hand, the 'plans' which we are discussing here are not necessarily the object of explicit calculation; and on the other, they can at any moment be refashioned to a greater or lesser degree.

initial level, speakers must decide (vaguely or precisely) on the content of what they are going to say and the order in which they are going to present it. Each stage of the plan will (broadly speaking) correspond to a sentence. Once the semantic representation corresponding to a sentence has been constructed, it is necessary to programme its formulation. An overall syntactic framework has to be provided (to take a simple example, a schema of the form Agent–Action–Object–Time). Each of the slots in this framework will accommodate phrases which, in general, will consist of a combination of lexical units ('government ministers', 'for several months', etc.), each of which will also require planning. A phonological sequence is then constructed, and this makes it possible to establish a motor (articulatory) programme which concludes with the final realization of the sentence.

Although this analysis is, of course, theoretical, it does enable us to identify the two main types of problem which must be addressed by empirical studies. The first is connected with the *levels* of planning (their psychological reality, their interrelations, and the procedures which take place within them). The second relates to the *units* with which planning at these various levels is concerned.

I. An initial source of information regarding the levels of speech planning may be found in *speech errors*.

We can distinguish between two types of speech error. The most frequent are word *exchanges* ('As you *reap*, so shall you *sow*') or sound exchanges ('*spi*ctly *str*eaking') and *shifts* ('I'd forgot about*en* that'). *Anticipations* and *perseverations* generally affect sounds ('The song called Yank*le* Doodle Dandy', 'I dreamt that he *dr*oke his arm'). Finally, there are also *substitutions* of words ('I've got an *apartment* (appointment) now') and blends ('That's *to*rrible!' = terrible + horrible).[11]

These different speech errors testify to the simultaneous presence in the mental representation of two units between which there is an exchange or a substitution. Thus such errors can provide useful information about the organization of the different planning levels.

In studies of a large corpus (4,200 errors observed in spontaneous speech), Garrett (1980, 1982) has identified some interesting regularities. Thus word exchanges generally involve words of the same grammatical

---

11. The last two types of error (substitutions and blends) formed the object of Freud's famous analysis in *The Psychopathology of Everyday Life*. They can be thought of as deriving from the competition between different plans – at what Garrett (see below) describes as the 'functional' level.

category and almost always 'content' words (nouns, verbs, adjectives). They can also appear over large distances, extending from one phrase to another. In contrast, sound exchanges (and, similarly, anticipations and perseverations) generally occur within a single phrase and ignore grammatical categories. The same is true for shifts, which generally involve 'function' words (adverbs, prepositions, pronouns, etc.) or grammatical inflections.

These observations have led Garrett to distinguish between two levels in utterance planning:

- a *functional* level which involves both the selection of 'content' words (still in an abstract form which contains only their semantic and grammatical characteristics) and the definition of their grammatical function: at this level, which concerns units of sentence size, neither the surface order of the elements nor their phonological form is yet represented;
- a *positional* level at which the grammatical morphemes are inserted and the phonological form and the order of realization are specified.

In broad terms, this distinction may be compared to the two main types of classic aphasia: the first (Broca's aphasia) in which sufferers, while retaining their naming ability, have lost the use of functional morphemes and the capacity to combine words to form sentences (agrammatism); and the second (Wernicke's aphasia) in which sufferers remain capable of constructing sentences but are unable to retrieve 'content' words (which they often replace with neologisms while retaining the correct grammatical inflections).

However, the distinction may be less simple than this, and we should doubtless expect there to be interactions between these levels. An analysis of another corpus carried out by Dell and Reich (1981) has shown that word exchanges (which should derive from the 'functional' level alone) are significantly affected by phonological similarities (which relate to the 'positional' level) and, conversely, that sound-related errors tend, equally significantly, to produce real words rather than non-words (and are thus dependent on factors involved at the 'functional' level).

II. Further data are supplied by the study of *pauses* in spontaneous speech. In fact, pauses have a variety of functions. Clearly, one role is to permit the speaker to breathe. Another concerns the exigencies of communication and allows the listener time to understand what has been said. The subject's emotional state may also have a role to play here. However, pauses may also be indications of 'cognitive difficulty': these are moments at which speakers stop to plan the continuation of their speech.

The first and most important work to be carried out in connection with this subject was conducted by Frieda Goldman-Eisler from 1956 onwards.[12] A first result – which is by no means unexpected – is that pauses become more frequent as the difficulty of planning the semantic content of speech increases: for example, subjects hesitate less frequently and for shorter periods when they have to describe a humorous drawing than when they have to describe why it is funny. What is unexpected, however, is that the length of pauses is not affected by syntactic complexity: in contrast to semantic programming, which requires controlled cognitive activity, syntactic programming would appear to be the result of essentially automatic processes. This is confirmed by another of Goldman-Eisler's experiments (1968): the administering of a sedative (a barbiturate which acts at the cortical level) does not entail a modification of the syntactic complexity of subjects' utterances, whereas the administration of a neuroleptic (chlorpromazine, which acts on the reticular activating system and affects vigilance and arousal) brings about a significant fall-off in this syntactic complexity.

The main part of this cognitive work is thus performed at the level of semantic planning. Another important aspect manifested in connection with pauses is the question of *lexical selection*. Goldman-Eisler (1958) has shown that pauses almost always precede words of a higher degree of uncertainty.

Further detail is brought to these results by Butterworth (1980*b*) on the basis of a very precise analysis of spontaneous monologues. These reveal a quite regular organization into 'cycles' in which there is an initial phase characterized by a high proportion of hesitations and a second phase which is much more 'fluent'. Each cycle lasts between 20 and 30 seconds on average and extends over three to four sentences. The first phase essentially seems to correspond to a *semantic* planning stage concerned not only with the current sentence but also with the sentences which are to follow. During the second phase, semantic planning has been completed and hesitations correspond solely to word searches. At this stage, however, the pauses preceding words are shorter (by approximately a third). Butterworth interprets this with the supposition that the semantic representation of the words has been acquired, and only their phonological representation remains to be found. An interesting study conducted by Beattie (1980) confirms this interpretation. This has as its object a parallel analysis of the pauses, gestures and ocular fixations of subjects who are speaking to a listener. Gestures – which, during the first period (hesitant), essentially have the role of punctuating the speech – become 'iconic' during the second (they precede the emission of a word and 'mime' it in some way – this would suggest that the semantic characteristics of the word are already available). Moreover, the speaker frequently looks away from the listener during the first phase (which

---

12. For a detailed review of research into this subject, see Butterworth (1980*b*).

would indicate the existence of a search stage) only to concentrate his gaze on him during the second.

III. To sum up: the data available to us – somewhat limited in scope, it is true – allow us to distinguish between various planning levels bearing on units which differ in nature and size:

- At an initial level, semantic planning progresses over a domain which may exceed the scope of the sentence. At this level, the representation is conceptual and pre-verbal in nature.
- We should probably distinguish between this initial level and Garrett's 'functional' level, which would correspond to an 'interface' between the cognitive representation and its verbalization. The representation enters this level in the form of discrete, still unlinearized units. The units on which processing focuses at this level might correspond to the clause.[13] At this level, lexical elements are still represented only in their semantic form.
- Finally, a third level – Garrett's 'positional' level – involves the phonological realization of the words, the addition of the functional morphemes and the ordering of the utterance into its linear form. At this level the programming unit would appear to be phrase-sized.

It is noteworthy that this description contains no level corresponding to autonomous *syntactic* processing. Neither in comprehension nor in production are any effects of syntactic complexity observed. The programming units at the 'functional' level seem to be essentially semantic, whereas at the 'positional' level they seem to have a phonological character.

A number of studies of this subject conducted by Gee and Grosjean (1983) have revealed a remarkable agreement between very diverse experimental data (sentence recall, segmentation, judgement of word associations, length of pauses in slow reading or in spontaneous speech). The 'performance structures' they identify do not correspond to the syntactic structure which the linguist would describe. Rather, they comprise a hierarchical and symmetrical organization involving basic units of equal length. These units could be defined as *phonological phrases*, centred around a stressed 'content' word and constituting the units of both production and comprehension.

---

13. Ford and Holmes's observations (1978) might be of relevance at this level. These authors, who asked their subjects to detect clicks produced at regular intervals while they were speaking, observed that reaction times were longer at the end of clauses that is to say, at the point where the work of planning the next clause would be carried out.

Syntactic processing thus appears to be largely automatic and, in any case, essentially subordinate to semantic and lexical decisions (see Bock, 1982), and doubtless also, as we shall now see, to functional determinations.

The speaker's choices

There is one essential aspect of verbal production which we have not yet looked at. A given semantic content does not correspond to *a single* linguistic realization. The speaker must make a choice – or, more precisely, a series of choices – between a number of possible formulations. How are these choices determined?

I. *Lexical selection* may depend on a number of factors. First of all, we cannot ignore an automatic activation effect: the word chosen is in fact the first one that comes to mind – or (in more technical terms) the one which is activated most quickly. This activation speed depends primarily on the frequency of use, but what is it that determines this frequency?

The work of Rosch *et al.* (1976), for example, demonstrates the existence of a 'basic level' which is the preferred recourse of subjects in naming tasks. For example, subjects choose the word 'apple' rather than a more general term ('fruit') or a more specific one ('pippin'). The terms corresponding to this basic level are, in general, used more frequently and are the first to be learned by children. However, Rosch has shown that at the same time these words correspond to an optimum level of categorization at which the members of the category possess the maximum number of similarities to other members of the category and the maximum number of differences from members of neighbouring categories. Seen in this light, frequency of use reflects a functional preference. In many cases, the 'basic level' terms are those which guarantee the most effective communication.

The choice of a term therefore depends essentially on its functional value. As Olson and Clark in particular have demonstrated (see above, p. 87), this function is to differentiate an element of the representation from other elements (present or potential) within the particular field on which speech is focused. This derives partly from the speaker's current representation of the field and partly from the representation which the speaker attributes to the listener. We shall return to this problem in the next chapter.

II. The problem of the *order of utterance* may be approached in a similar manner. Here again, automatic activation phenomena may have a role to play.

For example, Bock (1982) has adduced a number of experimental arguments to show that – in some cases, at least – the syntactic structure of utterances is determined by the variable speed of lexical access. The most accessible word (either because of its frequency or because it has been pre-activated by the context) will be placed at the beginning of the utterance. The subsequent construction of the sentence will be adapted to this word through the implementation of largely automated syntactic patterns.

This lexical activation may depend on a simple phenomenon of 'priming' (which, as Bock says, would help to account for the fact that 'old' or 'given' information is often found at the start of an utterance where it precedes 'new' information)? However, there can be no doubt about the involvement of other effects associated with attention and, more generally, the orientation of the discourse and the speaker's awareness of the listener's point of view. Here, too, we are in the presence of problems which are no longer semantic but pragmatic, and we shall return them in greater detail in the next chapter.

III. Finally, an utterance is not limited to a simple formulation of the (informational) content of a representation. It constitutes an *act of uttering* through which the speaker creates a certain relationship between himself, his listener and the content of his speech:

- First, the speaker must decide on the type of *speech act* to perform: statement, question, order, wish, promise, threat, etc.; these will give rise (on the basis of the same semantic content) to different forms (syntactic and/or intonational) of utterance. Furthermore, a given type of speech act – an order, for example – can be expressed directly ('Close the door!') or more or less indirectly ('Would you mind closing the door?' or even 'What a draught there is in here!').
- Second, even a simple statement is not the straightforward verbal actualization of a representation. Instead, the speaker is stating a position and then acting, in some way, as its guarantor. This statement of position must itself be qualified in some way by a *modality* ('perhaps', 'I think that', 'it's clear', 'of course', etc.), the absence of modal markers being simply one of the possible choices.[14]
- Finally, the utterance does not generally occur in isolation but has a function within the discourse. The speaker can employ a variety of methods to mark this function, the use of *connectives* ('but', 'since', 'therefore', etc.) being particularly frequent.

From this we can see that a study of the processes of verbal production cannot do without either determinants of a *pragmatic* nature (which concern

14. We can also consider acts of reported speech in connection with this question of 'taking responsibility'. In such instances, speakers assign the responsibility for an utterance to sources other than themselves, or indeed to a series of nested sources: 'According to BBC reports, the lawyer said his clients felt embarrassed about the problems they had brought upon their country' (*Daily Telegraph*, 18.4.92).

the relations between utterance, speakers and situation of utterance) or the organization of discourse, of which the utterance is only one element. Before considering these two sets of problems we must return to the processes of comprehension, in which connection we shall see that the same problems arise.

The semantic representation

The idea of propositional representation

Sentence processing leads to the construction of a semantic representation. As we saw in the last chapter, the idea that has gained the most general acceptance is that this representation is abstract and conceptual in nature. It is thought to be 'amodal' – that is to say, independent of the modality – verbal or pictorial – in which the information can be materialized and transmitted.

It is easy to observe that meaning is independent of its verbal substrate. When we listen to a conversation or follow a speech we can, in general, repeat word for word the last sentence (or at least the last clause) we have heard. Of what has gone before, however, we retain only the general meaning, without normally being able to repeat it accurately.

Some now classic experiments by Fillenbaum (1966) and Sachs (1967, 1974) have shown that the literal formulation of a sentence is forgotten very quickly, while its meaning is retained precisely. Thus, a sentence located in the middle of a paragraph can no longer be distinguished from its various paraphrases (change of syntactic form, replacement of a word by a synonym) once it has been followed by a text of about 40 syllables. In contrast, subjects readily detect even a minimal change to its meaning.

An interesting experiment conducted by Potter, Valian and Faulconer (1977) shows that during the comprehension process itself, meaning is independent of both the verbal substrate and the pictorial representation. These authors asked subjects to listen to sentences (for example, 'The jungle shrilled with the cries of exotic birds') immediately followed by the visual presentation of a word or a picture (for example, 'monkey' or a picture representing a monkey). The subjects had to decide quickly whether or not the word or picture coincided with the meaning of the sentence. If this meaning was mentally represented in a specific 'format' (verbal or pictorial), then it should be possible to observe longer response times in connection with those cases (words or pictures) which had to be translated from one modality to the other. However, no such time difference was observed. Moreover, response times were affected neither by the capacity of the sentence to evoke an image nor by the semantic (linguistic) relationship between the test word and the sentence. This indicates that a sentence is comprehended in the form of a representation which is neither verbal nor pictorial, but can equally easily be translated into either of these two modalities.

The semantic representation of a sentence must therefore be thought of as a set of information recorded in an abstract form. As we saw in the last chapter, the detailed formulation of this representation is conceived of in a great variety of ways (lists or networks, various types of 'labelled relations', conceptual units which may or may not be deconstructed into primitive elements). There is, however, general agreement about the *propositional* character of this representation. In other words, it is accepted that the basic unit is *predication*, the position of a relation bearing on one or more concepts.

A sentence generally contains a number of hierarchically organized propositions. For example (Kintsch and Van Dijk, 1978), the sentence: 'A series of violent, bloody encounters between police and Black Panthers Party members punctuated the early summer days of 1969' can be divided into seven propositions:[15]

1. (SERIES, ENCOUNTER)
2. (VIOLENT, ENCOUNTER)
3. (BLOODY, ENCOUNTER)
4. (BETWEEN, ENCOUNTER, POLICE, BLACK PANTHER)
5. (TIME: IN, ENCOUNTER, SUMMER)
6. (EARLY, SUMMER)
7. (TIME: IN, SUMMER, 1969)

Proposition 4 governs all the others (level 1); 1, 2, 3 and 5 are directly subordinate to it (level 2), while 6 and 7 are dependent on 5 (level 3).

Numerous experiments have been conducted in an attempt to establish the psychological reality of this propositional representation. Thus Kintsch (1974), who presented subjects with sentences containing an equal number of words but a different number of underlying propositions, noted that reading time is a function of the number of propositions present. Moreover, the higher the position of a proposition in the hierarchical structure of the sentence, the easier it is to recall. Other experiments have shown, for example, that the effect of semantic priming is more marked between words belonging to the same proposition than between words belonging to different propositions (Ratcliff and McKoon, 1978), etc.

The interest of the propositional representation of meaning – apart from

15. Of course, the way in which the propositions are presented is purely a matter of conventional – and convenient – notation.

its psychological plausibility – lies in the fact that it also lends itself to a description of units larger than the sentence. The hierarchical organization of propositions can extend to the level of the text – we shall return to this question in Chapter 7.

However, can this representation alone provide us with a satisfactory account of comprehension? In other words, have we understood a sentence when we have reduced it to an organized set of predicative relations between concepts? As we shall see, a number of experimental data suggest that we should take our investigation further.

Semantic integration

Understanding a sentence does not consist solely of extracting the information it contains but also of identifying what this information relates to and integrating it into a coherent whole. This process of *semantic integration* has been demonstrated by a group of experiments conducted by Bransford and colleagues.

Let us take the example of a complex sentence containing four propositions (for example, 'The ants in the kitchen ate the sweet jelly which was on the table'). Bransford and Franks (1972) constructed a set of sentences derived from this but containing only one, two or three propositions (for example: 'The jelly was sweet', 'The ants ate the jelly which was on the table', etc.). They presented their subjects with a list of sentences constructed in this way and then submitted them to a recognition task in which they were asked to judge their degree of certainty (on a scale of 5). Not only do subjects 'recognize' sentences which have not actually been presented to them (but can be constructed from those which they have listened to), but also the degree of certainty with which they claim to recognize the sentence increases with the number of propositions contained in the presented sentence – the highest certainty rating being conferred on a four-proposition sentence which has never been presented to the subjects! In fact, the subjects have constructed an integrated representation on the basis of the separate items of information presented to them, and it is this representation that is stored in memory.

If no such integration can be performed, comprehension becomes difficult and, in some cases, impossible. A group of experiments cited by Bransford and McCarrell (1974) consists of presenting paragraphs describing either an unusual scene or a general topic. When these paragraphs were presented in the absence of any context which would clarify the object of the commentary, they were judged to possess a low level of comprehensibility by subjects, who also enjoyed little success in tasks of recalling them. However, when the paragraphs were presented together with a title or a picture depicting the scene, the scores obtained in the recall and comprehension tasks more than doubled. It is important to note that no improvement was observed when the title or picture was presented *after* the reading of the text. It therefore appears that semantic integration is performed during the reading of the text.

During the construction of this integrated representation, verbal information is frequently complemented by other information which is not provided directly but which comes from the general or specific knowledge already possessed by the subject. In other words, comprehension involves *inference*, to such an extent that it is sometimes impossible to distinguish between what has actually been read or heard and what has been inferred. We shall return to these inferences in a later chapter, and limit ourselves here to a number of examples which are immediately relevant to the nature of the semantic representation.

In another recognition task, Bransford, Barclay and Franks (1972) noted that when subjects were presented with, for example, the sentence 'Three turtles rested on a floating log and a fish swam beneath them', a high level of false recognitions was observed in reaction to the modified sentence: ' . . . and a fish swam beneath it'. In contrast, this confusion does not arise when the first sentence starts: 'Three turtles rested beside a floating log . . . '. The authors conclude that the subjects have used the heard sentence to construct a global representation of the described scene and that they compare the sentence which is to be recognized with this representation.

But this is not always so. An experiment conducted by Mani and Johnson-Laird (1982) investigated series of sentences describing spatial relations, some of which are 'determinate' – that is to say, permit only a single representation – such as:

(1) The spoon is to the left of the knife, the plate is to the right of the knife, the fork is in front of the spoon, the cup is in front of the knife.

and others which are 'indeterminate' (and allow a number of possible representations):

(2) The spoon is to the left of the knife, the plate is to the right of the *spoon*, the fork is in front of the spoon, the cup is in front of the knife.

In a recognition task, subjects who had been given description (1) were able to retain its meaning but not its form, whereas the opposite was true of subjects who had been presented with description (2). The former thus appear to have constructed a mental model, while the latter have formed a simple propositional representation.

We must therefore accept that full comprehension requires not only a propositional representation which is drawn directly from the sentence, but also the construction of a *mental model* which integrates the various items of available information (possibly complemented by already known or probable information). In *Mental Models* (1983), Johnson-Laird showed how this idea of mental models can account for a large number of cognitive activities, from reasoning through to understanding of texts.

'Mental models' clearly possess certain characteristics of the *image*: on the one hand, they integrate a set of information within a single representation; on the other, they are structurally analogous to the reality they represent. However, they lack the pictorial nature of *images*: they are able to represent an abstract reality and, more significantly, they can underlie thought processes without themselves having to form the object of a conscious representation. It is preferable to think of them as a sort of schema of a greater or lesser degree of abstraction, on which the various mental procedures can be executed.

The function of the utterance

Furthermore, the verbal substrate of the utterance is not necessarily completely forgotten. Even if we ignore those – relatively exceptional – cases where a text is remembered 'by heart' over many years, or even for an entire lifetime (poems, prayers, etc.), the literal formulation of an utterance may be retained for longer than Sachs's experiments would suggest.

This fact is already observable in Sachs's own experiments, in which subjects who incorrectly recognize a paraphrase still attribute to it a lower level of certainty than the original sentence. In the same way, latencies observed in a verification task are longer for paraphrases, even after a ten-minute interval (Hayes-Roth and Hayes-Roth, 1977). A 'trace' of the verbal form of the utterance must therefore be retained for a certain period in long-term memory.

But a more interesting result has been brought to light by Keenan, McWhinney and Mayhew (1977), who first recorded a spontaneous discussion and then, 30 hours later, subjected the participants in the discussion to a recognition task. Sentences which are purely informative are scarcely distinguished from their paraphrases, whereas the distinction between sentences with a 'high interactional content' (jokes, personal criticism, etc.) is excellent. Kintsch and Bates (1977) obtained a similar result in connection with jokes, incidental remarks, etc., incorporated into a course attended by the subjects.

Why should this type of sentence be better recorded in its literal form than others? Keenan *et al.* think it is because information associated with this form has a special significance – not on account of the semantic content itself, but because of the *relations between interlocutors* which the sentence establishes. If a sentence functions in a way which directly affects such relations, it is natural that its form should be better recorded.

Therefore, if the literal form of an utterance can be remembered after a fairly long interval, this reflects the extent to which the form itself contributes to the meaning of the utterance. This observation invites us to *extend the notion of meaning itself*: this notion is not concerned solely with the (descriptive) semantic content of the utterance, but also with its (pragmatic) function in communication.

Utterances, therefore, carry two different types of information, and propositional notation runs the risk of obscuring these differences by failing to distinguish between the treatment of psychological representations which are not of the same type. On the one hand, the utterance transmits a certain informational content (the description of a state of affairs), while on the other it establishes certain relations between this content, the speakers, the situation of utterance and the rest of the discourse. We have already considered this second aspect in our discussion of the 'speaker's choices' in the production of an utterance.

Thus understanding an utterance also means identifying the speaker's choices and, through them, the 'intention' behind the utterance. This does not simply involve interpreting what is being said, but also identifying what *is being done* when it is being said and grasping 'what is being got at'. All this is expressed by means of linguistic processes and forms the object of psycholinguistic study. The study of the sentence, which started at the level of syntactic considerations and passed through the level of semantic considerations, has finally brought us to the problems of the pragmatics of language.

Conclusion

The study of the syntactic aspects of language processing has long held pride of place in the field of psycholinguistics. Today, the primacy of syntax is scarcely more than an outgrown stage of development. In the first place, this is because new theoretical methods and models have enabled researchers to investigate other types of problem (lexical access, semantic representation, speech processing). A second and more important reason is that syntactic issues have been subjected to a kind of internal deconstruction, both at the level of the psychological procedures involved in processing and in the conception of syntax itself.

1. Although the idea of an autonomous *'syntactic component'* may still have its supporters, it has been seriously undermined. It is hardly possible any longer to accept that comprehension of a sentence involves a stage at

which its syntactic structure is fully computed in order to be sent to a subsequent 'semantic component' in which its meaning is interpreted. In the first place, a body of work in the field of artificial intelligence has shown that it is possible to construct the meaning of a sentence directly, without passing through an intermediate stage in which a formal grammatical structure is determined (see Johnson-Laird, Schank). More important, however, is the fact that techniques of *on-line* analysis have shown that the elaboration of meaning commences at the very beginning of the sentence (see Marslen-Wilson). Subjects do not apply a series of analyses which tamely follow the sequence of analytic levels prescribed by the linguist. Instead, they use the various available information sources in parallel. This *interactive* character of processing, now fairly well established for the processes of comprehension, also appears probable at the (currently less well known) level of production processes.

2. At the same time, the conception of syntax as a *formal system* has become psychologically debatable. Syntactic features (word order, grammatical categories, functional morphemes) are signs just as much as words are. They indicate the existence of semantic relations (the 'roles' of the various elements: agent, action, instrument, etc.) on the one hand, and pragmatic relations (the function of elements, and of the utterance itself, in the act of communication) on the other. From a formal conception, we have moved on to a *functional* conception of syntax, which is no longer thought of as a system of rules for combining symbols but as a set of devices used in realizing the aims of communication.

Syntax, semantics and pragmatics no longer appear as independent, successive levels of analysis and processing. The structure of an utterance is inseparable from its meaning which, itself, is indissociably linked to the way in which it is used.

Recommended reading

Apart from the source works explaining the initial forms assumed by Chomsky's theory (Chomsky, 1957, 1965, 1972), a review of the psycholinguistic studies to have been inspired by generative grammar may be found in Greene's slender volume (1972). A more elaborate presentation is given in Fodor, Bever and Garrett (1974).

For the current form of the theory (Government–Binding), see Chomsky (1981). Cook (1988) has written a very clear presentation of the theory.

The different approaches to language processing in artificial intelligence are presented in a very simple form in Garnham (1988). For a more detailed and technical review, see Charniak and McDermott (1985).

An original and stimulating approach to the problems of semantic representation may be found in Johnson-Laird's important book *Mental Models* (1983).

Finally, Levelt (1989) provides a good summary of the work on language production.

CHAPTER 6

The Sentence 2: Pragmatics

The pragmatics of language

In the preceding chapters we have approached language as if we were dealing with a self-sufficient object: a system of signs possessing a certain structure, whose processing consists of operations regulated by this structure alone. We have frequently been forced to recognize the inadequacy of this approach.

Language is also an *instrument*. Speaking consists of more than simply combining signs; it is also the performance of an action: the production, in a particular context and intended for a particular listener, of utterances which have a particular objective. In other words, language does not just possess a specific structure, it is also used in a variety of ways. It is this *usage* of language that constitutes the field of study for pragmatics.

Interest in the pragmatic aspects of language has emerged relatively recently and is now represented in all the disciplines concerned with language: linguistics, sociolinguistics, the philosophy of language and artificial intelligence as well as, of course, psycholinguistics. However, there is still a long way to go before pragmatics can be said to constitute a coherent, unified field of study.

An initial difficulty arises when we try to define the *limits* of pragmatics. In fact, since language's conditions of use derive from the entirety of human experience and the factors which determine this, can pragmatics be said to represent anything other than a 'coverall' devoid of any theoretical unity?

A second problem arises when we try to situate pragmatics in relation to the other levels of analysis. Should we think of it as a complementary study which we can append to the analysis of the phonological, lexical, syntactic and semantic aspects of language? This approach considers language to be primarily a formal object with a certain structure which can be studied in isolation; besides that, it can also be used for various purposes. However, there is another way of looking at things. If language is primarily an instrument for communication and exchange, its structure will depend on this communicative function. Far from being supplementary, the pragmatic aspects would then constitute the very basis of language and language functioning.

The concept of 'pragmatics' has been approached in three different ways within the field of psycholinguistics.

I. First, language use clearly has recourse to a set of *extralinguistic knowledge*: general knowledge relating to the (physical or social) world and the general order of things; specific knowledge concerning the speaker (or listener); social rules associated with the relative status of the partners, etc.

We can thus speak of *pragmatic strategies* in the comprehension of sentences when, without performing a complete syntactic analysis, subjects simply rely on the probable relationship between the elements in the sentence in order to attribute a function to them. For example, the comprehension of a passive sentence can progress without syntactic analysis if the roles of agent and patient are obvious ('The flowers are being watered by the girl') (Slobin, 1966). It is this type of strategy which enables young children to understand certain passive sentences without difficulty, while at the same time they are unable to understand 'reversible' passives (that is to say, passives in which the roles of agent and patient can be reversed: 'The girl is being kissed by the boy') (Bronckart, 1983).

In the same way, aberrant utterances ('John dressed and had a bath'; 'Don't print that or I won't sue you') give rise to a *pragmatic normalization* (Fillenbaum, 1977). Subjects automatically correct such utterances and, when asked to undergo a recognition task, believe that it is the 'sensible' utterance which they have heard.

The largest body of work has concentrated on the question of *pragmatic inferences* – that is to say, on the information which is not explicitly transmitted in an utterance and is constructed (or activated) on the basis of the listener's knowledge of the general nature of things. Numerous experiments involving both recall (for example, Brewer, 1977) and recognition (for example, Johnson, Bransford and Solomon, 1973) have shown that these inferences are recorded in memory at the same time as the explicitly present information: for example, 'The absent-minded professor didn't have his car keys' is recalled as 'The absent-minded professor forgot his car keys' (Brewer, 1977); or again, subjects who have heard a sentence dealing with 'pounding a nail' think they recognize a sentence in which a 'hammer' is explicitly mentioned (Johnson *et al.*, 1973). These inferences play an important role in the comprehension of texts, where they are often indispensable if coherence is to be maintained. We shall discuss this question further in the next chapter.

This first meaning of the term 'pragmatic' is both very broad and very vague. It covers all those aspects in the interpretation of an utterance which do not derive from its 'purely linguistic' significance and is thus defined solely in negative terms.[1] If we are to define this term more precisely, we should note two points:

- First, listeners are selective about the inferences they make, performing only those which are determined by the context. The same sentence, uttered in different contexts, can give rise to different inferences (Plas and de Froment-Latour, 1981). These inferences therefore obey a principle of *relevance* which subordinates the interpretative activity to the goals of the discourse (or the representation which the listener constructs of it).
- Second, the inferential procedures presuppose a kind of tacit *contract* between the participants in the communication. The speaker is absolved of the necessity to provide information which the listener already knows and is in a position to retrieve. The listener supposes that what is being said makes sense, and that should certain items of information not be provided, this is because they can be supplied on the basis of the listener's own knowledge of the customary order of things.

Finally, the so-called 'pragmatic' inferences do not depend solely on the general knowledge of the listener but are also based on the *rules of conversation* which guarantee the regulation of the interpretative activities.

II. A second and more precise approach to the pragmatic aspects of language might therefore be based on this idea of *conversational rules*. This comes from the idea that all speech activity is shared and demands a reciprocal adaptation between the partners if it is to attain its goal. Speakers produce their words in accordance with what they presume their listeners will understand; listeners interpret these words in accordance with the assumed approach of the speakers.

Grice's maxims (see above, p. 24) represent the best-known and most frequently cited formulation of conversational rules. It is true that the *co-operative principle* on which they are based has attracted a certain amount of criticism: clearly, the partners do not necessarily share the same objective

1. We should add that the idea of 'inference', which is in widespread use, is itself very confused. On the one hand, it is used to describe a wide variety of phenomena which do not necessarily arise from identical psychological processes. On the other hand, we are dealing here with a purely descriptive idea which in no way explains how the listener constructs this 'non-explicit' information.

and the conversation may be aggressive, polemical, deceitful, etc. However, what appears to us to be valuable, fruitful and worthy of retention amongst Grice's ideas is the conception of conversation as a *shared, goal-orientated* activity. Each partner attempts to realize their objectives by inducing the other to construct a certain representation, and this implies, if not co-operation (which supposes a common aim), then at least mutual adaptation (which does not exclude opposed aims).

It was in this light that Sperber and Wilson (1986) suggested rejecting the maxim of co-operation and the rules which derive from it and replacing them with a single *axiom of relevance*: 'The speaker tries to make the utterance as relevant as possible to the hearer.' Clearly, however, we still need to find a precise definition of this concept of 'relevance'.[2]

The mutual adaptation of the interlocuters does not involve simply the comprehension of the message but also the reciprocal *status* of speaker and listener. Natural languages make it possible to mark this status in a variety of ways, most notably by the various degrees of *politeness* with which a particular speech act can be performed (a question, for example).[3]

These conversational rules, together with the 'implicatures' associated with them, have given rise to a large body of work and constitute one of the most frequently studied aspects of pragmatics. However, they remain external to language itself, regulating its use but unconcerned with its nature. It is possible to go a step further and search in the language system itself for pragmatic aspects – that is to say, aspects which refer to the activity of language use.

III. As we have already pointed out (p. 22), natural languages – unlike formal, logico-mathematical languages – are specifically characterized by the presence of a set of means through which the utterance can refer not to a simple conceptual content, but to the *utterance act* – that is, to the activity which produced the utterance.

We can divide these means into two main categories:

(a) First, the linguistic markers which relate the utterance to the situation in which it is produced – that is to say, which refer to the participants in the speech event (speaker and addressee), and to the place and time of utterance act. This is the field of *deixis* (from the Greek word δειξις, meaning 'act of pointing or indicating').

---

2. This is the object of Sperber and Wilson (1986).
3. In fact, the rules of politeness are peripheral to the field of psycholinguistics. The conditions under which it is *thought correct* to use a particular formula are clearly the object of sociolinguistic study. However, the *significance* of these formulae (the relative status they attribute to speaker and listener) clearly concerns the psycholinguist. Later, for example, we shall encounter Clark's interpretation of these formulae in terms of 'exchange of goods'.

(b) Second, the various ways (lexical or syntactic) in which the *function* of the propositional content of a particular act of communication can be specified: the type of speech act performed (statement, order, question, etc.), modalities specifying the speaker's attitude towards the utterance, putting information into perspective.

Here we are dealing with intrinsic characteristics of natural languages whose meaning and functioning cannot be understood without reference to the activity of language implementation. Seen in this light, pragmatics is no longer superimposed on language but is instead an integral part of it.

These three ways of approaching the problems of pragmatics actually derive from three very different conceptions of language, and we shall return to this issue at the end of this chapter. For the moment, we should simply note that they do at least agree on one fundamental idea: that the meaning of an utterance can be fully defined only with reference to its conditions of use.

In the following, we shall therefore turn our attention to the problems associated with the three main aspects of these conditions of use:

(i)   The utterance is produced within a certain *situation*: it contains a set of landmarks which relate it to this situation and, more generally, assumes its meaning on the basis of it.

(ii)   The utterance involves *speaking subjects* who stand in a certain relation to the utterance, on the one hand, and (mediated by the utterance) with each other, on the other.

(iii) Finally, the activity which produces the utterance is based on a certain *intention*. It aims to achieve a certain goal and organizes the elements of the communication as means to be used in attaining this objective.

Speech and the situation: 'Deixis' and reference

'Deixis'

The phenomenon of *deixis* is characteristic of natural languages. All such languages comprise a set of terms whose value can be specified only with reference to the particular situation in which they are spoken.

Let us suppose that on arriving at my office I find a note pinned to the door, reading: 'I'll come to visit you in an hour.' Since I do not know who wrote the message, or at what time, it is incomprehensible to me. In contrast, it would be perfectly clear if it were spoken by a physically present speaker.

The function of deictic markers is to *designate* what is being spoken about by situating this within a system of reference defined by the situation of utterance. This system of reference contains three essential elements:

(a) The *participants* in the utterance: the personal markers of the first or second person (pronouns: I, we, you; possessives; verbal markers) make this designation possible (the third person designates a non-participant). Other functions may be superimposed on this landmarking function, notably the indication of the reciprocal status of the partners which is effected by the use of familiar *versus* non-familiar personal pronouns in languages such as French or German, or by the much more complex and subtle 'honorary' forms used in some languages such as Japanese.

(b) The *place* of utterance also constitutes a landmark for the designation of positions (here, there) objects (this, that) and movements (come/go, bring/take). It is generally the position of the speaker that serves as the reference point (but some languages permit the use of far more complex landmarks).

(c) Finally, the *time of utterance* serves as the basis for a wide range of temporal landmarks marked by all kinds of adverbial expressions (now, soon, yesterday, next year, etc.) and, of course, by verb tenses.

The interest of *deixis* lies in the fact that it is a phenomenon which is specific to natural languages and totally absent from formal languages. Despite this, it has been the object of only a limited amount of psycholinguistic study. The majority of the available data relate to the *acquisition* of the deictic markers, and are essentially descriptive in nature.

We shall limit ourselves here to a study of the most important points. First of all, we should note the very primitive nature of *deixis*, which appears right at the start of the language-learning process (Brown, 1973) and even seems to have its roots in pre-linguistic communicative behaviour (Bruner, 1975; Bates, 1976). The first functioning of *deixis* appears as a simple undifferentiated 'pointing'. More specialized contrastive components appear later and initially designate binary contrasts (presence/absence, here/ elsewhere, now/not now) which subsequently give way to increasingly subtle distinctions (see Bates, 1976). Finally, this landmarking system which evolves from *deixis* gradually integrates other functions which are associated with more complex intradiscursive relations (we have seen an example above relating to the acquisition of the system of articles, studied by Karmiloff-Smith, 1979).

Hardly any work has been done on deictic functioning in adults. In the usual types of experimental situation, in which the situation of utterance is carefully neutralized, it is not surprising that deictic markers (if they are present at all) should generally be neglected by subjects. Thus Clark and Stafford (1969) have observed that verb tenses cause considerable confusion in the recall of a list of sentences. However, Harris and Brewer (1973) have demonstrated that the simple addition of explicit temporal landmarks ('tomorrow', 'last month') is enough to improve recall significantly.

Similarly (Brewer and Harris, 1974), there is a great deal of confusion between *this*, *that* and *the*, and between *come* and *go*, etc., in sentences which are unrelated to the context of utterance. However, these errors cease to occur when the sentences refer to the real situation,[4] – for example: 'The Chinese ping-pong team *came* to the United States', or 'Marijuana grows wild in *this* county.'

This is a very small body of work, and further studies are undoubtedly necessary. In fact, *deixis* brings to light a number of important characteristics of language:

(i) The use of language always implies a *point of view* with reference to which the representation is organized. This point of view can also change and give rise to a complex interplay of centrations and decentrations. The exact nature of the cognitive operations involved in the construction of this system of landmarks remains, for the most part, unstudied.

(ii) An important characteristic of many of the deictic markers is their *polyfunctionality*: more complex intradiscursive landmarks may be superimposed on or replace the spatiotemporal landmarks relating to the here-and-now of the utterance.

We have already referred to the case of the system of articles. Another particularly fruitful example is provided by *verb tenses*. First, they situate the described event with reference to the moment of the utterance (later, earlier or simultaneous). They are also able to provide landmarks relating events to each other (for example, the contrast between pluperfect and simple past, etc.). A further type of landmarking is provided by *aspect* (perfective/imperfective, simple/ continuous). Finally, verb tenses also possess a *modal* value and thus express the speaker's attitude towards the utterance. For example, Benveniste (1966) has demonstrated the distinction, in French, between 'temps du récit' (narrative tenses) which mark the narrator's distance from the object of the narrative ('passé simple', 'imparfait', 'plus-que-parfait') and 'temps du discours' (speech tenses) which indicate the speaker's involvement ('présent', 'passé composé', 'futur').

With the exception of a small number of studies of children (for example, Bronckart, 1976) which show, in particular, that the aspectual value of tenses emerges later than their relational uses, this domain remains largely unexplored.

(iii) *Deixis* is thus clearly intimately linked to problems of *reference*. It

---

4. That is to say – to quote the authors – if the sentences were formulated in such a way that 'the dicictic elements were appropriate for a sentence being spoken by Richard Harris in experimental room 679, on the sixth floor of the Psychology building at the University of Illinois in Champaign, Illinois, on July 5–6, 1973.'

represents the most elementary type of reference, in which linguistic determination is reduced to a minimum. But is there a difference in nature between simple verbal 'pointing' ('Give me that!') and the more elaborate forms of linguistic description ('Give me that paper!' – 'Give me the paper you are holding!')? This is the problem to which we shall turn next.

'Common ground', reference and meaning

To understand an utterance is not simply to grasp its meaning – that is to say, to translate it into a conceptual representation. It is also to identify *what* the speaker is talking about. How is this identification of the referent performed?

In tackling this problem, H. Clark has proposed the idea of *common ground*.[5] For comprehension to be possible, the two speakers – let us call them A and B – must share some degree of mutual knowledge (or belief). Furthermore, A must think not only that B possesses this knowledge but also that B thinks that A possesses the same knowledge, and *vice versa*. In other words, the 'common ground' represents the set of *shared* knowledge, beliefs and assumptions possessed by the participants at the moment of the utterance.

It is on the basis of this 'common ground' that the speaker is able to choose the formulation which allows the listener to identify the intended referent unambiguously, and it is on the basis of this presumed approach that the listener can make the inferences necessary for such an identification.

In an experiment conducted by Clark, Schreuder and Buttrick (1983), for example, students were shown a picture of President Reagan with David Stockman, Director of the Office of Management and Budget, and asked one of two questions:

You know who this man is, don't you?
Do you have any idea at all who this man is?

The first question presupposes that the experimenter expects the subject to know the answer, and therefore that it is very likely that the person named forms part of the *common ground*. In contrast, the second question suggests that the speaker considers that it is unlikely that the listener will know the person referred to. This is, in fact, the way in which the subjects understood these questions. Fourteen out of 15 subjects interpreted the first question as referring to Reagan, and 7 subjects out of 15 thought that the second question referred to Stockman.

5. Of Clark's many articles on this subject, see, for example, Clark and Murphy (1982).

The referent is thus identified on the basis of a very general principle, which Clark calls *the principle of optimal design*. It may be explained as follows:

> The speaker designs his utterance in such a way that he has good reason to believe that the addressees can readily and uniquely compute what he meant on the basis of the utterance along with the rest of their common ground. (Clark, Schreuder and Buttrick, 1983, p. 246.)

How is this common ground formed? It is possible to envisage three sources for it. First of all, there is *physical co-presence*: the section of the environment simultaneously perceived by the participants constitutes a knowledge set which each participant may assume to be available to the partner, and which further entitles individual participant to assume that the partner knows that this knowledge is also available to them, etc. Second, there is *linguistic co-presence*: anything said by either of the participants forms part of the common ground in the communication that follows. Finally, there is *community membership*, which involves the common possession of a certain degree of knowledge and belief.

Clark's analyses (and the experimental data which accompany them) bring to light a number of important points:

1. First, language use implies an *interaction*. The speaker does not simply encode a mental representation in the form of a message which is subsequently decoded by the listener. The utterance is designed in the light of knowledge about the addressee, who understands it in the light of this presumed intention.

2. This implies that all verbal communication is performed with reference to a certain *domain* and does not extend to include the whole universe of discourse. A conversation, a discourse, a text always imply a limitation to a certain domain which may vary in size and precision, and it is with reference to this domain that the relevance of utterances is judged. However, the idea of 'common ground' proposed by Clark would no doubt require us to take this explanation further. In any given conversation the participants do not bring the entirety of their potential *common ground* into play. The way the particular domain to which the verbal exchange refers is constructed, delimited and represented is a question which has still to be explored.[6]

3. Finally, progressing beyond the problem of reference, it is the problem of *meaning* which Clark's analyses call into question. If comprehension of

---

6. On this topic, see also Clark's more recent works (Clark and Wilkes-Gibbs, 1986; Isaacs and Clark, 1987). The role of 'topic' in the comprehension of a text has been examined by Bransford and McCarrell (1974) and by Garrod and Sanford (1983).

an utterance (that is to say, what is said by a certain speaker to a certain addressee in a certain situation) depends on understanding the speaker's *intention*, then we are justified in asking whether there is anything apart from *contextual* meaning. In other words, the meaning of the utterance could be constructed at the time of the utterance itself, without any possibility of defining any 'literal', context-independent meaning.

It is true that Clark's analyses do not go this far. It remains the fact that *neologisms*, for example (Clark, 1983; Clark and Gerrig, 1983), which cannot *by definition* be present in subjects' 'internal lexicons', are generally understood unproblematically on the basis of the *common ground*. In such cases we are clearly dealing with a creation of meaning rather than with the selection of a meaning previously recorded in the internal lexicon. The same contextual construction of meaning appears in 'shorthand expressions' such as 'a Picasso', 'a beer', etc., and the same process can account for the phenomena of semantic flexibility observed by Bransford and colleagues (Clark, 1978). Here, we are once again in the presence of the considerations we examined above, at the end of Chapter 4.

In conclusion, the relationship between the utterance and the situation of its production – its context – brings to light a number of essential characteristics of speech activity. These are characteristics which long remained inaccessible to experimental observations that concentrated on isolated sentences, devoid of any communicative function. However, as soon as attention is shifted to the effective use of language, such characteristics become inescapable:

- the fact that all speech activity is linked to a particular *point of view* and implies a complex interplay of landmarks relating to this;
- the *intersubjective* character of this activity, which requires the participants to construct a shared representation and to adapt their approaches in a controlled way;
- finally, the relativity of meanings to a certain *field* of reference.

Each of these aspects presents the psycholinguist with a range of problems, the study of which has scarcely begun.

Speech and speakers: Taking responsibility

An utterance is not a simple object (which would symbolize or represent a certain state of affairs). It is the product of an utterance *act* which involves at least two individuals and establishes certain relations between them. Seen in this perspective, the utterance expresses (and, through its articulation, realizes) not only its propositional content but also a particular endorsement[7] for what has been said – that is to say, for:

- the type of *act* that has been performed: statement, question, order, promise, greeting, etc.;
- the type of *commitment* the speaker brings to this act: modalities expressing certainty, doubt, likelihood, etc.;
- finally, the *source* of the utterance (which is not necessarily the speaker).

Speech acts and illocutionary force

The idea of *speech act* – which, as we have seen, was proposed by Austin (1962) – constitutes one of the most thoroughly studied areas of linguistic pragmatics. All utterances possess a certain *illocutionary force* – that is to say, they realize a certain act on the basis of conventional rules. The fact of being defined by rules distinguishes illocutionary acts (for example, advising, promising, affirming) from the *perlocutionary* effects of the utterance which, for their part, derive from causal factors and depend on the empirical circumstances (for example, persuading, consoling, upsetting, etc.).

The theory of speech acts raises all sorts of problems which we are unable to develop here.[8] We should, however, note the following:

(a) All languages possess particular syntactic and morphological means of distinguishing between various types of utterance: declarative, imperative, interrogative, optative, etc.

(b) Language can be used to perform all types of acts, of which statement (or the description of a state of affairs) is only one particular case. The reality of these acts is confirmed by the existence of specific formulations (performative verbs) which can qualify them explicitly as such: 'I declare . . . ', 'I order . . . ', 'I advise you . . . ', 'I congratulate you', etc.

These two observations justify the introduction of the idea of illocutionary acts. However, they also raise a problem. There is no simple correspondence between the form of an utterance and its illocutionary force. On the one hand, a given illocutionary act can be uttered in a variety of ways: for example, a question can, of course, be formulated in the interrogative mode, but also in the declarative ('I should like to know . . . ') or imperative ('Tell

---

7. This notion of endorsement ('prise en charge'), which was proposed by Culioli, has been reused by Grize (see, for example, Grize, 1983) in a model of argumentative operations.
8. For a discussion, see, for example, Levinson (1983, ch. 5).

me ... ') forms. On the other hand, one and the same utterance may, depending on context, correspond to a variety of illocutionary acts: for example, 'Do you know what the time is?' might express a request for information, advice to hurry up, etc.

A point of view which is currently in favour is that an utterance can have a 'literal' illocutionary value (for example, 'Would you type this letter for me?' is, literally, a question) and can, depending on context, assume an 'indirect' value (in the above case, that of an order). We then speak of *indirect speech acts*.

The first psychological works to take an interest in this subject concentrated primarily on showing that the illocutionary force was recorded in memory as an integral part of the meaning of an utterance. Thus (Jarvella and Collas, 1974) subjects who have been asked to produce or listen to a dialogue containing a sentence possessing a certain illocutionary value (for example, 'The food is on the table' as an invitation to come and eat) often fail to recognize the same sentence if the context confers a different value on it (for example, the above sentence occurring in a description). In the same way (Schweller, Brewer and Dahl, 1976), when asked to recall a sentence describing a speech act (for example, 'The housewife spoke to the manager about the increased meat prices'), subjects tend to emphasize its implicit illocutionary force ('The housewife complained to the manager about the increased meat prices').

The greatest problem, however, is to know how this illocutionary force is identified. This is a problem which is clearly raised by all those speech acts which are said to be indirect.

A first hypothesis would be simply to accept that the various ways of expressing a single speech act are purely conventional and are learned as such. According to this hypothesis, they would be present in the 'internal lexicon' of speakers in the same way as idiomatic expressions such as 'break the ice' or 'kick the bucket'. However, this solution is unsatisfactory.

There is no doubt that some expressions are highly conventional: for example, sentences of the type 'Can you X?' or 'Would you X?' are very widely used as a request to perform action X and are probably learned as such by young children. However, that this is not a question of arbitrary conventions is shown by the fact that the same procedures appear in very different languages. Moreover, the considerable variety of possible formulations of one and the same illocutionary act makes it difficult to believe that they are all recorded in memory.[9] Finally, there are cases where the 'literal' interpretation is the correct one (In some cases 'Do you know the

9. Thus, alongside conventional forms such as 'Would you close the door?', Levinson (1983, 265) quotes far more indirect formulations such as: 'Now, Johnny, what do big people do when they come in?'.

time?' may simply be a way of making sure that the listener possesses the information in question). We therefore have to accept that the interpretation of speech acts requires a certain type of computation.

We can now think in terms of processing involving several stages. The literal meaning of the utterance will be computed first and the interpretation which this yields will be compared with the context, and its relevance verified. If the interpretation proves not to be relevant, the listener progresses to an indirect interpretation based on the general rules of conversation. For example, 'Have you got ten pounds?' will initially be interpreted as a question (does the listener possess this sum?). Second stage: can the speaker be assumed to be ignorant of whether the listener possesses the sum in question, and to have reasons for wishing to know this? As this is not a very plausible interpretation, it is necessary to compute an indirect interpretation: the fact that B possesses the object X is a prior condition for A being able to ask B to give him X. The utterance must therefore be interpreted as an indirect request.

The calculation of the illocutionary value of an utterance would thus appear to be a sequential type of process. However, the experimental data do not allow us fully to accept this hypothesis.

An experiment performed by Clark and Lucy (1975) provided arguments in support of this model. It consisted of measuring the time taken by subjects to verify whether or not a picture satisfactorily corresponded to a request made either directly ('Please colour the circle blue') or indirectly ('Can you make the circle blue?' – 'I would hate to see you not colour the circle blue', etc.). The response times were clearly longer for the indirect requests, a result which appears to show that they require additional processing. Furthermore, a request phrased in the negative form (but with a positive indirect meaning – for example, 'I'll be very sad unless you make the circle blue') takes longer still to respond to, thus proving that the literal meaning is also considered (the negative sentences require an additional processing time).

However, Gibbs (1979) has shown that these results are valid only for isolated sentences. When he presented subjects with indirect requests which occurred within the context of a narrative, he observed that the time required for comprehension and verification was no longer for these, and that they were actually understood more quickly than when they had to be interpreted literally. This suggests that the 'indirect' meaning is, in fact, constructed *directly* without passing through an initial 'literal' meaning stage.

What is called into question here is the very notion of literal meaning itself – as we have already seen in connection with metaphor and, more generally, semantic flexibility (see above, p. 86).

Even if we have to reject the sequential processing hypothesis, however, this does not exclude the idea of multiple processing proceeding in parallel at various levels. A single speech act can be formulated in many different ways, and if these different formulations possess the same illocutionary function – that is to say, if they translate the same intention on the part of the speaker – then there is another level at which they differ. This is the *status* which such formulations attribute to the interlocutors.

In more recent work (Clark, 1979; Clark and Schunk, 1980), Clark accepts that the 'literal' and 'indirect' meanings can be computed simultaneously, but retains the principle of the dual significance of indirect speech acts. Proof of this is seen in the fact that the *response* to an indirect request is itself often dual: the response to the question 'Can you tell me the time?' will be 'Yes, I can, it's six.' In this example the listener responds to both the direct question ('yes') and the indirect question ('it's six').

More generally, a series of experiments conducted by Clark show that the response's degree of politeness is adapted to that of the request. This suggests that the addressee interprets not only the meaning of the request but also the way it is formulated (and therefore its 'literal' meaning). This degree of politeness can be defined within the framework of what Clark terms an 'exchange of goods': to ensure that communication is effective, the speaker offers his partner the recognition of a certain status (for example, a certain decision-making power) in exchange for what is asked of him (an item of information, a service, or simply his attention). In this way, he allows him to 'save face' (here, Clark refers to the well-known analyses of Goffman, 1967).

It may be seen that the value of a speech act involves not only a certain intention on the part of the speaker, but also a set of relations which obtain between the partners within the framework of this intention. These relations are linguistically encoded, and the associated procedures of construction and interpretation are the subject of psycholinguistic study just as much as the purely informational aspects of the utterance.

The analysis of these procedures has scarcely begun. To take it further we would clearly need to deepen the study of the contextual parameters which are involved in interpretation, as well as to investigate more intensively the psychological operations which correspond to what is called – perhaps inappropriately – the 'literal meaning' of the various types of utterance. What mental operations correspond to interrogative, imperative, exclamatory utterances, etc.? So far, psycholinguistic research has barely started to investigate this type of problem. This is a surprising omission, and rectifying it should be a matter of urgency.

Modalities

Another characteristic feature of natural languages is the variety of possibilities they offer for marking the relationship established between the speaker and the utterance formulated. In saying, 'The light bulb must be burnt out' or 'I think it's going to rain', the speaker is not being limited to the verbal encoding of a state of affairs. A certain position is also being taken with regard to the utterance act by its being coloured with a certain *modality*.

Logical thought regarding modalities goes back as far as Aristotle and has given rise to a considerable body of work.[10] Essentially, such thought has concentrated on formalizing the notions of *possible* and *necessary* in so far as they qualify the truth value of a proposition (*alethic* modalities). However, there are other types of modality, possessing similar formal properties, which have also been the object of attempts to construct logical theories: *deontic* modalities (permitted, obligatory), *epistemic* modalities (plausible, certain; or again: to know/to believe).

Here we shall content ourselves with indicating three major problems which confront the psycholinguistic approach:

1. It is important to make a logical distinction (which goes back to Abélard) between modalities *de re* (which bear on the predicate alone) and modalities *de dicto* (which bear on the proposition itself). For example, 'Peter may come' signifies either 'Peter is able to come' (modality *de re*) or 'It may happen that Peter will come' (modality *de dicto*). The *de dicto* modality comes solely from the speaker's 'taking responsibility for' the utterance. However, as the above example shows, the distinction does not rest on any explicit linguistic marker. This ambiguity raises two problems: first, why does it exist? (that is to say, why is the same term used with two different values?); second, how is it resolved?

2. A second type of ambiguity, which raises the same problems, concerns the type of modality to be expressed. Thus in the above example, apart from the epistemic meaning (*de dicto*) which we have paraphrased, we can also imagine a quite different deontic meaning: 'Peter is permitted to come' (which itself gives rise to a double interpretation: 'I permit Peter to come' or 'X permits Peter to come').

3. More generally, the association of a modality with an utterance depends on operations quite different to those which construct the proposition itself. What is the psychological nature of these operations?

While the development of modal notions in children has been the topic of an interesting body of work (Piéraut-Le Bonniec, 1974; Piaget, 1981, 1983), psycholinguistic study in this field has only just started. Some data are available on the comparative development of the epistemic and deontic modalities in children (Hirst and Weil, 1982) and on the development of operations associated with the verbs 'know' and 'believe' (Bassano, 1982;

10. For a brief summary, see Piéraut-Le Bonniec (1974).

Bassano and Champaud, 1983).[11] The psycholinguistics of modalities in adults has, as yet, been poorly studied.[12]

Reported speech

Finally, a third aspect of this taking responsibility for the utterance concerns its attribution to a *source*, which need not necessarily be the speaker.

The utterance act can be explicitly attributed to another speaking subject. This may take the simple, neutral form of quotation or may assume the more complex forms of 'indirect speech' which require specific landmarking operations, notably in the temporal perspective. Speakers can also show agreement ('As X said ... ') or distance themselves from the material they are reporting ('According to X, the government has the intention of ... ').

However, reference to another source can also be performed in a more implicit way. Ducrot (1984) has developed a number of analyses in support of what he calls the *polyphony* of speech – that is to say, the possible plurality of speakers to which an utterance may refer. In French, for example, the difference in meaning between *puisque* and *car* lies in the fact that the first of these connectors attributes the proposition it introduces to a source other than the current speaker, whereas the second identifies the current speaker as the source (*Sortons puisqu'il fait beau* → '(Yes) Let's go out, since (as you say) it's a nice day' and *Sortons, car il fait beau* → 'Let's go out, since it's a nice day'). Another example is provided by negation which, according to Ducrot, implies a double operation: the utterance (attributed to another source) of the affirmative proposition and the rejection (by the speaker) of this affirmation.[13]

Once again, the psycholinguistic study of this type of operation is still in its infancy. We can, however, cite a number of studies of reported speech in children (Hickmann, 1983; Berthoud-Papandropoulou and Kircher, 1987). Ducrot's analyses, for their part, have inspired research into the comprehension of the French conjunctions *mais* (but) (Kail and Weissenborn, 1984) and *si* (if) (Caron, 1987).

In conclusion, the various aspects of this 'taking responsibility for' the utterance involve a complex set of operations for the construction of various

---

11. The verbs of opinion (think, believe, know, etc.) have mostly been studied within the framework of investigations of the comprehension of presuppositions (see, for example, McNamara, Baker and Olson, 1976). We can also quote the work of Wing and Scholnick (1981) on the subject of 'beliefs' associated with certain connectors (because, if, although, unless).
12. We should, however, mention a few studies on the semantics of verbal uncertainty expressions (see D.A. Clark, 1990, for a review).
13. It is interesting to note that Wason and Johnson-Laird (1972) attribute the additional difficulty in utterance processing caused by negation to the necessity of reconstructing the corresponding affirmative utterance. They base this interpretation on the fact that certain contexts can facilitate the processing of negation (Wason, 1965).

relationships between the participants in the utterance on the one hand, and between these participants and the utterance itself on the other. The study of these operations, neglected until recently, has only just started. For the most part, they represent a *terra incognita* whose exploration may well lead to important discoveries.

Putting information into perspective: Presupposition and topicalization

Finally, a third aspect bearing on the pragmatics of natural languages is the fact that such languages make it possible to establish a *functional organization* of information with reference to the objectives of the communication. In effect, an utterance is not limited to encoding information. It can also indicate the function intended to be conferred on it in the speaker's speech.

If Alan tells Bernard, 'My upstairs neighbour has stopped beating his wife', his utterance contains several items of information. First of all, that the neighbour is not currently beating his wife (this is the explicitly stated part of the utterance), but also that he has beaten her before, that Alan has an upstairs neighbour, and that this neighbour is married. Although these last three items of information are not directly stated in the utterance, they nevertheless contribute to its meaning, and it may be that Bernard is now learning them for the first time ('What! He used to beat her?' or 'What! I didn't know he was married!'). In such cases we speak of the *presuppositions* of the utterance.

Furthermore, Alan could have said, 'My upstairs neighbour has stopped being beaten by her husband.' Although the situation described is exactly the same, the utterance no longer has the same function. The information it contains now refers to the female, not the male neighbour. The element on which attention is focused is no longer the same. This process is called *topicalization*.

This 'putting into perspective' of information is absent from formal (logico-mathematical) languages.

Presuppositions

Together with the speech act, the idea of presupposition constitutes one of the most widely studied topics in pragmatics, and has been of equal interest to both philosophers of language and linguists. It has been, and remains, the object of considerable debate, the detail of which we are unable to discuss here.[14] Instead, we shall limit ourselves to pointing out some important problems.

14. For a review of the problems and the current state of the issue, see Levinson (1983, ch. 4).

Let us take an example. If we say, 'Philip is sorry he's moved', we provide two pieces of information. The first is the object of an explicit statement: the unfavourable judgement passed by Philip on his move. The second is presupposed and holds that Philip has actually moved. If we put the utterance into the negative form ('Philip isn't sorry he's moved') the statement is modified, but the presupposition remains the same.

I. An initial problem concerns the *status* which is to be attributed to the presupposition.

Should we see in it a (logical) *implication* of the utterance? Unfortunately, the presupposition remains true even if the proposition is negated, and this entails considerable logical difficulties. Another solution is to see here a 'conversational implicature' based on rules such as Grice's. However, these 'implicatures' are only probable, which is not the case with presuppositions.

The solution proposed by Ducrot (1972) is to consider presupposition as a special type of *illocutionary act* by means of which the speaker defines the framework which has to be accepted by the listener (the 'price to pay') if communication is to proceed. In this light, the presupposition becomes an element in the 'language-game' in which the participants are engaged. This conception – which challenges the purely logical approach to the question of presuppositions – currently appears to us to be the most satisfactory.

II. A second problem concerns the *unity* of the idea of presupposition. Starting from a precise case (the presupposition of existence associated with 'definite descriptions' such as 'The King of France is bald'), this idea has been gradually extended to embrace numerous other cases: factive verbs (know, regret, notice, etc.) which presuppose the truth of their complement; or contrafactives (pretend, wish) which presuppose its falsity; cleft sentences ('It's X who's done Y' presupposes that someone has done Y); certain adverbs ('Even X was there' or 'X was there too' presuppose that other people were present), etc. (for a list, refer to Levinson, 1983, pp. 181–4). This leads us to ask ourselves whether in all these different cases, we are really dealing with the same phenomenon.

Psycholinguistic studies of presupposition[15] have generally approached the question as a particular case of *inference* – that is to say, as an item of information which, without being explicitly furnished by the utterance, is constructed on the basis of it.

15. For an excellent critical review, see Kail and Plas (1979).

This is the perspective which embraces the majority of the developmental research, which has primarily investigated children's comprehension of presuppositions associated with factive or contrafactive verbs (know, forget, pretend, etc.). At first sight, the results show very little coherence. Some works show an early comprehension from the age of 4 onwards (McNamara, Baker and Olson, 1976), whereas others find a gradual development from the age of 6–7 onwards (Harris, 1975), and still others find no comprehension of presuppositions before adolescence (Lehalle and Jouen, 1977). In fact, the diversity of the results is most certainly due in part to the diversity of the experimental situations and, in particular, to the fact that the utterances are sometimes presented in isolation and sometimes (as in McNamara *et al.*) in context. Such diversity can also be partly explained by the variable complexity of the operations which permit the construction of presuppositions. These are the two directions taken by the most interesting research. In a series of studies, Kail has been able to show that the comprehension of presuppositions associated with certain French adverbs such as *même* (even), *aussi* (also), *seulement* (only) and *encore* (again) (Kail, 1978, 1979) or a connector such as *mais* (but) (Kail and Weissenborn, 1984) emerges gradually as a function of the degree of complexity of the required operations, in so far as these can be defined on the basis of Ducrot's analyses. Moreover, interesting research by Ackerman (1978, 1979) has demonstrated children's early capacity – from 5 years of age onwards – to interpret the presuppositions of an utterance as a function of the intentions which the context makes it possible to attribute to the speaker.

Studies involving adults have tended to focus more on demonstrating a *difference* in the way the presupposed information and the other information communicated by the utterance is *processed*.

An experiment by Offir (1973) investigated the memory representation of this information. The subjects were presented with short stories containing sentences in which a relative subordinate introduced a presupposed element: for example, 'A Sioux Indian he befriended represented the chief' contains the presupposition 'he befriended a Sioux Indian', the statement being 'The Sioux Indian represented the chief'; in contrast, 'He befriended a Sioux Indian who represented the chief' contains the same information, but the distribution of the asserted and presupposed information is inverted. In a recognition task, Offir observed that subjects confused these two sentences far less than sentences in which a change of formulation brought about no change of presupposition. The status – asserted or presupposed – of the information must therefore be recorded in memory, at least temporarily.

If presuppositions constitute information indirectly provided by the utterance, then we should also ask ourselves whether they are psychologically differentiated from the implications of this utterance. For example, 'At 6.00 the bullfighter departed from the arena' *presupposes* that just before

6.00 he was in the arena, and *implies* that a little after 6.00 he was no longer there.[16] In a memory task, Harris (1974) observed no difference between these two types of information. However, Just and Clark (1973), who used a more sensitive method of measuring response times, were led to conclude that the implications of an utterance (for example, 'John forgot to let the dog out' implies that the dog is not out) are examined before the presuppositions (in this case, 'John was supposed to let the dog out').

This last observation is corroborated by those of Hornby (1974), who asked subjects to listen to sentences of the type 'It is the girl that is petting the cat', followed by a picture presented at the tachistoscope for a twentieth of a second. This picture either matched the sentence or differed from it in the presupposed element (a girl petting a dog) or the asserted element (a boy petting a cat). The error rate among the subjects was approximately double when the presupposed element was misrepresented on the picture. Similar results have been obtained by Singer (1976): the presupposed information (in a sentence such as 'It was the king who led the troops') is memorized less well than the 'asserted' information.

These data suggest that we should interpret presuppositions within a functional perspective: the items of information provided by an utterance do not all have the same status. A number of authors have proposed interpreting this difference in terms of an opposition which has already been suggested by linguists: that between 'given' and 'new' information.

Given and new information

When utterances contain presupposed information, it is rare (except in psycholinguistic experiments) for this information to be new to the listener. In most cases, listeners already possess the information and simply have to retrieve it from memory and integrate it with the new information provided by the 'asserted' part of the utterance.

As Haviland and Clark (1974) have emphasized, this implies a co-operative strategy on the part of both speaker and listener. The former syntactically marks both the old information which it is thought the listener already possesses (*given information*) and the *new information* in a way which allows his or her partner to distinguish between the items. The listener, acting in the belief that his or her partner is behaving co-operatively, identifies the two types of information, searches his or her memory for the 'address' corresponding to the given information, and integrates the new information into it.

In cases where the information presented as given does not figure

16. Negating the utterance leaves the presupposition unchanged, but causes the negation of the implication.

explicitly in memory, this interpretative strategy, which is based on the tacit *given–new contract*, leads the listener to make *bridging inferences* to associate it with what is already known. This has been verified by Haviland and Clark (1974), who presented subjects with pairs of sentences, such as:

(1) We got some beer out of the trunk. The beer was warm.
(2) We checked the picnic supplies. The beer was warm.

The reading time for the second sentence of the pair ('The beer was warm') was longer (by approximately 0.2 s) in case (2) than case (1). This proves that the subjects actually made the expected inference.

Moreover, Hupet and Le Bouedec (1977) were able to show that the semantic integration described by Bransford and Franks (see p. 119 above) is based on this *given–new strategy*.

That the same strategy can also be shown to be at work in the production of utterances has been demonstrated by Bock (1977), who asked her subjects to read lists of sentences containing, for example:

(3) The Old Water Tower is the oldest building in Chicago.

She then asked them questions, such as:

(4) Michigan Avenue was built around the Old Water Tower so that it wouldn't have to be destroyed. Why?
(5) Because of the Chicago fire, there are very few old buildings in Chicago. What is the oldest building?

In responding to question (4), subjects repeated sentence (3). In responding to question (5), however, they inverted sentence (3): 'The oldest building in Chicago is the Old Water Tower.' In other words, they spontaneously reordered the sentence to give it a given–new structure corresponding to the question.

The 'given–new' distinction has prompted a large body of work, particularly in the study of text comprehension (to which we shall return in the next chapter) and children's acquisition of grammatical structures (Bates, 1976; Greenfield, 1979). Although it clearly plays an important role in the processes of language production and comprehension, it none the less raises certain difficulties.

First of all, we should note that the two types of information can be linguistically marked in a great variety of ways – lexical, syntactic, intonational – each of which can also fulfil other functions (landmarking, emphasis, etc.). Moreover, the given–new strategy, as described by Clark, supposes that the given information is identified before the new information.

This, however, accords badly with Hornby's observations which we have cited above. All in all, Clark's model, however interesting it might be, is certainly too simple.[17]

Topicalization and focusing

Another distinction – related to those mentioned above, although it should not be confused with them – is that between *topic* and *comment*.[18] The topic represents what the utterance is about; the comment what is said about it.

Different languages use different procedures to mark the topic of an utterance. In Japanese, for example, the particle *wa* is reserved for this purpose. In languages such as English or French, the topic is marked by being placed in *initial position* (Halliday, 1985). It follows that the function of the topic will often be assumed by the grammatical subject. This is not always the case, however, and other elements in the sentence can take on the role, as is demonstrated by the following examples, taken from Halliday: '*After tea*, will you tell me a story?', '*A bag-pudding* the King did make.'

Although the topic–comment distinction often coincides with the opposition between given and new information, it is important not to confuse them. As Halliday (1985) has pointed out, the given–new distinction depends on the point of view of the listener, whereas the topic–comment distinction relates to that of the speaker. The 'given' element is that which the speaker presents as already being known to the listener, while the topic element is the one the former decides to take as the starting point. We are therefore dealing with two different functions.

The effects of topicalization on the comprehension of utterances have been widely studied. They first become evident at the level of listener expectation. Yekovich, Walker and Blackman (1979) have demonstrated this by measuring the time taken to comprehend a sentence, for example:

The craft made *the landing* near the crater

which had been preceded by one of the following four sentences:

(1) The astronaut readied *the craft* for the descent
(2) The scientists watched *the landing* on the screen
(3) *The craft* relayed the data to the scientists
(4) *The landing* represented a triumph for the scientists.

---

17. The given–new distinction is discussed in Jarvella and Engelkamp (1983).
18. Other terms have been used by different authors. Halliday (1985), to whom we shall be referring, prefers to talk about *theme* and *rheme*. However, the terms *topic* and *comment* are the ones most frequently used by psychologists.

The target sentence gave rise to the shortest comprehension times when it followed sentence (1). Comprehension time was longest after (4), with cases (2) and (3) coming in between. The most natural sequence, therefore, is when the comment of the first sentence is repeated as the topic of the second.

A frequently used case in the study of the effects of the topic/comment structure is the active/passive opposition. In effect, both an active sentence and its corresponding passive sentence describe the same situation. However, one places the agent (the 'logical subject') in initial position, while in the other it is the object of the action (the 'logical object') that is topicalized. As a result, there is a difference in the emphasis accorded to the elements in the sentence. However, it is necessary to specify which of the two elements, topic or comment, is emphasized in this way.

Johnson-Laird (1968) thought he had demonstrated that the topicalized element (in this case, the grammatical subject) was the one which the speaker judged to be most important. He presented his subjects with strips of coloured paper containing variable proportions of blue and red, and asked them to choose the one which best corresponded to one of these two descriptions:

(1) There is a blue area that precedes a red area.
(2) There is a red area that is preceded by a blue area.

The observed choices revealed a tendency to take the colour occupying the greater surface area as the grammatical subject (that is to say, as the topic). However, Costermans and Hupet (1977) have used similar results to propose the opposite interpretation: it is the least evident item of information (in this case, the smaller surface area) which constitutes the important element to which the speaker wishes to attract the listener's attention. The 'assertional focus' of the sentence would thus be the comment.

This latter interpretation is supported by the observations of Klenbort and Anisfeld (1974). If subjects are asked to complete a sentence such as:

I thought that the principal had been angered by the president of the PA, but I was mistaken. Rather . . .

the correction tends to bear on the complement (' . . . it was the union representative who angered the principal') rather than on the grammatical subject (' . . . the president of the PA angered the president of the teachers' association'). The topicalized element thus tends to be retained.[19]

---

19. Hupet and Le Bouedec (1975), who repeated the same experiment, showed that the results are modified if the articles are varied: it is the element marked by the indefinite article that tends to be chosen as the 'assertional focus', irrespective of its position.

In fact, it is not the vague notion of 'importance' that is significant here, but the idea of a *functional asymmetry* of the utterance. The topic plays the role of a landmark in relation to which information is situated, while the comment constitutes the specific information supplied by the utterance. Bates and McWhinney (1979) have suggested that we should consider this *topic/comment* relationship as a fundamental pragmatic relationship,[20] and have emphasized the diversity and complexity of the effects to which it can give rise:

- It can be applied recursively, producing embedded structures of varying complexity.
- It can result from a variety of motives (to distinguish between given and new information, choose a point of view, express a contrast, emphasize an element, etc.).
- Finally, it can be expressed in a great variety of ways: apart from the order of utterance, the speaker can manipulate intonation, the use of definite or indefinite articles, pronominalization, ellipsis, etc.

The use of these procedures can vary between languages. The problem – resolved by each language in its own way – is to use the four types of available linguistic means (lexical elements, morphological markers, word order and intonation) to realize an optimal representation of the various types of semantic and pragmatic information which the utterance is intended to transmit. The different ways in which this 'competition' is resolved should make it possible to understand both the grammars of different languages (thought of from a 'functional' perspective) and the stages in which children acquire them.

The model proposed by Bates and McWhinney has given rise to a vast programme of interlanguage research, which is currently still being conducted.[21]

The functional organization of information

In conclusion, the observations which we have presented above reveal a fundamental characteristic of language: to put the information it provides *into perspective*, assigning it different functions in speech. And in this, natural language differs from the formal 'languages' in which every piece of information is placed, so to speak, on the same level. This functional

20. It can be compared with the much more general operation of location ('repérage'), proposed by Culioli (see Desclés, 1982).
21. For a presentation of the 'competition' model and the research connected with it, see Kail (1983).

differentiation leads, as we have seen, to different types of processing on the part of the listener.

That having been said, however, the works we have presented here still testify to a certain amount of confusion. In fact, we should distinguish between at least three types of functional opposition:

- The presupposed/asserted distinction concerns the way the speaker *takes responsibility for* the information (the presupposed element is introduced without being explicitly stated).
- The opposition of given and new information refers to the *integration of information* by the listener (given information constituting the fixed point in memory to which new information can be anchored.
- Finally, the topic/comment opposition concerns the *landmarking* which the speaker provides for the utterance.

These functions may frequently be intermixed: the 'co-operative' speaker chooses as a landmark (as topic) an element already known to the listener which, because of this, does not have to be explicitly stated. In reality, however, these are distinct functions which can be combined in various ways. More detailed research is necessary if we are to analyze the way these various aspects are processed.

Conclusion

Language performs a dual function. On the one hand, it has the function of *representation*: it serves to encode information. Seen from this perspective, it can be described as a code, containing a basic vocabulary (the lexicon of the language), syntactic rules for the construction of well-formed expressions, and semantic rules of interpretation which make it possible to match each expression to a meaning.

On the other hand, however, language is an instrument of *communication*. That is to say, it involves subjects acting within a certain situation and interacting with each other with the intention of realizing certain aims. Any approach to the pragmatic aspects of language must take account of this communicative function.

How, then, are these two functions linked?

I. The easiest path to follow would be to think of the pragmatic dimension as superimposed on the 'purely' linguistic processing of utterances. These utterances would possess a context-independent 'literal meaning' which would be defined by the rules of the language alone. Once this meaning had been constructed at the end of a syntactico-semantic processing stage, a 'pragmatic component' would use it to compute an interpretation which takes into account the available contextual information.

It is this idea which is currently most commonly adhered to. It has the advantage of retaining the experience gained by the syntactic and semantic approaches, and maintaining their autonomy. Seen from this perspective, the field of pragmatics is assimilated into the set of extralinguistic factors which are involved in the production and comprehension of language:

- either in the restricted form of rules of language use: Grice's conversational maxims provide the most elaborate example of such rules; however, it is possible to think of others (rules of politeness, for example);
- or, more generally, in the form of the body of knowledge relating to the world, the situation, the participants, which is involved in the processing of utterances. Moreover, there is no reason why this point of view should not be extended to include not only knowledge but also motivations, emotional factors, etc.

Given such a viewpoint, psycholinguistics, in the strict sense, would need to concern itself only with the genuinely linguistic level (phonological, lexical, syntactic and semantic) of utterance processing. Pragmatics would then fall within the domain of a 'psychology of language' of much vaguer dimensions.

The difficulty with this conception is that it presupposes a level of language functioning at which language can be assimilated to a simple code independently of context and conditions of use. Whereas this might be the case for formal languages (which are constructed precisely in order to be pure instruments of representation), natural languages cannot be reduced to this type of processing.

As we have seen, it is a universal characteristic of natural languages to comprise a set of markers which refer to the activity within which they are used. These are markers of the utterance act which, on the one hand, ensure that the utterance can be situated with reference to the situation and, on the other, characterize its function in the act of communication. The communicative function of language is not superimposed on it (as, for example, the possible uses of a natural object are superimposed on its physical properties), but determines its very structure.

Moreover, the very general fact that there is never an unequivocal correspondence between linguistic form and meaning indicates that languages cannot be reduced to simple codes. On the one hand, the *ambiguity* inherent in all natural languages invests the context of utterance with a determining role in the construction of meanings. On the other, the multiplicity of possible *paraphrases* of the same propositional content can be interpreted only in terms of a diversity of communicative aims.

II. An alternative approach would consist in accepting that the pragmatic dimension is inherent in the very nature of language, which would then be an instrument of interaction between subjects who are situation-specific bearers of communicative intentions. The *structure* of language could then be understood only in terms of its *usage*. Pragmatics would no longer be a superimposed afterthought but, in contrast, would represent the principle on which the intelligibility of language is founded. This path has been followed by a number of linguistic researchers in reaction to the 'structuralist' approach which, from Saussure to Chomsky, has tended to define language as an autonomous object which can be studied in isolation.

The idea of *functional grammars* has been gaining influence in English-speaking countries. This idea has been inspired, in particular, by Halliday (1985), for whom the aim of linguistic theory is to explain the organization of language in terms of the way it is used and the human needs to which it must respond.

In France, Benveniste's *utterance-centred linguistics* has been illustrated by the work of Culioli in particular and, within a slightly different perspective, by Ducrot. The former is developing a most rigorous model of speech operations which is of great interest to the psycholinguist; while the latter, in the perspective of 'integrated pragmatics', is attempting to bring to light the way language, particularly in its argumentative function, organizes intersubjective relations.

These various studies may furnish psycholinguists with a rich collection of hypotheses – indeed, with a new set of theoretical models. In particular, the rigour of Culioli's operational model[22] lends itself especially well to experimental research.

Pragmatics *in* the language or *about* the language? 'Integrated' pragmatics (as proposed by utterance-centred linguistics) or superimposed pragmatics (in the form of usage rules)? These two approaches may not be mutually exclusive and might at least appear, given the current state of research, to be complementary. However this may be, the pragmatic dimension remains an unavoidable aspect of language for the psycholinguist. It is an aspect which, as this chapter has shown, has already prompted a large body of experimental research. This research remains diverse in nature and

---

22. The Genevan psycholinguists – Bronckart in particular – have drawn inspiration from this model. Unfortunately, the absence at the moment of a collective review, and the small number of publications released by Culioli, have limited its potential influence on psycholinguistic research.

frequently rests on an uncertain theoretical basis. In the future, work in this field will have to clarify the theoretical background and specify, in particular:

- a model of linguistic *representation* which is capable of taking into account not only the propositional content, but also the situation of utterance, the participants and the intersubjective function of utterances;
- a model of the constitutive *operations* of this representation.

If we are to achieve this goal, we must go beyond the level of the isolated sentence and concentrate on the concrete unit of communication: discourse.

Recommended reading

Pragmatics has its source in the philosophy of language. The classic works are Austin (1962), Searle (1969) and Grice (1975).

Green (1989) offers a clear introduction to the problems of linguistic pragmatics. A more detailed discussion may be found in Levinson's (1983) excellent work.

Verschueren's two collections (Verschueren and Bertuccelli-Papi, 1987; Verschueren, 1991) give an idea of the variety of current work in pragmatics. The *Journal of Pragmatics* (founded in 1977) publishes a large number of important articles.

The development of utterance-centred linguistics has been concentrated in France. The most important articles by Culioli have recently been gathered together in a single collection (Culioli, 1990) which contains a number of articles in English. A good presentation of Culioli's essential ideas has just been published in English (Bouscaren *et al.*, 1992).

CHAPTER 7

Discourse

An utterance is rarely isolated. It combines with other utterances to form a totality which has its own characteristics – text, conversation, etc. – and to which we give the generic term *discourse*. A discourse is not a simple set of utterances, but possesses a unity which can be characterized in three ways:

- Considered in its entirety, discourse comprises an *organization*: it is composed of a set of hierarchical and (more or less strictly) ordered elements; we can extract its plan, make a summary of it, give it a title, etc.
- As a process which progresses across time, discourse has a *coherence*: each new utterance is related in some way to those preceding and following it, thus allowing its integration to a continuous process.
- Finally, as an activity, discourse is *goal-orientated*: it aims to achieve a particular goal, to have a particular effect on the listener.

In this chapter we shall investigate each of these three aspects in turn.

The organization of discourse

The first psychological studies of discourse were developed within the framework of the study of memory. Some researchers – notably those approaching the question from a Gestaltist perspective – who were working independently of the behaviourist study of *verbal learning*, which uses only lists of words and syllables as its material, became interested in the problems of organization in memory. In studying the memorization of texts, they have found a method of approach which is particularly well adapted to this area of investigation.

How is a text represented in memory? This problem, which Bartlett approached half a century ago, underwent a revival of interest in the 1970s with the renewal of research into memory (see Tulving and Donaldson, 1972). We can note that the emphasis here is on the *content* of the texts without the specifically linguistic (and psycholinguistic) aspects being taken into account. The texts most often used are narratives.

Bartlett and the notion of 'schema'

In his classic text *Remembering* (1932), Bartlett established some of the essential facts which later works were to investigate.

In the first place, subjects' recall of a narrative which they have read in no way constitutes a faithful reproduction of it. Not only is its literal form forgotten, along with a greater or lesser number of details, but above all the narrative becomes the object of an *elaboration* which increases in proportion with the interval between reading and recall. This elaboration is manifested, on the one hand, in the addition of new elements which are not in the text itself but render it more coherent and, on the other, in the suppression of details which are difficult to integrate.

The recall of a text thus appears to involve the substitution of a version which is at once simpler, more stereotypical and more coherent. This stereotypicality increases with the length of retention in memory and is also observed when the narrative is repeatedly passed from subject to subject.

In order to account for these observations, Bartlett introduced the idea of *schema* – that is to say, a very general subject-internal organization as a function of which recollection can be constructed. His observations raise two main problems:

I. Does the elaboration he describes take place during the actual process of understanding the narrative (in which case it would be the product of this which is recorded in memory)? Or is it produced at the time of recall (that is to say, in the form of a reconstruction by the subject on the basis of the incomplete traces that the subject has retained in memory)? Doubtless both are involved. However, it is obviously difficult to distinguish between elaborations produced at the time of storage and those which arise from a reconstruction at the time of recollection.

Nevertheless, an interesting experiment by Frederiksen (1975) throws some light on this problem. This author presented subjects with the same text several times and asked them to recall it after each presentation. The proportion of correct recollections increased regularly from one presentation to the next. However, the interesting result concerns the modifications introduced to the text. If they arise from a process of reconstruction in order to compensate for gaps in memory during recall, then they should diminish as correct recollection improves. This was indeed the case for one type of error, which Frederiksen calls 'elaborations', which consist of information absent from the original text being added by the subjects. However, the frequency of three other types of error remained virtually constant from one attempted recall to the next: generalizations, specifications and inferences drawn from the text. This indicates that these transformations must have been performed and recorded in memory during the reading of the text.

II. The second problem concerns the nature of the implementation of the 'schema'. The – rather vague – notion of schema in fact refers to two distinct things: on the one hand, a formal representation of the general structure of a story (a 'well-formed' story should contain certain types of element in a certain order); on the other, general knowledge concerning the normal sequence of events (here it is a question of the content, not the form, of the story). It is these two aspects of the idea of the schema which more recent studies have researched.

Story grammars

There are certain analogies between the structure of a story and that of a sentence. A story, like a sentence, comprises a certain number of elements – some obligatory, some optional – which should follow one another in a defined order. These elements can be represented in the form of hierarchically organized 'components'. If some obligatory elements are missing, or the order is not respected, then the story will be perceived to be 'badly formed'. Finally, the rules for the canonical organization of the narrative are tacitly shared by the members of any given cultural community, where they constitute a 'narrative competence' analogous to the 'grammatical competence' postulated by Chomsky. From this we derive the idea of formalizing this narrative competence in the form of rules (rewrite rules and transformational rules) analogous to those of generative grammar.

A number of story grammars have been proposed. The most elaborate, proposed by Mandler and Johnson (1977),[1] is presented in the form of two sets of rules.

(a) *rewrite* rules, such as:
    STORY $\rightarrow$ SETTING and EVENT STRUCTURE
    EVENT STRUCTURE $\rightarrow$ EPISODE (then EPISODE)^n

1. Later, the same authors (Johnson and Mandler, 1980) produced a reorganized version of this model, to which the reader should refer for a detailed presentation.

EPISODE → BEGINNING cause DEVELOPMENT cause ENDING
DEVELOPMENT → / SIMPLE REACTION cause ACTION
                        / COMPLEX REACTION cause GOAL PATH
    etc.;

(b) *transformational* rules, which make deletions and rearrangements possible.

A story can thus be represented in the form of a tree structure whose terminal nodes are events or states. It should be noted that the recursive nature of the rules permits highly complex chainings and nestings (thus, GOAL PATH can be rewritten as ATTEMPT cause OUTCOME and OUTCOME, in its turn, can be rewritten as EPISODE, which refers back to an earlier rule, etc.).

Other story grammars of similar inspiration have been proposed – by Thorndyke, Rumelhart, Stein and Glenn, etc.

These story grammars have given rise to a large body of experimental research (for an appraisal of this work, see Mandler, 1982). On the whole, the results reveal the following:

- Recall of a story is achieved more easily the closer the narrative adheres to the form prescribed by the grammar; moreover, subjects tend to move towards the 'canonical' form in their retelling (see, for example, Mandler and Johnson, 1977).
- The story components ('episodes' in particular) play the role of processing units, constituting 'chunks' in memory (Black and Bower, 1979); moreover, processing time is significantly higher at the beginning and end of an episode (Haberlandt, Berian and Sandson, 1980): this difference would seem to indicate the 'initialization' of a new unit in memory at the beginning of the episode, and an organization into a 'macro unit' at the end. In this way, the processing of narrative units would seem to resemble the processing of syntactic clauses.

However, while these results do provide incontestable evidence of the fact that a story constitutes a structured and ordered whole, they cannot be regarded as decisive arguments in favour of the text grammar model.

In the first place, even the idea of a story grammar raises quite serious theoretical objections (see Garnham, 1983); while sentence grammar presupposes a finite lexicon, whose elements belong to well-defined grammatical categories (noun, verb, determiner, auxiliary, etc.), the propositions which might appear in a story do not constitute a closed set, and there is no specific procedure for assigning a proposition (or set of propositions) to a given category. In fact it is the content of a proposition and its relation to other elements in the story which allow it to be classified as BEGINNING, DEVELOPMENT or ENDING, etc. The analogy with formal grammar is thus more apparent than real.

Mandler (1982) agrees, moreover, that his grammatical rules are only a 'notational system' and that there is no question of considering them to have any psychological reality. What subjects possess and implement is a *schema* which arouses certain expectations. The grammatical rules have the role of explaining the regularities reflected by the schema. However, we may ask ourselves what the nature of these regularities is. Are they specific to narrative texts? Or do they reflect a more general (extralinguistic) knowledge concerning the sequences of events and behaviour in everyday life?

For this reason, the 'story grammars' are equally able to 'predict' the structure of texts which are not stories at all, but sequences of goal-orientated courses of action (user instructions, cooking recipes, etc.). Moreover, they apply only to a fairly limited class of story – folk tales, children's stories – and fail to take account of narratives whose form is less stereotypical.

To sum up: while the notion of 'schema' incontestably has a certain psychological relevance, nothing useful appears to be added by representing it in the form of a grammar.

'Frames' and 'scripts'

As we have just noted, the regularities expressed by a 'schema', which guide the listener's expectations and inferences, are not specific to narrative texts. They also govern, more generally, the whole organization of human experience.

How are these regularities represented in memory? This problem was first approached by artificial-intelligence researchers who were confronted by the task of storing in a computer memory the knowledge necessary not only for understanding a text, but also for analyzing a visual scene. To this end, Minsky (1975) proposed the notion of *'frame'*.

A 'frame' is a structure for representing a typical situation – for example, celebrating a birthday, being in a room, etc. This structure assembles a set of information – for example, a room comprises walls, a ceiling, a floor; in the walls there are one or more windows and a door, etc.; there are various articles of furniture, etc. Empty 'slots' correspond to each of these elements, and these slots can then be filled by the available perceptual data. Where these data are absent, 'default' values are assigned to them (thus, for example, the part of a wall hidden by furniture is presumed to be present and to be similar to the visible parts of the wall).

Associated with each frame are rules of use and transformation which make it possible, for example, to perceive a room as remaining the same even when the observer moves to view it from a different perspective.

Frames can also be used to represent the syntactic or semantic structures of words or sentences, narrative schemas, typical sequences of events, etc.

The notion of *'script'* proposed by Schank and Abelson (1977) is more specifically designed to deal with the comprehension and production of narratives. A script is a structure describing a stereotypical sequence of events. A well-known example is the restaurant script: going to a restaurant entails a sequence of actions (entering, choosing a table, sitting down, reading the menu, ordering, eating, paying, leaving a tip, going), a set of objects (tables, chairs, place settings, menu, etc.) and people (waiter, chef, cashier, etc.); it is not necessary to make all these elements explicit; the mention of just one element is enough to activate the script, recorded in memory, on the basis of which the available information can be interpreted.

The script thus fulfils several functions: it guides the reader's expectations; it makes it possible to 'address' the received information (which fills the empty 'slots' in the script); it makes a set of inferences possible (for example, from 'John went to the restaurant and ordered steak and chips' we can infer that John ate steak and chips without explicitly being told that he did so); and finally, it ensures narrative coherence.

In fact the notion of script constitutes only one particular case of chaining: that of a sequence of actions frequently reproduced in a single, stereotypical form. The most general case is covered by the idea of *plans*. Plans refer to a sequence of actions intended to realize a particular *goal*, through the intermediary of a set of sub-goals. A plan can entail the implementation of one or more scripts (for example, the sub-goal 'go to New York', itself part of a larger plan, will call up a script for 'journey by aeroplane'). The goals themselves depend on *themes* (social roles, interpersonal relations, lifestyle): thus the theme 'ambition' or the theme 'love' allows us to predict the goals a person might wish to achieve.

More recently, Schank (1981) has been led to regard scripts as organizations constructed from more general modular elements which may belong to a number of different scripts: these are known as MOPs (*memory organization packages*).

The psychological reality of scripts has been the object of a number of experimental studies. In particular, these have demonstrated that after the presentation of a story, subjects show a marked increase in the number of times they incorrectly recognize sentences which are not in the story itself, but which refer to elements from the corresponding script. The subjects, therefore, do not distinguish between real information and information which is evoked on the basis of the script (Bower, Black and Turner, 1979).

Meanwhile, Schank and colleagues have used scripts in various computer programs for text comprehension. For example, the program FRUMP (De Jong, 1982) can read and summarize newspaper articles on the basis of about sixty scripts: it identifies the relevant script by looking for key words in the first sentence, then proceeds in a 'top–down' fashion, searching for information in the text with which to fill the empty 'slots'.[2]

Although these ideas of 'frame' and 'script' are interesting for the study of the representation of knowledge in memory, we must emphasize that they allow only a partial approach to the processing of texts. Without doubt, text comprehension is based on a set of reader (or listener) 'expectations' which are themselves determined by extralinguistic general knowledge. However, understanding a text is not simply recognizing an already known situation, or filling the 'slots' of an existing schema. It also consists in constructing a new representation which is specific to the particular text (or speech) in question. How is this representation constructed?

Microstructure and macrostructure: Text processing

The most elaborate model that has been proposed to account for the processes of text comprehension is Kintsch and Van Dijk's (1978).[3] The aim of this model is to account for the comprehension and memorization of any type of text (not only stereotypical narratives) as they are read on the basis of a representation of the semantic content in the form of a series of propositions. In this way, comprehension and memorization occur gradually during the course of reading the text.

The *microstructure* of the text is constituted by the series of propositions which represent the meaning of the sentence: that is to say, on the one hand, the propositions which are present explicitly and, on the other, those which have to be inferred in order to assure coherence – the whole constituting the 'text base'.

The text is processed sequentially in sections containing a number of propositions. The aim of processing is to establish textual coherence by linking propositions which share the same argument. When a processing cycle has been completed (that is to say, when a section has been processed) a new processing cycle begins on the next section, while a certain number of the propositions which have already been processed are retained (in the limited capacity of short-term memory). In this way, a 'coherence graph' is constructed which links the different propositions as and when they are presented. If a proposition does not share an argument with another proposition in short-term memory, then long-term memory has to be

2. This 'top–down' procedure can produce some surprising results. Thus in processing an article which began with the sentence: 'Pope's death shakes the Western hemisphere', FRUMP generated the following summary: 'There was an earthquake in the Western Hemisphere. The Pope died' (Riesbeck, 1982).
3. See also Miller and Kitsch (1980), who make some modifications to the initial model and provide a set of experimental data to support the newer model. We are unable to present the numerous other studies of text comprehension here, but for a critical review of the different models proposed, see De Beaugrande (1981).

searched for more distant propositions and, in the event of failure, the necessary inferences have to be made.

The probability of a proposition being recalled will be higher the greater the number of processing cycles in which it appears. Thus the model can predict the differences in recall between the propositions in the text on the basis of three parameters: n (maximum size of a section), s (number of propositions retained in short-term memory) and p (probability of reproduction after a processing cycle). These parameters vary, of course, depending on the subject and the type of text involved.

Similar processing is involved in the construction of the *macrostructure* of the text – that is to say, different levels of 'macro-propositions' are generated either by deleting the irrelevant propositions or by generalizing or integrating several propositions into a single proposition. This construction of the macrostructure is also performed in successive cycles. It depends essentially on the aims of the reader, which can be represented by a 'schema' which governs his or her anticipations and specifies the relevant propositions. Since these aims can vary considerably from one subject to another, Kintsch and Van Dijk decided to limit their research to cases where the reader's aims are strongly determined by conventional schemata (stories or research reports).

The interest of this model is that it permits certain precise empirical predictions to be made concerning both textual comprehensibility and subjects' performances in recall tasks. The observations which have been made correspond well with these predictions (see Miller and Kintsch, 1980). Moreover, it has been possible to implement certain facets of this model as a computer program (Kintsch, 1982).

In a more recent and much more elaborate version of their theory, Van Dijk and Kintsch (1983) have made several important improvements to their model. In the first place, a central role is accorded to *strategies* which function at multiple levels and make the model much more flexible and dynamic. In the second place, the aim of these strategies is to construct not only a propositional 'text base' but also a 'situation model', similar to Johnson-Laird's 'mental model', which integrates prior knowledge and constitutes the referential base for the discourse.

Many of the inadequacies which appeared in the earlier model have thus been corrected and the framework proposed by Van Dijk and Kintsch is, without a doubt, the most elaborated synthesis of the study of discourse. At the same time it constitutes a very rich and flexible model for future research.

Nevertheless, there is one criticism which can be levelled at this model – as, indeed, at all the studies of text processing. This concerns the purely *conceptual* level at which processing takes place. The specifically linguistic aspects of the text are ignored. Can the linguistic formulation of a discourse really be considered to have no role in its comprehension and memorization? We shall now turn our attention to studies associated with these aspects which are more truly psycholinguistic in nature.

Discourse cohesion

A discourse is coherent – if it were not, it would be a mere juxtaposition of utterances. However, this is not manifested only at the conceptual level (which goes beyond the domain of psycholinguistics in the strictest sense of the word). The relating of the successive elements which constitute discourse is also assured by linguistic procedures. This fact enables us to speak of *cohesion* rather than coherence: it is on the basis of linguistic markers that the listener establishes (and the speaker indicates) how elements are related to each other. We can interpret these markers either as *cues* provided by the speaker which the listener then uses to infer the relations intended by the speaker, or as *instructions* given by the speaker which govern the processing performed by the listener.

The 'given–new' contract

An initial aspect of this cohesion has already been mentioned in the previous chapter. As the discourse progresses, it must be possible to link each element to the one which has preceded it. Every utterance thus comprises two kinds of information: the 'new' information which is its *raison d'être*, its own contribution to the discourse, and the 'old' information which in some way gives it an 'address' by indicating where the new information should be integrated into the already constructed representation.

As Haviland and Clark (1974) have pointed out, this presupposes a kind of tacit *contract* between speaker and listener:

> The speaker must try to construct his utterances so that the given information actually *does* convey information he believes the listener actually knows or could know, and so that the new information actually *does* contain information he believes the listener doesn't actually know. The listener, for his part, agrees to interpret each utterance on the assumption that the speaker is trying to do this. (Clark, 1977)

The implementation of this contract calls for at least two things:

(a) In the first place, the listener must identify the 'old' information in the utterance, which presupposes that this is explicitly marked. As we have seen, the topic–comment structure can fulfil this role, although this can be augmented or replaced by other procedures: choice of article (indefinite article introducing a new element; definite article referring to an element introduced earlier); pronominalization (which refers to an already known element); intonation (new information can give rise to a particular emphasis); etc. The problem is that, as we have seen earlier, these linguistic markers can be used to fulfil a variety of functions.

(b) Having identified the 'old' information, the listener must retrieve it from memory. Inferences will often have to be made here, since the already recorded information is not always repeated word for word. A *bridging inference* has to be established between what is presented as already known, and what is actually known. Of course, these inferences rely on the listener's knowledge, but also on a general principle: to construct the simplest inference which is compatible with the data (Clark, 1977). We have seen elsewhere that the psychological reality of these inferences can be verified experimentally (Haviland and Clark, 1974; see p. 145 above).

There are two points to be made here:

(i) The communication is not necessarily 'co-operative': the speaker can present information as 'given' when it is in fact not known by the listener but is presented as part of the (presumed) 'common ground'. The entirety of Ducrot's theory about presupposition (1972) bears on this point.

(ii) The analysis based on the 'given/new' distinction is in fact a blend of two very different types of procedure: on the one hand, the *linguistic* markers (pronouns, articles, order of utterance, etc.) which play the role of search and insert instructions in the representation of the discourse; and, on the other, the inferential procedures which may be necessary for carrying out these instructions.

This distinction is well illustrated in the studies we shall turn to next.

Referential continuity and semantic integration

It is advisable to differentiate between the purely psycholinguistic aspects of the cohesion of discourse and the inferential aspects, for reasons which become apparent when we distinguish between *coherence* and *plausibility*. A discourse is coherent if its successive elements can be integrated into a unified representation. It is plausible if this representation accords with our knowledge of the normal order of things in the world in which we live.

The relevance of this distinction has been demonstrated in an experiment conducted by Garnham, Oakhill and Johnson-Laird (1982), who presented their subjects with three different versions of the same text. The first was an ordinary story. The second was constituted from the same story, but with the sentences changed around. The third also presented the story with the sentences changed around, but with linguistic markers inserted into each sentence so that the referent could be identified. For example:[4]

(1) Jenny was holding on tightly to the string of her beautiful new balloon. She had just won it and was hurrying home to show her sister. Suddenly, the wind caught it and carried it into a tree. The balloon hit a branch and burst. Jenny cried and cried.

(2) She had just won it and was hurrying home to show her sister. Suddenly the wind caught it and carried it into a tree. Jenny was holding on tightly to the string of her beautiful new balloon. Jenny cried and cried. The balloon hit a branch and burst.

(3) Jenny had just won a beautiful new balloon and was hurrying home to show her sister. Suddenly, the wind caught it and carried it into a tree. Jenny was holding on tightly to the string of her balloon. She cried and cried. It hit a branch and burst.

As one would expect, the subjects judged version (1) to be clearly more comprehensible than version (2) (the average score for comprehensibility fell from 8.8 out of 10 for the first version to 3.3 for the second) and, similarly, recall was far better for the first version (0.71) than for the second (0.30). The third version, however, gave intermediate results (comprehensibility: 4.6; recall: 0.43). The order of events, and thus their sequential plausibility, is nevertheless the same in (3) as in (2). The only difference is that in (3) the linguistic markers make it possible to construct a *referential continuity*, whereas this is not the case for (2). As the authors point out, a 'story grammar' is totally incapable of accounting for the difference observed between texts of types (2) and (3).

Referential continuity is not the only aspect which determines the cohesion of a text. Another important characteristic is the unity of the *point of view*. In a story, for example, the events are reported in relation to a certain point of view, that of the narrator. This landmarking is performed primarily by the choice of deictic markers. Black, Turner and Bower (1979) have been able to demonstrate that complex sentences or sequences of sentences in which this unity of point of view is assured are more quickly understood, better recalled and judged more comprehensible than those which contain a change in the point of view.

What all this brings to light is the essential role of linguistic markers in

4. This example is taken from a simplified version of the experiment designed for children. For adult subjects, the authors used longer texts (200–250 words).

the construction of an 'integrated' representation of discourse. Understanding a discourse is not a progressive construction of a network of propositions derived from the syntactico-semantic processing of each sentence; it is the elaboration of a *mental model* which is progressively reorganized and embellished. Thus linguistic markers play the role of instructions for performing these successive modifications to the mental model.[5]

The way is thus open for a truly psycholinguistic approach to the analysis of discourse, in which it is no longer a question of simply investigating how semantic representations are organized to form a coherent (or plausible) picture of the world, but also how the linguistic instruments are involved in directing the procedures for constructing this representation of discourse.

The processing of anaphora

Of all the linguistic tools which ensure discourse cohesiveness, it is *anaphoric expressions* that have given rise to the largest body of work.[6] The function of anaphora is to refer to an antecedent – that is to say, to a term introduced in another (generally earlier) part of the discourse. The study of the processes through which this antecedent is identified may thus provide valuable clues about the mechanisms for processing discourse.

Although there are syntactic constraints (see above, p. 99) operating on the selection of the antecedent, these can clearly operate only within the framework of the sentence. In most cases, the antecedent is situated in another sentence; therefore, its identification entails a memory search and the use of semantic or pragmatic cues.

It might be thought that the time required for this search will increase, the further removed the clause containing the antecedent is from that containing the anaphoric expression. This expectation seems to be confirmed by certain experimental data, notably that relating to reading time (Clark and Sengul, 1979) or ocular fixation (Ehrlich and Rayner, 1983). Nevertheless, this distance effect is no longer observed if the discourse topic remains unchanged between the sentence containing the antecedent and the sentence containing the anaphora (Lesgold, Roth and Curtis, 1979). It is not, therefore, the distance which is important but the fact of whether or not the relevant information is 'in focus'. In fact, a simple change of scene during a narrative can make a considerable difference to the accessibility of the antecedent. For example, in the following narrative (Sanford and Garrod, 1982):

5. This idea of 'mental model' may be found in various forms in the works of a number of linguists: Kamp (1981) writes of 'discourse representation'; Fauconnier (1984) of 'mental spaces'. In later formulations of their theory, we have seen that Van Dijk and Kintsch (1983) also introduce this idea under the name 'situation model'.
6. For a recent review of this work, see Garnham (1987); Sanford and Garrod (1989); Oakhill, Garnham and Vonk (1989).

At the cinema
 Jenny found the film rather boring. The projectionist had to keep changing reels. It was supposed to be a silent classic.
 (Seven hours)/(Ten minutes) later the film was forgotten. (He)/(She) had fallen asleep and was dreaming.

the time taken to identify the antecedent of *he* (the projectionist) is greater in the 'Seven hours later' version than in the 'Ten minutes later' version. In contrast, the antecedent of *she* is identified just as quickly in both versions. According to Sanford and Garrod, this difference can be explained by a change of 'focus' in the mental model which is constructed on the basis of the narrative.

Moreover, McKoon and Ratcliff (1980) note that the interpretation of an anaphor leads to the activation not only of the antecedent but also of all elements in the clause in which it occurred.

Finally, Marslen-Wilson and Tyler (1987) show that 'pragmatic' constraints (that is to say, those which are associated with the plausibility of the event described) intervene in the processing of the sentence just as quickly as the constraints of 'focus' or even the grammatical constraints themselves.

These various observations tend to support the idea of a direct 'mapping' of the lexical information on to a mental model which is constructed, reorganized and embellished throughout the discourse.

The orientation of discourse

Finally, we must remember that discourse is a goal-orientated process. That is to say, its aim is not solely to impart a certain volume of information which the listener needs only to weigh up in order to reconstitute the starting representation. It also constitutes a goal-orientated route which is designed to have a certain *influence* on the beliefs, attitudes and behaviour of the listener through the intermediary of a representation which is not simply enriched but also transformed and corrected as a function of the aims of the speaker (or the interlocutors).

In other words, a discourse always has a more or less *argumentative* function which is related not only to the content but also to the linguistic means employed.

Language and argumentation

There is currently a revival of interest among logicians and linguists in the study of argumentation, which was the object of classical rhetoric. We shall mention two notable bodies of work which are of direct interest to the psycholinguist.

J.-B. Grize and colleagues at the Neuchâtel Centre for Semiological Studies (see Borel, Grize and Miéville, 1983) sought to characterize the 'natural logic' of argumentative discourse – that is to say, 'the system of thought operations which permit an involved speaking subject to propose his representations to a listener, and to do so by means of a discourse' (Grize, 1976). The analysis of logico-discursive operations proposed by Grize is directly inspired by Culioli's linguistic work, and could constitute a very interesting framework for the psychological study of the processes of discourse production and comprehension.

In a very different – but, in our opinion, complementary – perspective, Ducrot and Anscombre have developed the idea of an 'argumentative force' which is inherent to language: 'The meaning of an utterance comprises, as an integral and constitutive part, that form of influence which we call argumentative force. For an utterance to have meaning, it has to be goal-orientated' (Anscombre and Ducrot, 1983, p. 5). In other words, the chaining of utterances in a discourse depends not only on their content but also on their linguistic form which defines a set of constraints which is imposed on the possible chainings. The fine analyses which Ducrot and colleagues have applied to a number of argumentative operators (*mais* ['but'], *d'ailleurs* ['moreover'] etc.; see Ducrot *et al.*, 1980) open up an important field of research for psycholinguistic study.[7]

An example: The functioning of connectives

The psycholinguistic study of discursive procedures thus leads to that of the *dynamic* of discourse. Through a series of reorganizations, embellishments, and also rectifications of the representation, discourse progresses towards a particular objective. This progression is directed by linguistic means, the study of which constitutes a topic for investigation which has as yet scarcely been approached. An interesting example of these 'discourse operators' is provided by the connectives whose very function it is to mark the links between the successive stages of discourse.

Most of the work on connectives has been exclusively devoted to their logical or semantic aspects – that is to say, to the relations which they were supposed to mark either between the truth values of the propositions linked by them (implication: *if*; disjunction: *or*; conjunction: *and*) or between the states of the items or events denoted by them (for example, causal relation: *because*; contrastive relation: *but*). The need to take pragmatic factors (intention of the speaker, type of speech act performed, conversational rules) into account has, nevertheless, had to be recognized (see Fillenbaum, 1977).

7. For a rather more detailed presentation of the works of Grize and Ducrot, and the perspectives which their work offers to psycholinguistics, see Caron (1983).

A number of studies have begun to show an interest in the functioning of connectives in so far as they order the procedures for processing utterances within the framework of discourse.

Haberlandt (1982) thus shows that the presence in a story of a causal connective (*therefore*, *consequently*, etc.) or an adversative connective (*but*, *however*, etc.) at the beginning of a sentence leads to a shorter reading time and therefore to a more rapid comprehension of the sentence. In a more detailed study, Townsend (1983) demonstrates that sentence processing depends on the type of relation expressed by the connective. Depending on whether or not the connective allows the prediction of a link which conforms with the (causal) expectations of the speaker, the proposition will either be integrated into what has preceded it or left in abeyance in its surface form.

However, these studies are still concerned with narrative texts whose aim is simply to provide a series of information chained in accordance with a causal or temporal succession. The role of the connectives appears to be more specific in argumentative texts, where the linking of utterances is governed more directly by the speaker's intentions. The memory representation of such a text, as far as can be shown in a recall task, appears to depend quantitatively and qualitatively on the connectives it contains (Caron, 1985).

Certain linguistic markers thus appear to act as *processing instructions* which order the way in which information is processed by the listener and integrated in the representation of the discourse (see Caron, 1984). Connectives probably do not constitute an isolated case. Other linguistic procedures (modalities, illocutionary markers, etc.) could also be studied from this perspective. The pragmatics of discourse – and the linguistic means on which it is based – offers a field of psycholinguistic study which as yet remains virtually unexplored.

Conclusion

The psycholinguistic study of discourse is still only in its infancy. The many works focusing on the comprehension – and, less frequently, on the production – of discourse are concerned almost exclusively with the purely conceptual aspects of the representation of discourse, but have hitherto paid little attention to the truly linguistic aspects of this representation. One consequence of this orientation towards content in these studies has been the almost exclusive use of narrative or didactic texts in which the pragmatic, interactive aspects of language are, for the most part, neutralized.

Without doubt, the fundamental mechanisms of language processing are to be found in situations where language is used not only to impart information but also to achieve interaction. In this connection, *argumentative discourse* on the one hand, and *conversation* on the other, provide a field of study which remains largely unexplored. Until now the first has primarily been of interest to logicians and philosophers, and the second to sociologists and psychosociologists. Psycholinguists certainly still have a great deal to do.

To produce or understand a discourse is, in effect, not only to encode or decode a set of information. It is to try to construct, using the means of language, a representation which is common to both speaker and listener. The aim of the discourse is that this representation should have some effect on the interlocuter. It is only at this level that we can adequately approach the twin problems of the language-based *representation* and the psycho-linguistic *operations* which construct it.

1. The representation constructed on the basis of the discourse (or which orders its production) is not a simple structured set of information concerning a referent. It is a complex, multidimensional organization in which are specified not only a set of 'propositions', but also their relation to the various actors in the communicative exchange and their function within the act of communication. It is an organization which is progressively constructed, embellished and modified during the exchange. Current models provide only a very impoverished image of this representation.

2. In the final analysis, it is the task of psycholinguistic procedures to construct and transform this representation. This task defines both their *raison d'être* and, without doubt, the key to their functioning. Seen from this perspective, language appears to be a system of *instructions* for controlling this construction rather than a set of formal objects to be recognized and interpreted.

Both the result of the psycholinguistic operations themselves and the 'top–down' control of these operations make the study of discourse not a simple extension of psycholinguistics but its essential facet. There is little doubt that it is in this domain that the most important research will be performed in the future.

Recommended reading

Discourse analysis is a very active field of multidisciplinary activity. For an overall view, the reader could consult the four volumes of the *Handbook of Discourse Analysis* (Van Dijk, 1985). The journal *Discourse Processes* traces some of the most important work in progress.

As far as the psychological perspective is concerned, a number of references have already been mentioned in the text of this chapter. Van Dijk and Kintsch (1983) presents a detailed exposition of the model proposed by the authors, together with a review of the most important studies. A rather different approach, inspired by procedural semantics (and similar to the one I propose at the end of this chapter), is presented in Sanford and Garrod (1982). For a similar perspective, the reader could also consult Johnson-Laird (1983) and Garnham (1988).

CHAPTER 8

The Position and Perspectives of Psycholinguistics

As an intermediary science which lies between two distinct disciplines – linguistics and cognitive psychology – psycholinguistics has been doubtful about its status during the thirty or so years of its existence. At one time it appeared content to be a simple appendage to linguistics, which at that point seemed to have found in generative grammar the prestige of a unified and rigorously formulated theory. The failure of this endeavour led to more specifically psychological preoccupations, and the discipline became increasingly integrated into the general current of cognitive psychology, of which it today constitutes a major branch. This evolution appears to be quite irreversible: language is a human activity which derives from the same principles and is based on the same type of procedures as the other cognitive activities.

It does, none the less, have certain characteristics of its own, and it is these that reveal the specific nature of psycholinguistics:

(a) The first is a matter of degree rather than nature, and lies in the great richness and complexity of language processing. The limited progress made by artificial intelligence programs in this field illustrates vividly the impossibility of confining ourselves to oversimple models. To this end, psycholinguistics can provide a favourable environment for the refinement of theories of information processing in humans.

(b) A second, more essential, point bears on the very nature of natural languages. On the one hand, language has a purely mental reality: it exists only by virtue of the activity of speech by which it is generated. At the same time, however, it is external to the individual subject, on whom it imposes its rules and structure. On this count, language is neither a simple external object nor a purely mental activity, but both at once. It is an activity which is subject to a system of rules, but is also made possible by these very rules. This status, which is unique to

170

language, is what gives psycholinguistics its specificity. Psycholinguistics must take account of this linguistic organization before it can explain the nature of processing in individuals. Psycholinguistics, a branch of cognitive psychology, remains firmly allied to linguistics.

Language processing

As we have seen on a number of occasions, there are currently two opposing conceptions regarding language processing in humans:

1. The simplest way of thinking about language processing is the one I presented at the beginning of this book. In this conception the subject identifies the successive phonemes in the soundstream, groups them into words, establishes their syntactic relations, constructs a semantic interpretation on the basis of this and, finally, brings to bear any available extralinguistic information and elaborates a meaning which is commensurate with the situation. Such a process would function in a 'bottom–up' fashion – that is to say, it would be data-driven. It would require a series of autonomous 'components' or 'modules', each specialized in one type of processing (phoneme identification, word recognition, syntactic analysis, etc.). Finally, these modules would function *in series* – that is to say, each one would receive information only from the preceding component in order to transmit it, duly processed, to the next component.

2. However, we have seen that processes of the 'top–down' variety have appeared at each level of analysis. These are processes which are driven by the subject's knowledge, hypotheses and expectations. Some authors consider that this phenomenon makes a purely sequential conception of processing impossible. Instead, it would become necessary to regard the processing of different types of information as occurring in parallel and operating in an *interactive* fashion.[1]

These two conceptions of processing are themselves associated with very different approaches to the functioning of the human mind.

---

1. This interactionist theory can appear in various guises. For example, we may retain the idea of distinct processors as long as we allow each processor to use the information provided by the others. According to a 'weak' version of the theory, information obtained at a certain processing level can simply interrupt the functioning of the lower-level processors if the product of these is deemed irrelevant to interpretation. However, the idea of independent processors may also be rejected altogether. Instead, we may consider, like Marslen-Wilson and Tyler (1980, 1987), that lexical representations are directly 'mapped' on to a 'mental model' as speech progresses, on the basis of all the information (grammatical, semantic and pragmatic) available to the subject. Thus, within such a view there is no longer any place for postulating intermediate levels of representation (syntactic structure, logical form, literal meaning).

The modularist theory

The modularist conception of language processing, as defended by Forster in particular, relies principally on methodological arguments: if everything interacts with everything else, scientific knowledge is impossible. Until there is proof to the contrary, therefore, we must start from the principle that the system is 'in practice' decomposable into distinct components, and study these components separately.

However, this theory has a wholly different significance in the form given to it by Fodor (1983), for whom the 'language faculty' constitutes an entire module in itself – that is to say, an input system which is independent of the central systems. Specialized exclusively in the processing of verbal data, this system is 'informationally encapsulated' – that is to say, impermeable to any other type of information (context, subject's expectations, general knowledge, etc.) and to any central control. This makes its functioning fast and mandatory.

As its input, this module receives the product of acoustic analysis carried out by the sensory transducers. As its output, it provides the linguistic form (and probably the logical form[2]) of the utterance. It will be the task of the central systems to interpret this output on the basis of the situation and general knowledge. (Let me add that according to Fodor these central systems are non-modular and cannot, therefore, be studied scientifically.)

Finally, this system is based on a fixed neuronal architecture – it is hard-wired – and its principles of functioning are innately specified: the faculty of language is 'biologically necessary' (Chomsky, 1980).

In this radical form, modularism is more a philosophical stance than a scientific theory. The assimilation of language into a formal system (in which syntax plays a predominant role) which it supposes is far from being unanimously accepted by linguists. Moreover, it implies a radical split between the purely linguistic and the extralinguistic aspects of processing which the empirical data do not justify (for a discussion, see Marslen-Wilson, 1987).

At least this approach draws attention to a number of interesting problems, in particular concerning the initial conditions of access to language: if this appears to be a specifically human faculty, it supposes the existence of biologically necessary capabilities in the human being (although we cannot confirm *a priori* that they are specific to language). This is the reason behind research into the linguistic abilities of the newborn baby (conducted in France, for example, by Mehler and colleagues).

As for the existence of specialized, modular processors, we have already

---

2. According to Chomsky, the logical form is the first stage in semantic interpretation: namely, the stage which is governed by the syntactic structure.

seen that the experimental data (concerning lexical access, on the one hand, and syntactic analysis, on the other) do not provide any decisive answers. All they allow us to confirm is a *partial* modularity of certain processing levels. This does not exclude their permeability, in particular cases, to certain higher-level information and in no way implies that these processing levels are innate (rather than the product of automation). The real problem appears to be not so much that of choosing between two extreme conceptions of processing as that of empirically studying how these two types of processing (modular and interactive) can be linked.

The connectionist models

This problem is posed in completely different terms within the framework of the connectionist models which have been developed in particular as a result of the work of McClelland, Rumelhart and their colleagues (see McClelland, Rumelhart and the PDP Research Group, 1986).[3]

This approach regards cognitive functioning not as sequential processing conducted by one central processor (classic computer model) or by a series of specialized processors, but as massively parallel processing occurring in a highly interconnected network of numerous elementary processors (PDP = parallel distributed processing).

Evidently, this kind of model is inspired by the functioning of the brain (even though the nodes on connectionist networks have only a rather remote similarity to neurons). This model presents a number of properties which are particularly interesting for the study of language processing:

- It can take account of a large number of diverse constraints simultaneously.
- It makes it possible to account for interactive processes (through the interplay of excitation and inhibition of elements in the network) without excluding certain effects of partial modularity (see Tanenhaus, Dell and Carlson, 1987).
- It has the capacity to process incomplete or deviant data competently.
- Finally, it can account for learning processes.[4]

We have already encountered several illustrations of this kind of model, in particular with regard to lexical access (the TRACE model). In fact, the connectionist approach primarily constitutes a very general descriptive

---

3. An accessible presentation of this work can also be found in McClelland (1988).
4. See the model for the acquisition of the German article presented by McWhinney *et al.* (1989).

framework which has so far been used to account for already known experimental results rather than as a basis for empirically testable predictions (the majority of the published work relates to simulations). This type of model appears to be well adapted to describing the initial levels of language processing (phonological analysis, lexical access). Beyond those levels, current realizations are less convincing. However, further research is developing apace.

The 'top–down' aspects of processing

To conclude, I wish to point out that whichever model we may prefer, one of the essential characteristics of language processing is the place accorded to the 'top–down' types of process. Therefore, two important aspects of language functioning must be emphasized.

1. The first is the decisive role played by *contextual factors*. The notion of context is, no doubt, one of the most confused of all, and one of the major tasks of future research will be to distinguish its various aspects and the influence they exert.[5] However, the omnipresence of these contextual influences raises the question of the very nature of linguistic signs themselves. Current thinking has it that the form and the meaning of these signs are determined intrinsically, with context intervening only to introduce distortions of greater or lesser importance (for example, in the form of a 'derived meaning' obtained from a 'literal meaning'). However, if we accept that this relationship to context is not simply superimposed on language but is an integral part of it, then an entirely different approach can be envisaged: the linguistic sign would not have the function of *evoking* a representation but of *operating* on it – that is to say, of activating the procedures of finding, organizing and transforming representations which are already present. In the face of the diversity of the context-linked 'meaning effects', one of the psycholinguist's tasks would therefore be to identify the procedural invariants attached to the linguistic signs and the cognitive operations to which they correspond.

2. A second consequence of the 'top–down' types of processing is that they suggest a close link between the processes involved in the *comprehension* of language and those involved in language *production*. To comprehend an utterance is – to a greater or lesser extent – to anticipate it: that is to say, to reproduce its conditions of production. We have seen an illustration of this in connection with speech perception. The motor theory of sound perception remains one of the most attractive of concepts, and the same idea occurs in the 'analysis by synthesis' models of syntactic

5. For a basic analysis, see Clark and Carlson (1981).

processing, in the processing of references on the basis of the 'common ground', etc.

This communality of production and comprehension brings to light a characteristic which is wholly specific to language: its *intersubjectivity*. The activity of speech involves not only the processing of a sequence of symbols by one subject but also the representation of this activity by another subject. Speech is a shared activity. This is why pragmatic aspects are so crucially important. It is through them that this intersubjective function of language is expressed. They may even govern the very organization of natural languages.

Psycholinguistics and linguistics

These natural languages through which the human language function is realized form the object of a specific discipline: linguistics. How are we to position psycholinguistics in relation to this?

Some twenty years ago the answer was self-evident. So great was the prestige of generative and transformational grammar that it was hard to envisage any other role for psycholinguists than to 'find the processes by which the competence described by linguists is acquired by children and is reflected in their performance' (Ervin-Tripp and Slobin, 1966, p. 436). Currently we seem to be witnessing a movement in the opposite direction: distrust of the linguistic schools has led a number of researchers to return to the former designation of psycholinguistics as the 'psychology of language' (for example, Costermans, 1980) and even to speak in terms of a 'psycholinguistics without linguistics' (Johnson-Laird, 1977).

Such a tendency, however, is not without its dangers. In wanting to do without linguistics, researchers run the risk of ignoring *the linguistic* – that is to say, the very reality of language. Such a tendency may be seen in the concentration on the elementary levels of language processing: recognition of words, letters or sounds, where it is perhaps possible to ignore linguistics;[6] or, in contrast, in the withdrawal from the domain of language, in the study of conceptual organization such as we have seen in the work on semantic memory or the comprehension of discourse. To my mind, however, it is precisely in the space between these two approaches – in the passage from form to meaning or meaing to form – that the essential object of psycholinguistics is to be found. It is the implementation of a language

---

6. This tendency appears clearly in the recent volume in the series *Attention and Performance*, which is devoted to language processing (Bouma and Bouwhuis, 1984); see Seidenberg's pertinent criticism in *Contemporary Psychology* (1985, pp. 946–7).

system which simultaneously permits the construction of meaning and the control of this construction.

So there can be no psycholinguistics without linguistics. Indeed, the latter discipline makes two contributions to the psychological study of language processing.

Its first contribution is at a *descriptive* level. The systematic and methodical observations of linguists and the regularities to which they testify provide an indispensable basis for study, for which the linguistic intuition of the psychologist is no substitute. In particular, the diversity of languages requires comparative studies which are the proper domain of the linguist and which alone are able to destroy the too-frequent illusion that it is possible to generalize the particularities of one's own language as the universal properties of the human mind.

However, linguistics does not have a purely descriptive objective. Taking the diversity of these languages as its base, it also aims to construct a general *theory* of language. Such a theory must of necessity mobilize psychological hypotheses. It also raises problems which psycholinguists cannot neglect. As we have seen, the difficulty is that there are a large number of linguistic theories. However, a certain amount of simplification makes it possible to group them into two broad orientations:

- The first group focuses on the formal *structure* of language: a language is a system of symbols which are combined in accordance with certain rules.
- The second group concentrates on the *function* of language: a language is a set of means for expressing and transmitting meanings.

1. According to the first of these approaches, the aim of a linguistic theory is to bring to light the *formal* constraints (universal in principle) which determine the rules for the combination of the signs and make it possible to construct well-formed expressions in the language. From this perspective, syntax plays a special role. Chomsky's theory can be thought of as the most elaborate form of this type of approach. The reduction of language to a formal system leads logically to the belief that the principles of Universal Grammar form part of the structure of the mind and that the 'language faculty' is an isolated system, independent of general cognitive functioning.

2. The second type of theory aims to account for the way the various languages establish a relationship between forms (linguistic) and meanings (mental). The structural or formal aspects of language are not held to be given *a priori* but are the result of a set of *cognitive* operations and representations. Syntax is thus no longer thought of as autonomous but is inseparable from semantics (and, to a certain extent, from pragmatics). This

type of approach, illustrated recently by the work of Langacker (1986, 1987) in the USA and Culioli (1990) in France, thus views language not as a formal object, the object of an abstract 'competence', but as an activity which can be analyzed as a regulated system of mental operations.

For reasons which, as we have seen, are essentially historical, Chomsky's formal approach has long monopolized the attention of psycholinguists and continues to attract a number of adherents today. However, the 'functional' or 'cognitive' linguistic theories are much closer to those on which cognitive psychology is concentrating. As we have seen, a number of studies are emerging which are based more or less directly on this approach. A systematic examination of the hypotheses which have been inspired by these theories – now sufficiently elaborated to permit precise experimental research – will undoubtedly provide psycholinguistics with a rich field of research as well as a chance to contribute in its turn to the development of linguistic theory itself.

Perspectives

Psycholinguistics, well established within the general framework of the cognitive sciences, has the most affirmedly interdisciplinary character of all the branches of psychology. It is closely associated with linguistics, as we have just observed, but it also has solid links with artificial intelligence and the neurosciences. There can be no doubt that these interdisciplinary exchanges will continue to develop in the years to come. Psycholinguistics can play an important role in linking these different disciplines, provided that it avoids spreading itself too thinly and concentrates its efforts on what constitutes its real field of research: the study of the processes through which the human mind brings a *form* (acoustic or graphic) into relation with a *meaning* through the intermediary of a *language* system.

The current state of research, whose course I have attempted to trace in this book, permits the definition of several major and as yet insufficiently explored directions which future research should take.

I. To comprehend the utterances of a language is, on the one hand, to *identify* the linguistic elements of which they are composed and, on the other, to *interpret* these elements in order to construct a meaning. A considerable body of work has been devoted to the first aspect of this activity (identification of phonemes, words and syntactic relations). However, little is yet known about the *construction of meaning* itself.

This requires, first of all, that the nature of the semantic representation is better explored. We have seen that the idea of a 'mental model' which is constructed and adapted as the discourse progresses is one which has enjoyed widespread acceptance. However, the organization of this mental model is certainly far more complex than a simple tableau representing an external state of affairs. It needs to be defined far more precisely if it is to embrace a range of phenomena to which I have already alluded – focalizations, direction of an argument, modalizations and the representation of belief systems and so on.[7]

Above all, if we agree with Marslen-Wilson (1987) that language comprehension consists of 'mapping lexical representations onto discourse models', then much remains to be achieved in analyzing the processes through which this mapping occurs – that is to say, in systematically studying the contribution of the various types of linguistic markers to this construction of meaning.

II. This implies that we must approach language functioning at levels which are much more complex than that of the simple descriptive sentence to which much research still limits itself.

There is no doubt that the field of *discourse* is currently the object of numerous studies. As we have seen, however, these studies often neglect or evade the truly linguistic aspects in favour of analyses conducted at a purely conceptual level. The study of the linguistic determinants of discourse operations has hardly begun. Such a study certainly promises to yield some important discoveries, provided that research delves beyond the level of narrative discourse and approaches more complex types of language activity such as argumentation and conversation.

The analysis of the *pragmatic* aspects of language functioning is also a very active field of research, although many studies limit themselves to examining the processing which is presumed to occur after the 'truly linguistic' processing. There is still too little research into the functioning of the verbal tools involved in the situational anchoring of discourse and the construction of referential values on the one hand, and in the functional organization of the discourse representation on the other.

III. Finally, the study of the processes involved in verbal *production* is still far from advanced and should attract the attention of researchers in the years to come. Here again, the data so far obtained relate more to formal aspects (syntactic, morphological and phonological) than to the processes by which meaning is translated into its linguistic form. The implementation of well-controlled situations of verbal production (which are not limited to simple

7. In this regard, some interesting suggestions have been made within both linguistics (for example, Fauconnier, 1984) and artificial intelligence (for example, Wilks, 1986).

situations of referential communication; for example, problem-solving situations) is likely to provide interesting information on this point (see Caron-Pargue and Caron, 1989).

The development of these areas of research may make an important contribution to the understanding of a number of aspects of cognitive psychology in general. This is because, first, the analysis of subjects' verbal commentaries during the performance of a task has become established as an important source of information in cognitive psychology (see Ericsson and Simon, 1980): a better knowledge of the psycholinguistic processes of production will allow a far more fruitful use of this kind of data. More generally, the analysis of the psychological operations linked to the functioning of discourse may be of help in understanding the progression of 'natural logic' in everyday thought. Finally, it is probable that study of these complex aspects of language will lead to an enrichment – and, no doubt, to a greater or lesser reorganization – of the models which have so far been proposed for the processing of information in humans.

During the thirty or so years of its existence, psycholinguistics has experienced several crises of development. It is fair to say that it has now reached adulthood and is in a position to address the whole sphere of research which is open to it. Of all human behaviour, language is perhaps the most complex, the most differentiated and the most rich. This is what makes psycholinguistics one of the most fascinating fields of psychology. I hope I have been able to convey this to my readers.

Bibliography

Abbreviated titles for journals most often mentioned:

L'Année psychologique	*An. psych.*
Annual Review of Psychology	*Ann. Rev. Psych.*
Archives de Psychologie	*Arch. Psych.*
British Journal of Psychology	*Br. J. Psych.*
Bulletin de Psychologie	*Bull. Psych.*
Cognition	*Cogn.*
Cognitive Psychology	*Cogn. Psych.*
Journal of Experimental Child Psychology	*J. Exp. Ch. Psych.*
Journal of Experimental Psychology	*J. Exp. Psych.*
Since 1975 this has appeared in various volumes entitled:	
General	*(Gen.)*
Human Learning and Memory	*(HLM)*
Human Perception and Performance	*(HPP)*
Journal de Psychologie normale et pathologique	*J. Psych.*
Journal of Verbal Learning and Verbal Behavior	*JVLVB*
Since 1985, *Journal of Memory and Language*	*J. Mem. Lang.*
Langages	*Lang.*
Memory and Cognition	*Mem. Cogn.*
Perception and Psychophysics	*Perc. Psychoph.*
Psychological Bulletin	*Psych. Bull.*
Psychological Review	*Psych. Rev.*
Quarterly Journal of Experimental Psychology	*Q. J. Exp. Psych.*

Ackerman, B.P. (1978) 'Children's comprehension of presupposed information: Logical and pragmatic inferences to speaker's belief', *J. Exp. Ch. Psych.* **26**, 92–114.

Ackerman, B.P. (1979) 'Children's understanding of definite descriptions: Pragmatic inferences to the speaker's intent', *J. Exp. Ch. Psych.* **28**, 1–15.

Akmajian, A., Demers, R.A., Farmer, A.K., Harnish, R.M. (1990) *Linguistics: An introduction to language and communication*, Cambridge, MA: MIT Press, 3rd edition.

Anderson, J.R. (1976) *Language, Memory and Thought*, Hillsdale, NJ: Erlbaum.

Anderson, J.R. (1984) *The Architecture of Cognition*, Cambridge, MA: Harvard University Press.

Anderson, J.R. (1990) *Cognitive Psychology and its Implications*, New York: Freeman, 3rd edition.

Anderson, J.R. and Bower, G.H. (1973) *Human Associative Memory*, Washington, DC: Winston.

Anderson, R.C., Pichert, J.W., Goetz, E.T., Schallert, D.L., Stevens, K.V. and Trollip, S.R. (1976) 'Instantiation of general terms', *JVLVB* **15**, 667–9.

Anscombre, J.-C. and Ducrot, O. (1983) *L'argumentation dans la langue*, Brussels: Mardaga.

Austin, J.L. (1962) *How to Do Things with Words*, Oxford: Oxford University Press.

Barclay, J.R., Bransford, J.D., Franks, J.J., McCarrell, N.S. and Nitsch, K. (1974) 'Comprehension and semantic flexibility', *JVLVB* **13**, 471–81.

Barclay, J.R. and Jahn, G. (1976) 'Distance sémantique variable et "la" structure de la mémoire sémantique', *in* Ehrlich and Tulving (1976), 85–91.

Bartlett, F.C. (1932) *Remembering*, Cambridge: Cambridge University Press.

Bassano, D. (1982) 'Etude sur la modalité *croire*: l'interprétation d'énoncés avec "croire que . . . " chez des enfants de six à onze ans', *Arch. Psych.* **50**, 165–90.

Bassano, D. and Champaud, C. (1983) 'L'interprétation d'énoncés modaux de type assertif (. . . savour que . . .) chez l'enfant de 6 à 11 ans', *An. psych.* **83**, 53–73.

Bates, E. (1976) *Language and Context: The acquisition of pragmatics*, New York: Academic Press.

Bates, E. and McWhinney, B. (1979) 'A functionalist approach to the study of grammar', *in* E. Ochs and B. Schieffelin (eds), *Developmental Pragmatics*, New York: Academic Press, 167–211.

Bates, E. and McWhinney, B. (1982) 'Functionalist approaches to grammar', *in* E. Wanner and L.T. Gleitman (eds), *Language Acquisition: The state of the art*, Cambridge: Cambridge University Press, 173–218.

Beattie, G.W. (1980) 'The role of language production processes in the organisation of behaviour in face-to-face interaction', *in* Butterworth (1980*a*), 69–107.

Benveniste, E. (1966) *Problèmes de linguistique générale*, Paris: Gallimard. (Engl. transl, *Problems in General Linguistics*, Coral Gables, FL: University of Miami Press, 1971).

Benveniste, E. (1970) 'L'appareil formel de l'énonciation', *Lang.* **17**, 12–18.

Berthoud-Papandropoulou, I. and Kircher, H. (1987) 'Que faire quand on me dit de dire? L'enfant messagert des paroles d'autrui dans une situation de communication: recherche exploratoire', *Arch. Psych.* **55**, 219–39.

Bever, T.G. (1970) 'The cognitive basis for linguistic structures', *in* J.R. Hayes (ed.), *Cognition and the Development of Language*, New York: Wiley, 279–362.

Bever, T.G., Lackner, J.R. and Kirk, R. (1969) 'The underlying structures of sentences are the primary units of immediate speech processing', *Perc. Psychoph.* **5**, 225–34.

Black, J.B. and Bower, G.H. (1979) 'Episodes as chunks in narrative memory', *JVLVB* **18**, 309–18.

Black, J.B., Turner, J.T. and Bower, G.H. (1979) 'Point of view in narrative comprehension, memory and production', *JVLVB* **18**, 187–98.

Blumenthal, A.L. (1967) 'Prompted recall of sentences', *JVLVB* **6**, 203–6.

Blumenthal, A.L. (1970) *Language and Psychology: Historical aspects of psycholinguistics*, New York: Wiley.

Blumenthal, A.L. and Boakes, R. (1967) 'Prompted recall of sentences: A further study', *JVLVB* **6**, 674–6.

Bock, J.K. (1977) 'The effect of a pragmatic presupposition on syntactic structure in question answering', *JVLVB* **16**, 723–34.

Bock, J.K. (1982) 'Toward a cognitive psychology of syntax: Information processing contributions to sentence formulation', *Psych. Rev.* **89**, 1–47.

Borel, M.-J., Grize, J.-B. and Miéville, D. (1983) *Essai de logique naturelle*, Bern: P. Lang.

Bouma, H. and Bouwhuis, D.G. (eds) (1984) *Attention and Performance X: Control of language processes*, Hillsdale, NJ: Erlbaum.

Bouscaren, J., Chuquet, J. and Danon-Boileau, L. (1992) *A Linguistic Grammar of English: An utterer-centered approach*, Paris: Ophrys.

Bower, G.H., Black, J.B. and Turner, T. (1979) 'Scripts in memory for texts', *Cogn. Psych.* **11**, 177–220.

Bradley, D. (1978) unpublished PhD dissertation, MIT, Massachusetts (quoted in Butterworth, 1983*b*).

Bransford, J.D., Barclay, J.R. and Franks, J.J. (1972) 'Sentence memory: A constructive versus interpretive approach', *Cogn. Psych.* **3**, 193–209.

Bransford, J.D. and Franks, J.R. (1972) 'The abstraction of linguistic ideas: A review', *Cogn.* **1**, 211–49.

Bransford, J.D. and McCarrell, N.S. (1974) 'A sketch of a cognitive approach to comprehension: Some thoughts about understanding what it means to comprehend, *in* W.B. Weimer and D.S. Palermo (eds), *Cognition and the Symbolic Processes*, New York: Wiley, 189–230.

Bransford, J.D., McCarrell, N.S. and Nitsch, K.E. (1976) 'Contexte, compréhension et flexibilité sémantique: quelques implications théoriques et méthodologiques', *in* Ehrlich and Tulving (1976), 335–45.

Bresnan, J. (ed.) (1982) *The Mental Representation of Grammatical Relations*. Cambridge, MA: MIT Press.

Brewer, W.F. (1977) 'Memory for the pragmatic implications of sentences', *Mem. Cogn.* **5**, 673–8.

Brewer, W.F. and Harris, R.J. (1974) 'Memory for deictic elements in sentences', *JVLVB* **13**, 321–7.

Bronckart, J.-P. (1976) *Genèse et organisation des formes verbales chez l'enfant: de l'aspect au temps*, Brussels: Mardaga.

Bronckart, J.-P. (1983) 'La compréhension des structures à fonction casuelle', *in* Bronckart, Kail and Noizet (1983), 19–50.

Bronckart, J.-P., Kail, M. and Noizet, G. (eds) (1983) *Psycholinguistique de l'enfant: recherches sur l'acquisition du langage*, Neuchâtel: Delachaux & Niestlé.

Brown, R. (1973) *A First Language: The early stages*, Cambridge, MA: Harvard University Press.

Brown, R. and McNeill, D. (1966) 'The "tip of the tongue" phenomenon', *JVLVB* **5**, 325–37.

Bruner, J.S. (1975) 'From communication to language: A psychological perspective', *Cogn.* **3**, 255–87.

Butterworth, B. (ed.) (1980*a*) *Language Production*, vol. 1: *Speech and Talk*, London: Academic Press.

Butterworth, B. (1980*b*) 'Evidence from pauses in speech', *in* Butterworth (1980*a*), 155–76.

Butterworth, B. (ed.) (1983*a*) *Language Production*, vol. 2: *Development, Writing and other Language Processes*, London: Academic Press.

Butterworth, B. (1983*b*) 'Lexical representation', *in* Butterworth (1983*a*), 257–94.

Carey, S. (1982) 'Semantic development: The state of the art', *in* E. Wanner and L.R. Gleitman (eds), *Language Acquisition: The state of the art*, Cambridge: Cambridge University Press, 347–89.

Caron, J. (1979) 'La compréhension d'un connecteur polysémique: la conjonction "si" ', *Bull. Psych.* **32**, 791–801.

Caron, J. (1983) *Les régulations du discours: psycholinguistique et pragmatique du langage*, Paris: PUF.

Caron, J. (1985) 'Le rôle des marques argumentatives dans le rappel d'un texte', *Bull. Psych.* **38**, 775–84.

Caron, J. (1987) 'Processing connectives and the pragmatics of discourse', *in* Verschueren and Bertuccelli-Papi (1987), 567–80.

Caron-Pargue, J. and Caron, J. (1989) 'Processus psycholinguistiques et analyse des verbalisations dans une tâche cognitive', *Archives de Psychologie*, **57**, 3–32.

Carr, T.H. (1981) 'Research on reading: Meaning, context effects and comprehension', *J. Exp. Psych. (HPP)* **7**, 592–603.

Carroll, J.M., Tanenhaus, M.K. and Bever, T.G. (1978) 'The perception of relations: The interactions of structural, functional, and contextual factors in the segmentation of sentences', *in* Levelt and Florès d'Arçais (1978), 187–218.

Chapin, P., Smith, T. and Abrahamson, A. (1972) 'Two factors in perceptual segmentation of speech', *JVLVB* **11**, 164–73.

Charniak, E. and McDermott, D. (1985) *Introduction to Artificial Intelligence*, Reading, MA: Addison-Wesley.

Chomsky, N. (1957) *Syntactic Structures*, The Hague/Paris: Mouton.

Chomsky, N. (1965) *Aspects of the Theory of Syntax*, Cambridge, MA: MIT Press.

Chomsky, N. (1972) *Studies on Semantics in Generative Grammar*, The Hague: Mouton.

Chomsky, N. (1980) *Rules and Representations*, New York: Columbia University Press.

Chomsky, N. (1981) *Lectures on Government and Binding*, Dordrecht: Foris.

Church, K.W. (1987) 'Phonological parsing and lexical retrieval', *Cogn.* **25**, 53–69.

Clark, D.A. (1990) 'Verbal uncertainty expressions: A critical review of two decades of research', *Current Psychology: Research and Reviews* **9**, 203–35.

Clark, E.V. (1973) 'What's in a word? On the child's acquisition of semantics in his first language', *in* T.E. Moore (ed.), *Cognitive Development and the Acquisition of Language*, New York: Academic Press, 65–110.

Clark, H.H. (1970) 'Word associations and linguistic theory', *in* J. Lyons (ed.), *New Horizons in Linguistics*, Harmondsworth: Penguin, 271–86.

Clark, H.H. (1974) 'Semantics and comprehension', *in* T.A. Sebeok (ed.) *Current Trends in Linguistics*, vol. 12, The Hague: Mouton, 1291–1498.

Clark, H.H. (1977) 'Inferences in comprehension', *in* D. LaBerge and S.J. Samuels (eds), *Basic Processes in Reading: Perception and comprehension*, Hillsdale, NJ: Erlbaum, 243–63.

Clark, H.H. (1978) 'Inferring what is meant', *in* Levelt and Florès d'Arçais (1978), 295–322.

Clark, H.H. (1979) 'Responding to indirect speech acts', *Cogn. Psych.* **11**, 430–77.

Clark, H.H. (1983) 'Making sense of nonce sense', *in* Florès d'Arçais and Jarvella (1983), 297–331.

Clark, H.H. and Carlson, T.B. (1981) 'Context for comprehension', *in* J. Long and A. Baddeley (eds), *Attention and Performance IX*, Hillsdale, NJ: Erlbaum, 313–30.

Clark, H.H. and Clark, E.V. (1977), *Psychology and Language: An Introduction to Psycholinguistics*, New York: Harcourt, Brace, and Jovanovich.

Clark, H.H. and Gerrig, R.J. (1983) 'Understanding old words with new meanings', *JVLVB* **22**, 591–608.

Clark, H.H. and Lucy, P. (1975) 'Understanding what is meant from what is said: A study in conversationally conveyed requests', *JVLVB* **14**, 56–72.

Clark, H.H. and Murphy, G.L. (1982) 'Audience design in meaning and reference', *in* Le Ny and Kintsch (1982), 287–99.

Clark, H.H., Schreuder, R. and Buttrick, S. (1983) 'Common ground and the understanding of demonstrative reference', *JVLVB* **22**, 245–58.

Clark, H.H. and Schunk, D.H. (1980) 'Polite responses to polite requests', *Cogn.* **8**, 111–43.

Clark, H.H. and Sengul, C.J. (1979) 'In search of referents for noun phrases and pronouns', *Mem. Cogn.* **7**, 35–41.

Clark, H.H. and Stafford, R.A. (1969) 'Memory for semantic features in the verb', *J. Exp. Psych.* **80** 326–34.

Clark, H.H. and Wilkes-Gibbs, D. (1986) 'Referring as a collaborative process', *Cogn.* **22**, 1–40.

Cofer, C.N. (1978) 'Origins of the Journal of Verbal Learning and Verbal Behavior', *JVLVB* **17**, 113–26.

Cole, R.A. and Jakimik, J. (1978) 'Understanding speech: How words are heard', *in* G. Underwood (ed.), *Strategies of Information Processing*, London/New York: Academic Press, 67–116.

Collins, A.M. and Loftus, E.F. (1975) 'A spreading activation theory of semantic processing', *Psych. Rev.* **82**, 407–28.

Collins, A.M. and Quillian, M.R. (1972) 'How to make a language user', *in* Tulving and Donaldson (1972), 309–51.

Conrad, C. (1972) 'Cognitive economy in semantic theory', *J. Exp. Psych.* **92**, 149–54.

Cook, V.J. (1988) *Chomsky's Universal Grammar*, Oxford: Blackwell.

Cooper, F.S., Delattre, P.C., Liberman, A.L., Borst, J.M. and Gerstman, L.J. (1952) 'Some experiments on the perception of synthetic sounds', *Journal of the Acoustical Society of America* **24**, 597–606.

Corbett, A.T. and Chang, F.R. (1983), 'Pronoun disamtiguation: accessing potential antecedents', *Mem.Cog.*, **11**, 283–94.

Cordier, F. and Le Ny, J.-F. (1975) 'L'influence de la différence de composition sémantique de phrases sur le temps d'étude dans une situation de transfert sémantique', *J. Psych.* **72** (1), 33–50.

Costermans, J., *La psychologie du langage*, Brussels: Mardaga.

Costermans, J. and Hupet, M. (1977) 'The other side of Johnson-Laird's interpretation of the passive voice', *Br. J. Psych.* **68**, 107–12.

Crystal, D. (1991) *A Dictionary of Linguistics and Phonetics*, Oxford: Blackwell, 3rd edition.

Culioli, A. (1990) *Pour une linguistique de l'enonciation: opérations et représentations*, Paris: Ophrys.

Cutler, A. (1983) 'Lexical complexity and sentence processing', *in* Florès d'Arçais and Jarvella (1983), 43–79.

Cutler, A., Mehler, J., Norris, D. and Segui, J. (1986) 'The syllable's differing role in the segmentation of French and English', *Journal of Memory and Language* **25**, 385–400.

Cutting, J.E. (1976) 'Auditory and linguistic processes in speech perception: Inferences from six fusions in dichotic listening', *Psych. Rev.* **83**, 114–40.

Danks, J.H. and Glucksberg, S. (1980) 'Experimental psycholinguistics', *Ann. Rev. Psych.* **31**, 391–417.

De Beaugrande, R. (1981) 'Design criteria for process models of reading', *Reading Research Quarterly* **2**, 261–315.

De Jong, G. (1982) 'An overview of the FRUMP system', *in* W.G. Lehnert and M.H. Ringle (eds), *Strategies for Natural Language Processing*, Hillsdale, NJ: Erlbaum, 149–76.

Dell, G.S. and Reich, P.A. (1981) 'Stages in sentence production', *JVLVB* **20**, 611–29.

Desclés, J.-P. (1982) 'Programme interdisciplinaire de traitement formel et automatique des langues et du langage (PITFALL)', *Mathématiques et Sciences humaines* **77**, 43–92.

Diehl, R.L. (1981) 'Feature detectors for speech: A critical reappraisal', *Psych. Bull.* **89**, 1–18.

Donaldson, M. and Balfour, G. (1968) 'Less is more: A study of language comprehension in children', *Br. J. Psych.* **59**, 461–72.

Ducrot, O. (1972) *Dire et ne pas dire*, Paris: Hermann.

Ducrot, O. *et al.* (1980) *Les mots du discours*, Paris: Editions de Minuit.

Ducrot, O. (1984) *Le dire et le dit*, Paris: Editions de Minuit.

Ehrlich, K. and Rayner, K. (1983) 'Pronoun assignment and semantic integration during reading: eye movements and immediacy of processing', *in* K. Rayner (ed.), *Eye Movements in Reading: Perceptual and language processes*, London: Academic Press.

Ehrlich, S. (1979) 'Semantic memory: a free-elements system', *in* C.R. Puff (ed.), *Memory Organization and Structure*, New York: Academic Press, 195–218.

Erhlich, S. and Tulving, E. (eds) (1976) 'La mémoire sémantique', *Bull. Psych.*, special issue.

Eimas, P.D. (1982) 'Speech perception: A view of the initial state and perceptual mechanisms', *in* Mehler, Walker and Garrett (1982), 339–60.

Eimas, P.D. and Corbit, J. (1973) 'Selective adaptation of linguistic features detectors', *Cogn. Psych.* **4**, 99–109.

Ellman, J.L. and McClelland, J.L. (1986) 'Interactive processes in speech perception: the TRACE model', *in* McClelland, Rumelhart and the PDP Research Group (1986), vol. 2, 58–121.

Epstein, W. (1961) 'The influence of syntactical structure on learning', *America Journal of Psychology* **74**, 80–85.

Ericsson, K.A. and Simon, H.A. (1980) 'Verbal reports as data', *Psych. Rev.* **87**, 215–51.

Ervin-Tripp, S.M. and Slobin, D.I. (1966) 'Psycholinguistics', *Ann. Rev. Psych.* **17**, 435–74.

Fauconnier, G. (1984), *Mental spaces*, Cambridge, MA: MIT Press.

Fillenbaum, S. (1966) 'Memory for gist: Some relevant variables', *Language and Speech* **9**, 217–27.

Fillenbaum, S. (1970) 'Psycholinguistics', *Ann. Rev. Psych.* **22**, 251–308.

Fillenbaum, S. (1977) 'Mind your *p*'s and *q*'s: The role of content and context in some uses of *and*, *or*, and *if*', *in* G. Bower (ed.), *The Psychology of Learning and Motivation*, vol. 2, New York: Academic Press, 41–100.

Fillenbaum, S. and Rapoport, A. (1971) *Structures in the Subjective Lexicon*, New York: Academic Press.

Fillmore, C.J. (1968) 'The case for case', *in* E. Bach and G.T. Harms (eds), *Universals in Linguistic Theory*, New York: Holt, Rinehart & Winston, 1–88.

Florès d'Arçais, G.B. (1982) 'Automatic syntactic computation in sentence comprehension', *Psychological Research* **44**, 231–42.

Florès d'Arçais, G.B. and Jarvella, R.J. (eds) (1983) *The Process of Language Understanding*, New York: Wiley.

Fodor, J.A. (1983) *Modularity of Mind*, Cambridge, MA: MIT Press.

Fodor, J.A. and Bever, T.G. (1965) 'The psychological reality of linguistic segments', *JVLVB* **4**, 414–20.

Fodor, J.A., Bever, T.G. and Garrett, M.F. (1974) *The Psychology of Language*, New York: McGraw-Hill.

Fodor, J.A. and Garrett, M.F. (1967) 'Some syntactic determinants of sentential complexity', *Perc. Psychoph.* **2**, 289–96.

Fodor, J.D. (1989) 'Empty categories in sentence processing', *Language and Cognitive Processes* **4**, 155–209.

Ford, M. and Holmes, V.M. (1978) 'Planning units and syntax in sentence production', *Cogn.* **6**, 35–54.

Forster, K.I. (1976) 'Accessing the mental lexicon', *in* R.J. Wales and E. Walker (eds), *New Approaches to Language Mechanisms*, Amsterdam: North-Holland, 257–87.

Forster, K.I. (1979) 'Levels of processing and the structure of the language processor', *in* W.E. Cooper and E.C.T. Walker (eds), *Sentence Processing: Psycholinguistic studies presented to Merrill Garrett*, Hillsdale, NJ: Erlbaum, 27–85.

Forster, K.I. and Olbrei, I. (1973) 'Semantic heuristics and syntactic analysis', *Cogn.* **2**, 319–47.

Forster, K.I. and Ryder, L.A. (1971) 'Perceiving the structure and meaning of sentences', *JVLVB* **9**, 699–706.

Foss, D.J. (1988) 'Experimental psycholinguistics', *Ann. Rev. Psych.* **39**, 301–48.

Foss, D.J. and Swinney, D.A. (1973) 'On the psychological reality of the phoneme: Perception, identification and consciousness', *JVLVB* **12**, 246–57.

Fowler, C.A., Rubin, P., Remez, R.E. and Turvey, M.T. (1980) 'Implications for speech production of a general theory of action', *in* Butterworth (1980*a*), 373–420.

Fraisse, P. (1963) 'La perception des mots: étude sur les relations entre le seuil de reconnaissance et le seuil de dénomination', *in* J. de Ajuriaguerra *et al.*, *Problèmes de psycholinguistique*, Paris: PUF, 169–78.

Frazier, L. (1987) 'Sentence processing: A tutorial review', *in* M. Coltheart (ed.), *Attention and Performance*, vol. XII: The Psychology of Reading, Hillsdale, NJ: Erlbaum, 559–86.

Frazier, L. and Fodor, J.D. (1982) 'The sausage machine: a new two-stage parsing model', *Cogn.* **13**, 187–222.

Frazier, L. and Rayner, K. (1982) 'Making and correcting errors during sentence comprehension: eye movements in the analysis of structurally ambiguous sentences', *Cogn. Psych.* **14**, 178–210.

Frederiksen, C.H. (1975), 'Acquisition of semantic information from discourse: effects of repeated exposures', *JVLVB*, **14**, 158–69.

Garnham, A. (1983) 'What's wrong with story grammars', *Cogn.* **15**, 145–54.

Garnham, A. (1987a) *Mental models as representations of discourse and text*, New York: Wiley.

Garnham, A. (1987b) 'Understanding anaphora', *in* A.W. Ellis (ed.) *Progress in the Psychology of Language*, vol. 3, Hillsdale, NJ: Erlbaum.

Garnham, A. (1988) *Artificial Intelligence: An introduction*, London: Routledge & Kegan Paul.

Garnham, A., Oakhill, J, and Johnson-Laird, P.N. (1982) 'Referential continuity and the coherence of discourse', *Cogn.* **11**, 29–46.

Garrett, M.F. (1980) 'Levels of processing in sentence production', *in* Butterworth (1980*a*), 177–220.

Garrett, M.F. (1982) 'A perspective on research in language production', *in* Mehler, Walker and Garrett (1982), 185–200.

Garrod, S. and Sanford, A. (1983) 'Topic dependent effects in language processing', *in* Florès d'Arçais and Jarvella (1983), 271–96.

Gazdar, G., Klein, E. Pullum, G. and Sag, I. (1985) *Generalized Phrase Structure Grammar*, Oxford: Blackwell.

Gee, J.P. and Grosjean, F. (1983) 'Performance structures: a psycholinguistic and linguistic appraisal', *Cogn. Psych.,* **15**, 411–58.

Gibbs, R.W. (1979) 'Contextual effects in understanding indirect requests', *Discourse Processes*, **2**, 1–10.

Gibbs, R.W. (1984) 'Literal meaning and psychological theory', *Cognitive Science* **8**, 275–304.

Glass, A.L. and Holyoak, K.J. (1975) 'Alternative conceptions of semantic memory', *Cogn.* **3**, 313–39.

Goffman, E. (1967) *Interaction Ritual: Essays on face-to-face behavior*, Garden City, NY: Anchor.

Goldman-Eisler, F. (1958) 'Speech production and the predictability of words in context', *Q. J. Exp. Psych.* **10**, 96–106.

Goldman-Eisler, F. (1968) *Psycholinguistics: Experiments in spontaneous speech*, London: Academic Press.

Gordon, D. and Lakoff, G. (1971) 'Conversational postulates', *Papers from the 7th Regional Meeting of the Chicago Linguistic Society.*

Gough, P.B. (1965) 'Grammatical transformations and speed of understanding', *JVLVB* **4**, 107–11.

Green, G.M. (1989) *Pragmatics and Natural Language Understanding*, Hillsdale, NJ: Erlbaum.

Greene, J. (1972) *Psycholinguistics*, Harmondsworth: Penguin.

Greenfield, P.M. (1979) 'Informativeness, presupposition, and semantic choice in single-word utterances', *in* E. Ochs and B. Schieffelin (eds), *Developmental Pragmatics*, New York: Academic Press, 159–66.

Grice, H.P. (1975) 'Logic and conversation', *in* P. Cole and J.L. Morgan (eds), *Syntax and Semantics*, vol. 3: *Speech Acts*, New York: Academic Press, 41–58.

Grize, J.-B. (1976) *Matériaux pour une logique naturelle*, Neuchâtel, Travaux du Centre de Recherches sémiologiques, 29.

Grize, J.-B. (1983) 'Opérations et logique naturelle', *in* Borel, Grize and Miéville (1983), 97–146.

Grosjean, F. and Gee, J.P. (1987) 'Prosodic structure and spoken word recognition' *Cogn.* **25**, 135–55.

Haberlandt, K. (1982) 'Reader expectations in text comprehension', *in* Le Ny and Kintsch (1982), 239–49.

Haberlandt, K., Berian, C. and Sandson, J. (1980) 'The episode schema in story processing', *JVLVB* **19**, 635–50.

Halle, M. (1978) 'Knowledge unlearnt and untaught: What speakers know about the sounds of their language', *in* M. Halle, J. Bresnan and G.A. Miller (eds), *Linguistic Theory and Psychological Reality*, Cambridge: MIT Press, 294–303.

Halle, M. and Stevens, K.N. (1962) 'Speech recognition: a model and a program for research', *IRE Transactions of the Professional Group on Information Theory*, *IT*–8, 413–16

Halliday, M.A.K. (1985) *An Introduction to Functional Grammar*, London: Arnold.

Harris, R.J. (1974) 'Memory for presupposition and implication: A case study of 12 verbs of motion and inception-termination', *J. Exp. Psych.* **103**, 594–7.

Harris, R.J. (1975) 'Children's comprehension of complex sentences', *J. Exp. Ch. Psych.* **19**, 420–33.

Harris, R.J. and Brewer, W.F. (1973) 'Deixis in memory for verb tenses', *JVLVB* **12**, 590–7.

Haviland, S.E. and Clark, H.H. (1974) 'What's new? Acquiring new information as a process in comprehension', *JVLVB* **13**, 512–21.

Hayes-Roth, B. and Hayes-Roth, F. (1977) 'The prominence of lexical information in memory representations of meaning', *JVLVB* **16**, 119–36.

Hickmann, M. (1983) *Le discours rapporté: Aspects métapragmatiques du langage et de son développement*, Communication to the Romanistentag, Berlin, October 1983.

Hirst, W. and Weil, J. (1982) 'Acquisition of epistemic and deontic meaning of modals', *Journal of Child Language* **9**, 659–66.

Hollan, J.D. (1973) 'Features and semantic memory: Set-theoretic or network model?', *Psych. Rev.* **82**, 154–5.

Hörmann, H. (1971), *Psycholinguistics: An introduction to research and theory*, Berlin/New York: Springer Verlag.

Hornby, P.A. (1974) 'Surface structure and presupposition', *JVLVB* **13**, 530–8.

Howell, P. and Harvey, N. (1983) 'Perceptual equivalence and motor equivalence in speech', *in* Butterworth (1983a), 203–24.

Howes, D.H. and Solomon, R.L. (1951) 'Visual duration threshold as a function of word probability', *J. Exp. Psych.* **41**, 400–10.

Hupet, M. and Le Bouedec, B. (1975) 'Definiteness and voice in the interpretation of active and passive sentences', *Q. J. Exp. Psych.* **27**, 323–30.

Hupet, M. and Le Bouedec, B. (1977) 'The given–new contract and the constructive aspect of memory for ideas', *JVLVB* **16**, 69–75.

Isaacs, E.A. and Clark, H.H. (1987) 'References in conversation between experts and novices', *J. Exp. Psych. (Gen.)* **116**, 26–37.

Jakimik, J., Cole, R.A. and Rudnicki, A.I. (1985) 'Sound and spelling in spoken word recognition', *J. Mem. Lang.*, **24**, 165–78.

Jakobson, R. (1963) *Essais de linguistique générale*, Paris: Editions de Minuit.

Jarvella, R.J. and Collas, J.G. (1974) 'Memory for the intentions of sentences', *Mem. Cogn.* **2**, 185–8.

Jarvella, R.J. and Engelkamp, J. (1983) 'Pragmatic influences in producing and perceiving language: A critical and historical perspective', *in* Florès d'Arçais and Jarvella (1983), 225–70.

Johnson, M.K., Bransford, J.D. and Solomon, S.K. (1973) 'Memory for tacit implications of sentences', *J. Exp. Psych.* **98**, 203–5.

Johnson, N.S. and Mandler, J.M. (1980) 'A tale of two structures: Underlying and surface forms in stories', *Poetics* **9**, 51–86.

Johnson-Laird, P.N. (1968) 'The choice of the passive voice in a communicative task', *Br. J. Psych.* **59**, 7–15.

Johnson-Laird, P.N. (1974) 'Experimental psycholinguistics', *Ann. Rev. Psych.* **25**, 135–60.

Johnson-Laird, P.N. (1977) 'Psycholinguistics without linguistics', *in* N.S. Sutherland (ed.), *Tutorial Essays in Psychology*, vol. 1, Hillsdale, NJ: Erlbaum, 75–135.

Johnson-Laird, P.N. (1982) 'Propositional representations, procedural semantics and mental models', *in* Mehler, Walker and Garrett (1982), 111–31.

Johnson-Laird, P.N. (1983) *Mental Models*, Cambridge: Cambridge University Press.

Johnson-Laird, P.N. (1988) *The Computer and the Mind: An introduction to cognitive science*, London: Fontana.

Johnson-Laird, P.N., Gibbs, G. and de Mowbray, J. (1978) 'Meaning, amount of processing and memory for words', *Mem. Cogn.* **6**, 372–5.

Johnson-Laird, P.N., Herrmann, D.J. and Chaffin, R. (1984) 'Only connections: A critique of semantic networks', *Psych. Bull.* **96**, 292–315.

Jusczyk, P.W. (1982) 'Auditory versus phonetic coding of speech signals during infancy', *in* Mehler, Walker and Garrett (1982), 361–87.

Just, M.A. and Clark, H.H. (1973) 'Drawing inferences from the presuppositions and implications of affirmative and negative sentences', *JVLVB* 12, 21–31.

Kail, M. (1978) 'La compréhension des présuppositions chez l'enfant', *An. Psych.* 78, 425–44.

Kail, M. (1979) 'Compréhension de "seul", "même" et "aussi" chez l'enfant', *Bull. Psych.* 32, 763–71.

Kail, M. (1983) 'L'acquisition du langage repensée: les recherches interlangues', *An. Psych.* 83, 225–58, 561–96.

Kail, M. and Plas, R. (1979) 'Psycholinguistique des présuppositions: éléments pour une critique', *Semantikos* 3 (2), 1–26.

Kail, M. and Weissenborn, J. (1984) 'L'acquisition des connecteurs: critiques et perspectives', *in* M. Moscato and G. Piéraut-Le Bonniec (eds), *Le langage: Construction et actualisation*, University of Rouen, 101–18.

Kamp, H. (1981) 'Evénements, représentations discursives et référence temporelle', *Lang.* 64, 39–64.

Karmiloff-Smith, A. (1979) *A Functional Approach to Child Language*, Cambridge: Cambridge University Press.

Katz, J.J. and Fodor, J.A. (1963) 'The structure of a semantic theory', *Language* 39, 170–210.

Keenan, J.M., McWhinney, B. and Mayhew, D. (1977) 'Pragmatics in memory: A study of natural conversation', *JVLVB* 16, 549–60.

Kempson, R. (1977) *Semantic Theory*, Cambridge: Cambridge University Press.

Kintsch, W. (1972) 'Notes on the structure of semantic memory', *in* Tulving and Donaldson (1972), 247–308.

Kintsch, W. (1974) *The Representation of Meaning in Memory*, Hillsdale, NJ: Erlbaum.

Kintsch, W. (1980) 'Semantic memory: A tutorial', *in* R.S. Nickerson (ed.), *Attention and Performance VIII*, Hillsdale, NJ: Erlbaum, 595–620.

Kintsch, W. (1982) 'Aspects of text comprehension', *in* Le Ny and Kintsch (1982), 301–12.

Kintsch, W. and Bates, E. (1977) 'Recognition memory for statements from a classroom lecture', *J. Exp. Psych. (HLM)* 3, 150–9.

Kintsch, W. and Van Dijk, T.A. (1978) 'Toward a model of text comprehension and production', *Psych. Rev.* 85, 363–94.

Klenbort, I. and Anisfield, M. (1974) 'Markedness and perspective in the interpretation of the active and passive voice', *Q. J. Exp. Psych.* 26, 189–95.

Lachman, R., Lachman, J.L. and Butterfield, E.C. (1979) *Cognitive Psychology and Information Processing: An introduction*, Hillsdale, NJ: Erlbaum.

Lakoff, G. (1970) 'Linguistics and natural logic', *in* D. Davidson and G. Harman (eds), *Semantics of Natural Language*, Dordrecht: Reidel.

Langacker, R.W. (1986) 'An introduction to cognitive grammar', *Cognitive Science*, 10, 1–40.

Langacker, R.W. (1987) *Foundations of Cognitive Grammar*, Palo Alto, CA: Stanford University Press.

Lehalle, H. and Jouen, F. (1977) 'Quelques verbes d'opinion et leur présupposition: étude génétique de leur compréhension chez l'adolescent', *Enfance* 4–5, 237–45.

Le Ny, J.-F., Denhière, G. and Le Taillanter, D. (1973) 'Study time of sentences as a function of their specificity and of semantic exploration', *Acta Psychologica* **37**, 43–53.

Le Ny, J.F. and Kintsch, W. (eds) (1982) *Language and Comprehension*, Amsterdam: North Holland.

Lesgold, A., Roth, S. and Curtis, M. (1979) 'Foregrounding effects in discourse comprehension', *JVLVB* **18**, 291–308.

Levelt, W.J.M. (1978) 'A survey of studies in sentence perception: 1970–1976', *in* Levelt and Florès d'Arçais (1978), 1–74.

Levelt, W.J.M. (1989) *Speaking: From intention to articulation*, Cambridge, MA: MIT Press.

Levelt, W.J.M. and Florès d'Arçais, G.B. (eds) (1978) *Studies in the Perception of Language*, New York: Wiley.

Levinson, S.C. (1983) *Pragmatics*, Cambridge: Cambridge University Press.

Liberman, A.M., Cooper, F.S., Shankweiler, D.P. and Studdert Kennedy, M. (1967) 'Perception of the speech code', *Psych. Rev.* **74**, 431–61.

Liberman, A.M., Harris, K.S., Hoffman, H.S. and Griffith, B.C. (1957) 'The discrimination of speech sounds within and across phoneme boundaries', *J. Exp. Psych.* **54**, 358–68.

Liberman, A.M. and Mattingly, I.G. (1985) 'The motor theory of speech perception revised', *Cogn.* **21**, 1–36.

Lindsay, P.H. and Norman, D.A. (1977) *Human Information Processing: An introduction to psychology*, New York: Academic Press.

Lyons, J. (1977) *Semantics* (2 vols), Cambridge: Cambridge University Press.

McClelland, J.L. (1987) 'The case for interactionism in language processing', *in* M. Coltheart (ed.), *Attention and Performance*, vol. XII: *The Psychology of Reading*, Hillsdale, NJ: Erlbaum, 3 35.

McClelland, J.L. (1988) 'Connectionist models and psychological evidence', *J. Mem. Lang.*, **27**, 107–23.

McClelland, J.R., Rumelhart, D.E. and the PDP Research Group (1986) *Parallel Distributed Processing: Explorations in the microstructure of cognition* (2 vols), Cambridge: MIT Press.

McCusker, L.X., Hillinger, M.L. and Bias, R.G. (1981) 'Phonological recoding and reading', *Psych. Bull.* **89**, 217–45.

McDonald, J. and McGurk, H. (1978) 'Visual influence on speech perception processes', *Mem. Cogn.* **24**, 253–7.

McKoon, G. and Ratcliff, R. (1980) 'The comprehension processes and memory structures involved in anaphoric reference', *JVLVB* **20**, 204–15.

McNamara, J., Baker, E. and Olson, C.L. (1976) 'Four-year-olds' understanding of *pretend*, *forget* and *know*: Evidence for propositional operations', *Child Development* **47**, 62–70.

McWhinney, B., Leinbach, J., Taraban, R. and McDonald, J. (1989) 'Language learning: cues or rules?', *J. Mem. Lang.*, **28**, 255–77.

Mandler, J.M. (1982) 'Recent research on story grammars', *in* Le Ny and Kintsch (1982), 207–18.

Mandler, J.M. and Johnson, N.S. (1977) 'Remembrance of things parsed: Story structure and recall', *Cogn. Psych.* **9**, 111–51.

Mani, K. and Johnson-Laird, P.N. (1982) 'The mental representation of spatial descriptions', *Mem. Cogn.* **10**, 181–7.

Marslen-Wilson, W. (1984) 'Function and process in spoken word recognition: A tutorial review', *in* Bouma and Bouwhuis (1984), 125–50.

Marslen-Wilson, W. (1987) 'Functional parallelism in spoken word recognition', *Cogn.* **25**, 71–102.

Marslen-Wilson, W. (ed.) (1989) *Lexical Representation and Process*, Cambridge, MA: MIT Press.

Marslen-Wilson, W. and Tyler, L.K. (1980) 'The temporal structure of spoken language understanding', *Cogn.* **8**, 1–71.

Marslen-Wilson, W. and Tyler, L.K. (1987) 'Against modularity', *in* J.L. Garfield (ed.), *Modularity in Knowledge Representation and Natural Language Understanding*, Cambridge, MA: MIT Press, 37–62.

Martinet, A. (1967) *Eléments de linguistique générale*, Paris: A. Colin.

Mehler, J. (1963) 'Some effects of grammatical transformations on the recall of English sentences', *JVLVB* **2**, 346–51.

Mehler, J., Walker, E.C.T. and Garrett, M.F. (eds) (1982) *Perspectives on Mental Representation*, Hillsdale, NJ: Erlbaum.

Mervis, C.B. and Rosch, E. (1981) 'Categorization of natural objects', *Ann. Rev. Psych.*, **32**, 89–115.

Meyer, D.E. and Schvaneveldt, R.W. (1971) 'Facilitation in recognizing pairs of words: Evidence of a dependence between retrieval operations', *J. Exp. Psych.*, **90**, 227–34.

Miller, G.A. (1954) 'Communication', *Ann. Rev. Psych.* **5**, 401–20.

Miller, G.A. (1962) 'Some psychological studies of grammar', *American Psychologist* **17**, 748–62.

Miller, G.A. (1969) 'A psychological method to investigate verbal concepts', *Journal of Mathematical Psychology*, **6**, 169–91.

Miller, G.A. and Isard, S. (1963) 'Some perceptual consequences of linguistic rules', *JVLVB* **2**, 217–28.

Miller, G.A. and Johnson-Laird, P.N. (1976) *Language and Perception*, Cambridge: Cambridge University Press.

Miller, G.A. and Nicely, P.E. (1955) 'An analysis of perceptual confusions among some English consonants', *Journal of the Acoustical Society of America* **27**, 338–52.

Miller, J.R. and Kintsch, W. (1980) 'Readability and recall of short prose passages: A theoretical analysis', *J. Exp. Psych. (HLM)* **6**, 335–54.

Minsky, M. (1975) 'A framework for representing knowledge', *in* P. Winston (ed.), *The Psychology of Computer Vision*, New York: McGraw-Hill.

Morris, C. (1933) 'Foundations of the theory of signs', *in* O. Neurath, R. Carnap and

C. Morris (eds), *International Encyclopedia of Unified Science*, vol. 1, Chicago, IL: University of Chicago Press, 77–138.

Morton, J. (1979) 'Word recognition', *in* J. Morton and J.C. Marshall (eds), *Psycholinguistics Series*, vol. 2: *Structures and Processes*, London: P. Elek, 107–56.

Morton, J. (1982) 'Disintegrating the lexicon: An information processing approach', *in* Mehler, Walker and Garrett (1982), 89–109.

Morton, J. and Long, J. (1976) 'Effect of word transitional probability on phoneme identification', *J. Exp. Psych. (Gen.)* **106**, 226–54.

Neely, J.H. (1977) 'Semantic priming and retrieval from semantic memory: roles of inhibitionless spreading activation and limited capacity attention', *J. Exp. Psych. (Gen.)*, **106**, 226–54.

Nesdale, A.R., Herriman, M.L. and Tunmer, W.E. (1984) 'Phonological awareness in children', *in* W.E. Tunmer, C. Pratt and M.L. Herriman (eds), *Metalinguistic Awareness in Children: Theory, research and implications*, Berlin: Springer, 56–72.

Nicol, J. and Swinney, D. (1989) 'The role of structure in coreference assignment during sentence comprehension', *Journal of Psycholinguistic Research*, **18**, 5–19.

Norman, D.A. (ed.) (1979) *Perspectives on Cognitive Science*, Norwood, NJ: Ablex.

Norman, D.A. and Rumelhart, D.E. (1975) *Explorations in Cognition*, San Francisco: Freeman.

Oakhill, J., Garnham, A. and Vonk, W. (1989) 'The on-line constructions of discourse models', *Language and Cognitive Processes*, **4**, 263–86.

Offir, C.E., (1973) 'Recognition memory for presuppositions of relative clause sentences', *JVLVB* **12**, 636–43.

Olson, D.R., (1970) 'Language and thought: Aspects of a cognitive theory of semantics', *Psych. Rev.* **77**, 257–73.

Olson, G.M. and Clark, H.H. (1976) 'Research methods in psycholinguistics', *in* E. Carterette and M.P. Friedman (eds), *Handbook of Perception*, vol. 7: *Language and Speech*, New York: Academic Press.

Ortony, A., Reynolds, R.E. and Arter, J. (1978) 'Metaphor: Theoretical and empirical research', *Psych. Bull.* **18**, 919–43.

Ortony, A., Schallert, D.L., Reynolds, R.E. and Antos, S.J. (1978) 'Interpreting metaphors and idioms: Some effects of context on comprehensions', *JVLVB* **17**, 465–77.

Osgood, C.E. and Sebeok, T.A. (1954) *Psycholinguistics: A survey of theory and research problems*, Bloomington/London, Indiana University Press (2nd edition, 1965).

Parisi, D. and Antinucci, F. (1976) *Essentials of Grammar*, New York: Academic Press.

Piaget, J. (1981) *Le possible et le nécessaire*, vol. 1: *L'évolution des possibles chez l'enfant*, Paris: PUF.

Piaget, J. (1983) *Le possible et le nécessaire*, vol. 2: *L'évolution du nécessaire chez l'enfant,* Paris: PUF.

Piatelli-Palmarini, M. (ed.) (1979) *Théories du langage, théories de l'apprentissage*, Paris: Editions du Seuil (Engl. transl., *Language and Learning: The debate between Jean Piaget and Noam Chomsky*, Cambridge, MA: Harvard University Press, 1980).

Piéraut-Le Bonniec, G. (1974) *Le raisonnement modal*, Paris/The Hague: Mouton, (Engl. transl., *The Development of Modal Reasoning*, New York: Academic Press, 1980).

Plas, R. and de Froment-Latour, O. (1981) 'Effets du contexte et du délai sur la probabilité de stockage des inférences pragmatiques', *Ann. Psych.* **81**, 409–28.

Pollack, O. and Pickett, J.M. (1969) 'Intelligibility of excerpts from fluent speech: Auditory vs structural context', *JVLVB* **3**, 79–84.

Potter, M.C., Valian, V.V. and Faulconer, B.A. (1977) 'Representation of a sentence and its pragmatic implications: Verbal, imagistic, or abstract?', *JVLVB* **16**, 1–12.

Quillian, M.R. (1967) 'Word concepts: A theory and simulation of some basic semantic capabilities', *Behavioral Science* **12**, 410–30.

Ratcliff, R. and McKoon, G. (1978) 'Priming in item recognition: Evidence for the propositional structure of sentences', *JVLVB* **17**, 403–17.

Repp, B.H. (1982) 'Phonetic trading relations and context effects: New experimental evidence for a speech mode of perception', *Psych. Bull.* **92**, 81–110.

Rieber, R.W. (ed.) (1980) *Psychology of Language and Thought: Essays on the theory and history of psycholinguistics*, New York: Plenum Press.

Riesbeck, C.K. (1982) 'Realistic language comprehension', *in* W.G. Lehnert and M.H. Ringle (eds), *Strategies for Natural Language Processing*, Hillsdale, NJ: Erlbaum, 37–54.

Riesbeck, C.K. and Schank, R.C. (1978) 'Comprehension by computer: Expectation-based analysis of sentences in context', *in* Levelt and Florès d'Arçais (1978), 247–93.

Rips, L.J., Shoben, E.J. and Smith E.E. (1973) 'Semantic distance and the verification of semantic relations', *JVLVB* **12**, 1–20.

Rosch, E., Mervis, C.B., Gray, W.D., Johnson, D.M. and Boyes-Braem, P. (1976) 'Basic objects in natural categories', *Cogn. Psych.* **8**, 382–439.

Rubenstein, H. and Aborn, M. (1960) 'Psycholinguistics', *Ann. Rev. Psych.* **11**, 291–322.

Rubin, G.S., Becker, C.A. and Freeman, R.H. (1979) 'Morphological structure and its effects on visual word recognition', *JVLVB* **18**, 757–67.

Rumelhart, D.E., Lindsay, P.H. and Norman, D.A. (1972) 'A process model for long-term memory', *in* Tulving and Donaldson (1972), 198–246.

Sachs, J.S. (1967) 'Recognition memory for syntactic and semantic aspects of connected discourse', *Perc. Psychoph.* **2**, 437–42.

Sachs, J.S. (1974) 'Memory in reading and listening to discourse', *Mem. Cogn.* **2**, 95–100.

Sanford, A.J. and Garrod, S.C. (1982) *Understanding Written Language: Explorations in comprehension beyond the sentence*, New York: Wiley.

Sanford, A.J. and Garrod, S.C. (1989) 'What, when and how: Questions of immediacy in anaphoric reference resolution', *Language and Cognitive Processes*, **4**, 235–62.

Saussure, F. de (1916) *Cours de linguistique générale*, Paris: Payot.

Savin, H.B. and Bever, T.G. (1970) 'The non-perceptual reality of the phoneme', *JVLVB* **9**, 295–302.

Savin, H.B. and Perchonock, E. (1965) 'Grammatical structure and the immediate recall of English sentences', *JVLVB* **4**, 348–53.

Schank, R.C. (1972) 'Conceptual dependency: A theory of natural language understanding', *Cogn. Psych.*, **3**, 552–631.

Schank, R.C. (1981) 'Language and memory', *in* Norman (1981), 105–46.

Schank, R.C. and Abelson, R.P. (1977) *Scripts, Plans, Goals and Understanding*, Hillsdale, NJ: Erlbaum.

Schweller, K.G., Brewer, W.F. and Dahl, D.A. (1976) 'Memory for illocutionary forces and perlocutionary effects of utterances', *JVLVB* **15**, 325–37.

Searle, J.R. (1969) *Speech Acts: An essay in the philosophy of language*, Cambridge: Cambridge University Press.

Segui, J. (1984) 'The syllable: A basic perceptual unit in speech processing?', *in* Bouma and Bouwhuis (1984), 165–81.

Seidenberg, M.S. (1985) 'Low-level language processing', *Contemporary Psychology* **30**, 946–7.

Simpson, G.B. (1984) 'Lexical ambiguity and its role in models of words recognition', *Psych. Bull.* **96**, 316–40.

Simpson, G.B. and Krueger, M.A. (1991) 'Selective access of honograph meanings in sentence context', *J. Mem. Lang.*, **30**, 627–43.

Sinclair de Zwart, H. (1967) *Acquisition du langage et développement de la pensée*, Paris: Dunod.

Sinclair de Zwart, H. (1973) 'Language acquisition and cognitive development', *in* T.E. Moore (ed.), *Cognitive Development and the Acquisition of Language*, New York: Academic Press.

Singer, M. (1976) 'Thematic structure and the integration of linguistic information', *JVLVB* **15**, 549–58.

Slobin, D.I. (1966) 'Grammatical transformations and sentence comprehension in childhood and adulthood', *JVLVB* **5**, 219–27.

Smith, E.E. (1978) 'Theories of semantic memory', *in* W.K. Estes (1978), *Handbook of Learning and Cognitive Processes*, vol. 6: *Linguistic Functions in Cognitive Theory*, Hillsdale, NJ: Erlbaum, 1–56.

Smith, E.E., Shoben, E.J. and Rips, L.J. (1974) 'Structure and process in semantic memory: A featural model for semantic decision', *Psych. Rev.* **81**, 214–41.

Sperber, D. and Wilson, D. (1981) 'Pragmatics', *Cogn.* **10**, 281–6.

Sperber, D. and Wilson, D. (1986) *Relevance: Communication and cognition*, Oxford: Basil Blackwell.

Stanners, R.F., Neiser, J.J., Hernon, W.P. and Hall, R. (1979) 'Memory representation for morphologically related words', *JVLVB* **18**, 399–412.

Steedman, M.J. and Johnson-Laird, P.N. (1980) 'The production of sentences, utterances and speech acts: Have computers anything to say?', *in* Butterworth (1980*a*), 111–41.

Steinberg, D.D. and Jakobovicz, L.A. (1971) *Semantics: An interdisciplinary reader in philosophy, linguistics and psychology*, Cambridge: Cambridge University Press.

Stevenson, R.J. (1988) *Models of Language Development*, Philadelphia: Open University Press.

Swinney, D.A. (1979) 'Lexical access during sentence comprehension: (Re)consideration of context effects', *JVLVB* **18**, 645–59.

Swinney, D.A. and Cutler, A. (1979) 'The access and processing of idiomatic expressions', *JVLVB* **18**, 523–34.

Swinney, D, Ford, R., Frauenfelder, U. and Bresnan, J. (1988) 'On the temporal course of gap-filling and antecedent assignment during sentence comprehension', *in* B. Grosz, R. Kaplan, M. Macken and I. Sag (eds), *Language Structure and Processing*, Stanford, CA: CSLI.

Tabossi, P. (1988) 'Accessing lexical ambiguity in different types of sentential contexts', *J. Mem. Lang.*, **27**, 324–40.

Taft, M. and Forster, K.I. (1975) 'Lexical storage and retrieval of prefixed words', *JVLVB* **14**, 638–47.

Taft, M. and Forster, K.I. (1976) 'Lexical storage and retrieval of polymorphemic and polysyllabic words', *JVLVB* **15**, 607–20.

Tanenhaus, M.K., Dell, G.S. and Carlson, G. (1987) 'Context effects and lexical processing: A connectionist approach to modularity', *in* J.L. Garfield (ed.), *Modularity in Knowledge Representation and Natural Language Understanding*, Cambridge, MA: MIT Press, 83–108.

Tanenhaus, M.K., Leiman, J.M. and Seidenberg, M.S. (1979) 'Evidence for multiple stages in the processing of ambiguous words in syntactic contexts', *JVLVB* **18**, 427–40.

Taraban, R. and McClelland, J.L. (1988), 'Constituent attachment and thematic role assignment in sentence processing: Influences of content-based expectations', *J. Mem. Lang.* **27**, 597–632.

Townsend, D.J. (1983) 'Thematic processing in sentences and texts', *Cogn.* **13**, 223–61.

Treiman, R. (1986) 'The division between onsets and rimes in English syllables', *J. Mem. Lang*, **25** 476–91.

Treiman, R. and Chafetz, J. (1987) 'Are there onset- and rhyme-like units in printed words?', *in* M. Coltheart (ed.) (1987), *Attention and Performance XII: The psychology of reading*, Hillsdale, N.J.: Erlbaum, 281–98.

Tulving, E. (1972) 'Episodic and semantic memory', *in* Tulving and Donaldson (1972), 381–403.

Tulving, E. and Donaldson, W. (eds) (1972) *Organization of Memory*, New York: Academic Press.

Tyler, L.K. and Frauenfelder, U.H. (eds) (1987) *Spoken Word Recognition*, Special Issue of *Cogn.* **25**.

Tyler, L.K. and Marslen-Wilson, W. (1987) 'The on-line effects of semantic context on syntactic processing', *JVLVB* **16**, 683–92.

Van Dijk, T.A. (1985) *Handbook of Discourse Analysis* (4 vols), New York: Academic Press.

Van Dijk, T.A. and Kintsch, W. (1983) *Strategies of Discourse Comprehension*, New York: Academic Press.

Van Orden, G.C., Pennington, B.F. and Stone, G.O. (1990) 'Word identification in reading and the promise of subsymbolic psycholinguistics', *Psych. Rev.* **97**, 488–522.

Van Petten, C. and Kutas, M. (1987) 'Ambiguous words in context: an event-potential analysis of the time course of meaning activation', *J. Mem. Lang.*, **26**, 188–208.

Verbrugge, R.R. and McCarrell, N.S. (1977) 'Metaphoric comprehension: Studies in remembering and resembling', *Cogn. Psych.* **9**, 494–533.

Verschueren, J. (ed.) (1991) *Pragmatics at Issue (Selected Papers from the 1987 International Pragmatics Conference)*, Amsterdam: Benjamins.

Verschueren, J. and Bertuccelli-Papi, M. (eds) (1987) *The Pragmatic Perspective (Selected Papers from the 1985 International Pragmatics Conference)*, Amsterdam: Benjamins.

Walker, E., Gough, P. and Wall, R. (1968) 'Grammatical relations and the search of sentences in immediate memory', *Proceedings of the Midwestern Psychological Association* (quoted in Fodor, Bever and Garrett, 1974, p. 256).

Wanner, E. and Maratsos, M. (1978) 'An ATN approach to comprehension', *in* M. Halle, J. Bresnan and G.A. Miller (eds), *Linguistic Theory and Psychological Reality*, Cambridge, MA: MIT Press, 119–61.

Warren, R.A. and Obusek, C.J. (1971) 'Speech perception and phonemic restoration', *Perc. Psychoph.* **9**, 358–62.

Warren, R.M. and Warren, R.P. (1970) 'Auditory illusions and confusions', *Scientific American*, **223**, 30–6.

Wason, P.C. (1965) 'The contexts of plausible denial', *JVLVB* **4**, 7–11.

Wason, P.C. and Johnson-Laird, P.N. (1972) *Psychology of Reasoning: Structure and content*, London: Batsford.

Wilks, Y. (1986) 'Relevance and beliefs', *in* T. Myers, K. Brown and B. McGonigle (eds), *Reasoning and Discourse Processes*, New York: Academic Press, 265–89.

Wing, C.S. and Scholnick, E.K. (1981) 'Children's comprehension of pragmatic concepts expressed in "because", "although", "if", and "unless" ', *Journal of Child Language*, **8**, 347–65.

Winograd, T. (1972) 'Understanding natural language', *Cogn. Psych.* **3**, 1–191.

Wittgenstein, L. (1951) *Philosophical Investigations (Philosophische Untersuchungen)*, Oxford: Basil Blackwell.

Yekovich, F.R., Walker, C.H. and Blackman, H.S. (1979) 'The role of presupposed and focal information in integrating sentences', *JVLVB* **18**, 535–48.

Index

Abelson, R.P. 79, 158
Aborn, M. 5n, 15
Abrahamson, A. 98
access *see* lexical access
Ackerman, B.P. 143
acquisition of language 8, 8–9, 29, 65–6, 130
action *see* speech acts
active/passive approach 147
adaptation
 adaptive control of thought (ACT) 79–80
 selective 37
Akmajian, A. 31, 59
alethic modalities 139
ambiguity 58, 139, 150
 polysemy 20–1, 49, 83
analysis
 by synthesis 38–9, 102
 see also levels of analysis
anaphora 26
 processing 99–100, 164–5
Anderson, J.R. 11, 31, 80
Anderson, R.C. 85
Anisfield, M. 147
Anscombre, J.-C. 166
anticipations 111
Antinucci, F. 101
Antos, S.J. 86
aphasia 50, 112
argumentation 165–6, 167–8
articles 81–2
artifical intelligence 13n
aspect of verb tenses 131

associative links 73
asymmetry 148
ATNs (augmented transition networks) 104–6
auditory level 44
Austin, J.L. 10, 23, 24, 135, 152
automatic process 28–9
 and lexical access 57–8
autonomy of syntactic processing 106–8

Baker, E. 140n, 143
Balfour, G. 66
Barclay, J.R. 85, 120
Bartlett, F.C. 154–5
basic perceptual unit 42–3
Bassano, D. 139–40
Bates, E. 69, 121, 130, 145
Beattie, G.W. 113
Benveniste, E. 10, 23, 131, 151
Berthoud-Papandropoulou, I. 140
Bertucelli-Papi, M. 152
Bever, T.G. 42, 96n, 97, 98, 103
Bierwisch, M. 62
bit 4–5
Black, J.B. 156, 158, 163
Blackman, H.S. 146
Bloomfield, L. 2, 4
Blumenthal, A.L. 15, 97, 98
Boakes, R. 98
Bock, J.K. 114, 115–16, 145
Borel, M.-J. 166
bottom-up procedure 28, 33, 40
Bouma, H. 175n
Bouscaren, J. 152

Bouwhuis, D.G. 175n
Bower, G.H. 11, 156, 158, 163
Bradley, D. 50
Bransford, J.D. 126, 133n
　on meaning and reference 87–8
　on semantic flexibility 85, 134
　on semantic integration 119–20, 145
Bresnan, J. 102
Brewer, W.F. 126, 136
bridging inferences 145, 162
Bronckart, J.-P. 126, 131, 151n
Brown, R. 8n, 46n, 130
Bruner, J.S. 130
Butterworth, B. 48n, 50, 113
Buttrick, S. 132, 133

Carey, S. 66
Carlson, G. 173
Carlson, T.B. 174n
Carnap, R. 63
Caron, J. 82n–3n, 140, 166n, 167, 179
Caron-Pargue, J. 179
Carroll, J.M. 98
cases 21, 77
categorical phoneme perception 36
Chafetz, J. 43
Champaud, C. 140
Chang 100
channel and channel capacity 4–5
Chapin, P. 98
choices, speaker's 30, 110, 115–17
Chomsky, N.
　on anaphora 99–101
　on biological necessity of language
　　172
　on competence and performance 8,
　　155
　on deep and surface structures 21, 96,
　　97–9
　on generative grammar 6–7, 19
　Government-Binding (new) theory
　　95n, 98–101, 102
　on kernel sentence 93
　on language acquisition 8–9, 29
　Standard Theory 6–12, 21, 91–8, 123,
　　176–7
　on Universal Grammar 99
Clark, D.A. 140n
Clark, E.V. 31, 65–6

Clark, H.H.
　on anaphora 164
　on 'common ground' 87, 132–4
　on contextual factors 174n
　on given-new contract 144–6, 161–2
　on politeness 128n, 138
　on presuppositions 144
　on production of utterances 115
　on semantic complexity 65
　on speech acts 137–8
　on verb tenses 130
　on word association 64
codes 4–6, 94
cognitive grammar 101
coherence/cohesion 26, 161
　of discourse 153, 161–5
cohort model 54–6
Cole, R.A. 41, 46
Collas, J.G. 136
Collins, A.M. 72–4, 75, 76
comment 27
　and topic 146–8
commitment 135
'common ground' 87, 132–4
communication 149
community membership 133
commutation 17
competence 8, 29, 90, 92, 155
complexity 65, 92–6
component 106
componential semantics 62, 64–7, 71, 88
comprehension 16–27, 50, 68, 178
　experiments 12
　and processing 174–5
　and syntax and semantics 94, 109,
　　119–20, 122
　and topicalization 146–7
computation of information 75
computers 11
concepts 62–3, 77–8, 160
connectionist models 40, 59, 173–4
connectives 82–3, 116
　functioning of 166–7
connotations 63
Conrad, C. 74
constituents 96
constructive conception 87, 177
content 87
context 21, 107–8, 174
　contextual meaning 134
　and continuous speech 40–2

context (*continued*)
  and meaning 81–8
  and phonemes 37–8
continuity
  referential 162–4
continuous speech, perception of 32,
  40–5
contract 127
  'given-new' 144–6, 161–2
controlled process 29
  and lexical access 57–8
conversation/conversational 168
  implicature 25
  logic 24–5
  rules 127–8
Cooper, F.S. 35n
co-operative principle 24, 127–8
co-presence 133
Corbett 100
Corbit, J. 37
Cordier, F. 66
Costerman, J. 147, 175
Crystal, D. 31
Culioli, A. 10, 152
  on endorsement 135n
  on location 148n
  on utternace operation 101, 151, 177
Curtis, M. 164
Cutler, A. 43n, 49, 65
Cutting, J.E. 44n
cybernetics 3

Dahl, D.A. 136
Danks, J.H. 15
De Beaugrande, R. 159n
de Froment-Latour, O. 127
De Jong, G. 158
de Mowbray, J. 55–7
decision task, lexical 46
declarative knowledge 80
deep structure 8–9, 21, 96, 97–8, 99
deixis 22–3, 23, 128, 129–32
Dell, G.S. 112, 173
deontic modalities 139
derivational theory of complexity 93
Desclés, J.-P. 148n
description 176
designation 129–30
detection
  detector hypothesis 35–7
  phonemes and words 42, 43, 46
diachronic approach 2

Diehl, R.L. 37n
difference 143
differentiation 35, 87
discourse 26–30, 153–69, 178
  cohesion 161–5
  defined 26n
  organization of 153–61
  orientation 165–7
distance, semantic 64–5
distinctive features 17, 35–7, 88
distributionalism 2
domain 133
Donaldson, M. 66
Donaldson, W. 154
Ducrot, O. 10
  on argumentation 166
  on illocutionary act 24, 142
  on polyphony 140
  on presuppositions 162
  on utterance-centred linguistics 151
dynamic of discourse 166–7

economy of storage 73–4
Ehrlich, K. 164
Ehrlich, S. 80–1
Eimas, P.D. 37
elaboration 154–5
elimination 56
Ellman, J.L. 40, 51, 57
empty categories 100–1
endorsement 135
Engelkamp, J. 146n
episode 78
epistemic modalities 139
Epstein, W. 96
Ericsson, K.A. 13n, 179
errors, speech 111–12
Ervin-Tripp, S.M. 15, 175
exchanges 111
experimental procedures 12–13, 14–15
extralinguistic knowledge 126

Fauconnier, G. 164n
Faulconer, B.A. 117
features model of lexical meaning 74–6
field of reference 131–2
Fillenbaum, S. 15, 65, 117, 126, 166
Fillmore, C.J. 21, 22, 77, 80, 101
flexibility, semantic 83–7, 134, 137
Florès, d'Arçais, G.B. 108
focusing and topicalization 146–8

Fodor, J. 10, 123
  on componential theory 62
  on empty categories 101n
  on language faculty model 172
  on meaning and reference 87n
  on perceptual strategies 103
  on selectional restrictions 84
  on syntactic structure 97
  on transformations 95
Ford, M. 114n
form 87, 177
formal/formality
  constraints 176
  grammar 123
  system 123
formants 34–5
Forster, K.I.
  on modularist theory 172
  on prefixes 48
  on sequential search 50, 51–3, 60
  on syntactic processing 106
Foss, D.J. 15, 42, 43
Fowler, C.A. 40n
Fraisse, P. 47n
'frames' 157–9
Francis, W.N. 47
Franks, J.R. 119, 120, 145
Frauenfelder, U.H. 59
Frazier, L. 103–4, 106–7
Frederiksen, C.H. 154–5
Frege, G. 62
frequency effect and lexical access 46–7
Freud, S. 111n
function/functional 129, 176
  asymmetry 148
  conception of syntax 123
  functionalism 11, 102
  grammars 151
  organization of information 141,
    148–9
  planning level 112, 114
  of utterance 121–2
  words 49–50, 81–3

Garnham, A. 156, 162–3, 164n, 169
Garrett, M.F. 95, 103, 111–12, 114
Garrod, S.C. 86, 133n, 164, 169
Gazdar, G. 102
'general problem-solver' (GPS) 53
generative grammar 7, 19–20, 96, 102
generative semantics 101

Gerrig, R.J. 134
Gibbs, G. 55–7
Gibbs, R.W. 86, 137
'given-new' contract 144–6, 161–2
Glas, A.L. 74
Glenn, C.G. 156
Glucksberg, S. 15
goal-orientated discourse 153
Goffman, E. 138
Gough, P. 97
grammar 21–2, 151
  generative 7, 19–20, 96, 102
  language as 6–9
  story 155–7
  and syntax and semantics 96, 99,
    101–2, 123
Griffith, B.C. 36
Grize, J.-B. 166

HAM (human associative memory) 79
Harris, K.S. 36
Harvey, N. 39, 40n
heuristics 102, 103
Hirst, W. 139
Hjelmslev, L. 62
Hoffman, H.S. 36
Hollan, J.D. 75
Holmes, V.M. 114n
Holyoak, K.J. 74
Hörmann, H. 5n
Hornby, P.A. 144, 146
Howell, P. 39, 40n
Howes, D.H. 47
Hull, C.L. 3
Hupet, M. 145, 147n, 147

identification 46, 54, 177
idiomatic expressions 49–50
illocutionary force/act 24, 135–8, 142
implication 25–6, 142
incompleteness of speech 33
indirect speech acts 136, 138
inferences 120
  bridging 145, 162
  pragmatic 126–7, 142–3
influence 165
information 3
  'given-new' contract 144–6, 161–2
  integration of 149
  in perspective 141–9
  storage 75

information (*continued*)
  technology 104–6
  theory 4–6
  transmission 6
initial position 146
instructions 161, 168
instrument, language as 125
integration
  of information 149
  perceptual 37–8
  semantic 119–21, 145, 162–4
intention 23–6, 129, 134
interaction 133, 171
  interactive conception 108
  levels 27–9
internal lexicon 19, 45–6
  contents 48–9
  frequency and priming 46–8
interpretation 87, 108, 177
intersubjectivity 134, 175
IPN transformations 93–5
Isaacs, E.A. 133n
Isard, S. 40–1, 96

Jahn, G. 85
Jakimik, J. 41, 46
Jakobovicz, L.A. 89
Jakobson, R. 2, 4, 17
Jarvella, R.J. 136, 146n
Johnson, M.K. 126
Johnson, N.S. 155–6
Johnson-Laird, P.N. 15, 89, 123, 169
  on artifical intelligence 13n
  cognitive science approach 31
  on coherence and plausibility 162–3
  on learning and memory 66–7
  on linguistics 175
  on mental models 87n
  on procedural semantics 69–70
  on reported speech 140n
  on semantic flexibility 84, 86
  on semantic processing 98, 108–9
  on topicalization 147
Jouen, F. 143
Jusczyk, P.W. 37n
Just, M.A. 144

Kail, M. 140, 143, 148n
Kamp, H. 164n
Karmiloff-Smith, A. 82, 130
Katz, J.J. 62, 84, 87n
Keenan, J.M. 121

Kempson, R. 89
kernel sentence 7, 93–4
Kintsch, W. 89
  on function of utterance 121
  on learning and memory 67
  on mental model 164n
  on propositional conception 67–8, 71,
    78–9, 118
  on semantic complexity 65
  on semantic integration 120–1
  on semantic representation 118
  on text processing 121, 159, 160
  on verification time 76&n
Kircher, H. 140
Kirk, R. 98
Klenbort, I. 147
knowledge 63, 80
  extralingusitic 126
  representation *see* networks
  shared 87, 132–4
Krueger 58
Kucera, H. 47
Kutas, M. 58

Lachman, R. 31
Lackner, J.R. 98
Lakoff, G. 101
landmarking 22–3, 130–2, 149
Langacker, R.W. 101, 177
language acquisition *see* acquisition
Late Closure 103–4
Le Bouedec, B. 145, 147n
Le Ny, J.-F. 66
learning 66
  see also acquisition
Lehalle, H. 143
Leibnitz, G.W. 62
Lesgold, A. 164
levels of analysis 16–31
  comprehension of verbal message
    16–27
  processing and interaction 27–9
  verbal production 29–30
Levelt, W.J.M. 12n, 124
Levinson, S.C. 23, 135n, 136n, 142n,
  152
lexical access and perception of speech
  33, 45–58, 59
  mechanisms of 50–8
lexical ambiguity *see* polysemy
lexical decision task 46

lexical elements 8
lexical level of analysis 18–19
lexical meaning 45, 61–4, 72–6, 81–8
lexical selection 113, 115
lexical semantics 61–89
  meaning, context and reference 81–8
  meaning, problems of 61–4
  organization of semantic memory
    72–81
  psychological 64–72
Liberman, A.M. 33–6, 39, 40
Lindsay, P.H. 11, 28n, 31, 89
  on semantic networks 77–9, 80
linguistic co-presence 133
linguistics and psycholinguistics 175–7
location 148n
Locke, J. 62, 88n
locutionary act 24
Loftus, E.F. 75, 76
logic 24–5
logogen activation 51, 53–4
Long, J. 43
Lucy, P. 137
Lyons, J. 89

McCarrell, N.S. 85, 86, 119, 133n
McCawley 101
McClelland, J.L. 40, 51, 57, 59, 107
McClelland, J.R. 173
McCuster, L.X. 50n
McDonald, J. 38
McGurk, H. 38
McKoon, G. 118, 165
McNamara, J. 140n, 143
McNeill, D. 46n
macrostructure of text 160–1
McWhinney, B. 69, 121, 148, 173n
Mandler, J.M. 155–6, 157
Mani, K. 120
Maratsos, M. 104, 105
markers *see* landmarking
Marlsen-Wilson, W. 51
Marslen-Wilson, W. 60, 123
  on anaphora 165
  cohort model 54–6
  on comprehension 178
  on modularist theory 172
  on syntactic processing 107–8, 109
Martinet, A. 17n
Mattingly, I.G. 40
Mayhew, D. 121

meaning 20–2, 59, 122
  construction of 177
  lexical 45, 61–4, 72–6, 81–8
  and pragmatics 133–4, 137–8
  and propositional representation 117
  and reference 61, 81–2, 87–8, 132–4
Mehler, J. 172
  on coding hypothesis 94
  on syllables 42–3
memory 11, 66–7, 79–80, 144
  experiments 13
  lexical 89
  organization packages (MOPs) 158
  and presupposition 143
  semantic 72–81, 80–1
mental models 120–1, 164
Mervis, C.B. 69n
message 4
metaphor 86
methodology 12–15
Meyer, D.E. 47
microstructure of text 159–60
Miéville, D. 166
Mill, John Stuart 88n
Miller, G.A. 5n, 6, 15, 89
  on context 40–1
  on distinctive features 35
  on IPN transformations 93
  on lexical representation 171n
  on procedural semantics 69–70
  on semantic distance 64
  on syntactic structure 96
Miller, J.R. 159n–60
Minimal Attachment 103–9
Minsky, M. 157
mispronunciations 41–2
modalities 116, 131, 138–40
modularist theory 52, 171, 172–3
morpheme 18–19, 48–9
Morris, C. 10
Morton, J. 43, 50, 60
  on logogen activation 51, 53–4
motor theory of speech 39–40
'move' rules 99
Mowrer, O.H. 3
multiplicity
  of cues 37–8
  of languages 13–14
Murphy, G.L. 132n

necessary 139
Neely, J.H. 57–8

neologisms 134
Nesdale, A.R. 42
networks
    model of lexical meaning 72, 74–6
    semantic 76–81, 88–9, 109
new information 144–6
Newell, A. 6
Nicely, P.E. 35
Nicol, J. 100, 106
normalization, pragmatic 126
Norman, D.A. 11, 28n, 31, 77–80, 89
Norris, D. 43n

Oakhill, J. 162–3, 164n
objectives and methods 1–15
    birth and evolution 1–12
    methods 12–15
Obusek, C.J. 41
Offir, C.E. 143
Olbrei, I. 106
Olson, C.L. 140n, 143
Olson, D.R. 87
Olson, G.M. 12n, 115
operations 96, 101, 151–2, 168, 176–7
optimal design 133
optional transformations 95n
order of utterance 30, 115–16
organization
    of discourse 153–61
    of units 19–20
orientation of discourse 165–7
Ortony, A. 86
Osgood, C.E. 3–4

parallel functioning 28
    processing 43, 173
paraphrases 151
Parisi, D. 101
partial modularity 173
participants 130
pauses 112–13
perception of speech 32–60
    continuous 40–5
    phonemes 29, 33–40
    problems, general 32–3
    see also lexical access
perceptual strategies 103–4
Perchonock, E. 94
performance 8, 90, 92
    strategies 9

perlocutionary act 24, 135
permissible/impermissible sequences 44n
perseverations 111
perspective 177–9
    information in 141–9
phonemes 62
    detection 42, 43
    perception 29, 33–40
    phonemic restoration 41
phonetics 17n
phonology/phonological 17n–18, 44, 62
    level of analysis 16–18
    phrases 114
phrase-structure rules 7
physical co-presence 133
physiological measurements 13
Piaget, J. 8n, 92, 139
Piatelli-Palmarini, M. 8n
Pickett, J.M. 33
Piéaut-Le Bonniec, G. 139
place of utterance 130
planning utterances 29–30, 110–14
Plas, R. 127
plausibility 162–3
point of view 131, 134, 163
'pointing' *see* landmarking
politeness 128&n, 138
Pollack, O. 33
polyfunctionality 81, 131
polyphony 140
polysemy 20–1, 49, 83
position and perspectives 170–9
    language processing 171–5
    linguistics and psycholinguistics
        175–7
    perspectives 177–9
positional planning level 112, 114
possible 139
Postal 101
Potter, M.C. 117
pragmatics 10, 70, 91, 116, 125–52, 178
    defined 126–7
    information in perspective 141–9
    language 125–9
    speech and situation 129–34
    taking responsibility 134–41
predication 118
prefixes 48
presupposition 25–6, 141–4, 162
priming 47–8, 116

procedures/procedural
    conception of meaning 69–71, 89
    knowledge 80
processing/processes 143, 171–5
    anaphora 99–100, 164–5
    experiments 13
    levels 27–9
    lexical access 46
    parallel 43
    sentences 101–10
    'top-down' aspects of 174–5
production 13, 29–30, 50, 110–17,
    174–5, 178
proposition/propositional 77
    conception 67–8, 71
propositional conception 67–8, 71, 78–9
    representation 117–19
prosodic aspects 18, 43
prototype 63, 68–9
psycholinguistics *see* discourse; levels;
    lexical; objectives; perception;
    position; semantics;
    syntax; pragmatics
psychology
    psychological semantics 64–72
    scientific 3–12

Quillian, M.R. 72–4, 75, 78, 125

Rappoport, A. 65
Ratcliff, R. 118, 165
Rayner, K. 107, 164
redundancy 5
reference
    continuity and semantic integration
        162–4
    and deixis 131–2
    landmarks 22–3
    and meaning *see under* meaning
Reich, P.A. 112
relations 77, 121
relevance 127–8
reported speech 116n, 140–1
Repp, B.H. 38
representation
    and discourse 168
    of knowledge *see* networks
    and pragmatics 149, 152
    semantic 117–22
response 138
responsibility for speech, taking 134–41,
    149

restoration, phonemic 41
reversibility 106
rewrite rules 155–6
Reynolds, R.E. 86
Rieber, R.W. 15
Riesbeck, C.K. 109, 159
Rips, L.J. 69, 74, 75
Rosch, E. 63, 69, 115
Ross, J.R. 101
Roth, S. 164
Rubenstein, H. 5n, 15
Rubin, G.S. 48
Rudnickik, A.I. 46
Rumelhart, D.E. 11, 89, 156, 173
    semantic networks 77–9, 80
Ryder, L.A. 106

Sachs, J.S. 117, 121
Sanford, A.J. 86, 133n, 164, 169
Saussure, F. de 2, 20, 62
Savin, H.B. 42, 94
Schallert, D.L. 86
Schank, R.C. 11, 79, 109, 158
Scholnick, E.K. 140n
Schreuder, R. 132, 133
Schunk, D.H. 138
Schvaneveldt, R.W. 47
Schweller, K.G. 136
scientific psychology 3–12
'scripts' 158–9
Searle, J.R. 10, 24, 152
Seboek, T.A. 3
Segui, J. 42, 43n
Seidenberg, M.S. 175n
selection
    lexical 113, 115
    restrictions 84
selective adaptation 37
semantic(s) 8, 10
    complexity 65
    distance 64–5
    flexibility 83–7, 134, 137
    integration 119–21, 145, 162–4
    networks 76–81, 88–9, 109
    transition networks (STNs) 109
    see also lexical semantics; syntax and
        semantics
Sengul, C.J. 164
sentence 21
    kernel 7, 93–4

sentence (*continued*)
verification 73–4
see also pragmatics; syntax and
semantics
sequential processing 137
sequential search model 51–3
series, modules in 171
shadowing 12, 54–5
Shannon, C.E. 3, 4, 6
shared knowledge 87, 132–4
Shaw, J.C. 6
Shoben, E.J. 69, 74, 75
signs 2, 10, 18, 62
Simon, H.A. 6, 13n, 179
Simpson 58
Sinclair de Zwart, H. 92
Singer, M. 144
situation and speech 129–34
Slobin, D.E. 15, 175
Slobin, D.I. 94, 106, 126
Smith, E.E. 69, 74, 75, 89
Smith, T. 98
Solomon, R.L. 47
Solomon, S.K. 126
sound and phoneme 33–5
source 135, 140
specific procedures 14
speech
acts 23–4, 116, 134–8
errors 111–12
speaker's choices 115–17
see also perception of speech
speed of speech 32
Sperber, D. 128
Stanners, R.F. 48
status of speaker 128
Steedman, M.J. 13n
Stein, N.L. 156
Steinberg, D.D. 89
Stevenson, R.J. 99n
story grammars 155–7
strategies 160
perceptual 103–4
pragmatic 126
structure/structural 96, 151, 176
description 92
structuralism 2–3, 11
syntactic 96–9
substitutions 111
surface structure 96–7, 98
Swinney, D.A. 43, 49, 58, 100, 101, 106
syllables 42–3

synchronic approach 2
syntax and semantics in sentence 8, 10,
90–124
Chomskyan 91–102
syntax and semantics in sentence
(continued)
processing 101–10
production of utterances 110–17
semantic representation 117–22
verification 85
synthesis, analysis by 38–9, 102

Tabossi, P. 58
Taft, M. 48, 52
Tanenhaus, M.K. 58, 98, 173
Taraban, R. 107
text processing 159–61
theme and rheme 146n
theoretical interpretations and phonemes
38–40
theory 176
Thorndyke, P.W. 156
time
and comprehension 12
and verification 76&n
time of utterance 130
token node 73, 78
top-down processes 28, 33, 40, 45, 59,
174–5
topic/topicalization 27, 146–8
Townsend, D.J. 167
TRACE model 57, 173
traces 100–1

transformation 92, 93–6
rules 7, 156
transitions 34–5
transmission of information 6
Treiman, R. 43
Tulving, E. 72, 154
Turner, J.T. 158, 163
Tyler, L.K. 54, 59, 60, 107–8, 165, 171
type node 73, 78
typical examples 63
typicality 71, 74

units
basic perceptual 42–3
identification of 16–19
organization of 19–20
unity 142

universal grammar 99
usage *see* pragmatics
use of word 64
utterance
  act 128
  -centred linguistics 151
  function of 121–2
  landmarks 22–3
  operational *see* operations
  production of 110–17

Valian, V.V. 117
Van Dijk, T.A. 118, 159, 160, 164n, 168
Van Orden, G.C. 50n
Van Petten, C. 58
variability, acoustic 32
verbal learning 153
verbal message, comprehension of
  16–27
verbal production 29–30
Verbrugge, R.R. 86
verbs 48
  of opinion 140n
  tenses 130, 131
verification 76&n, 85
Verschueren, J. 152
visual information 38

voice onset time 36
Vonk, W. 164n

Walker, C.H. 146
Walker, E. 97
Wall, R. 97
Wanner, E. 104, 105
Warren, R.A. 41
Warren, R.M. 41
Warren, R.P. 41
Wason, P.C. 95, 140n
Watson, J.B. 3
Weil, J. 139
Weinreich, V. 62
Weissenborn, J. 140, 143
Wilkes-Gibbs, D. 133n
Wilson, D. 128
Wing, C.S. 140n
Winograd, T. 11
Wittgenstein, L. 64, 87
word associations 64
written language 50
Wundt, W. 15

Yekovich, F.R. 146

Zipf, G.K. 47